COLUMBIA COLLEGE CHICAGO

3 2711 00144 8384

D1776998

DATE DUE

JAN 0 5 2012		
MAR 2 1 2013		
~~DISCARD~~		
		1 1 2009

Demco, Inc. 38-293

IMMIGRATION

Recent Titles in
The Ilan Stavans Library of Latino Civilization

Latina Writers
Ilan Stavans, editor

Spanglish
Ilan Stavans, editor

The Ilan Stavans Library of Latino Civilization

IMMIGRATION

Edited by Ilan Stavans

GREENWOOD PRESS
Westport, Connecticut • London

Library of Congress Cataloging-in-Publication Data

Immigration / edited by Ilan Stavans.
    p. cm. — (The Ilan Stavans library of Latino civilization, ISSN 1938–615X)
  Includes bibliographical references and index.
  ISBN 978–0–313–34802–0 (alk. paper)
  1. Hispanic Americans—Social conditions. 2. Hispanic Americans—Biography.
3. Immigrants—United States. 4. United States—Emigration and immigration.
5. Latin America—Emigration and immigration. I. Stavans, Ilan.
  E184.S75.I36 2008
  973'.0468—dc22   2008017230

British Library Cataloguing in Publication Data is available.

Copyright © 2008 by Ilan Stavans

All rights reserved. No portion of this book may be
reproduced, by any process or technique, without the
express written consent of the publisher.

Library of Congress Catalog Card Number: 2008017230
ISBN: 978–0–313–34802–0
ISSN: 1938–615X

First published in 2008

Greenwood Press, 88 Post Road West, Westport, CT 06881
An imprint of Greenwood Publishing Group, Inc.
www.greenwood.com

Printed in the United States of America

The paper used in this book complies with the
Permanent Paper Standard issued by the National
Information Standards Organization (Z39.48–1984).

10 9 8 7 6 5 4 3 2 1

Contents

	Series Foreword *by Ilan Stavans*	vii
	Preface	ix
I	**CONSIDERATIONS**	**1**
	The Baby Bust: Who Will Do the Work? Who Will Pay the Taxes? *Rodolfo O. de la Garza*	3
	Proposition 187: Misrepresenting Immigrants and Immigration *Otto Santa Ana*	17
	Face the Nation: Race, Immigration, and the Rise of Nativism in Late-Twentieth-Century America *George J. Sánchez*	54
	Do Home-Country Political Ties Limit Latino Immigrant Pursuit of U.S. Civic Engagement and Citizenship? *Louis DeSipio*	69
	Theses on the Latino Bloc: A Critical Perspective *Rosaura Sánchez and Beatrice Pita*	90
II	**VOICES**	**115**
	The Coyote and the Chicken *Luis Alberto Urrea*	117
	A Soccer Season in Southwest Kansas *Sam Quinones*	125
	Gladys: An Immigrant Story *Ilan Stavans*	166
	"Headed North" and "The Runner" *Ramón "Tianguis" Pérez*	180

Conversations with Ilan Stavans   188
Rubén Martínez

Selected Bibliography   197
Index   199
About the Editor and Contributors   205

Series Foreword

The book series The Ilan Stavans Library of Latino Civilization, the first of its kind, is devoted to exploring all the facets of Hispanic civilization in the United States, with its ramifications in the Americas, the Caribbean Basin, and the Iberian Peninsula. The objective is to showcase its richness and complexity from a myriad perspective. According to the U.S. Census Bureau, the Latino minority is the largest in the nation. It is also the fifth largest concentration of Hispanics in the globe.

Out of every seven Americans, one traces his or her roots to the Spanish-speaking world. Mexicans make up about 65 percent of the minority. Other major national groups are Puerto Ricans, Cubans, Dominicans, Ecuadorians, Guatemalans, Nicaraguans, Salvadorans, and Colombians. They are either immigrants, descendants of immigrants, or dwellers in a territory (Puerto Rico, the Southwest) having a conflicted relationship with the mainland United States. As such, they are the perfect example of *encuentro:* an encounter with different social and political modes, an encounter with a new language, an encounter with a different way of dreaming.

The series is a response to the limited resources available and the abundance of stereotypes, which are a sign of lazy thinking. The 20th-century Spanish philosopher José Ortega y Gasset, author of *The Revolt of the Masses,* once said: "By speaking, by thinking, we undertake to clarify things, and that forces us to exacerbate them, dislocate them, schematize them. Every concept is in itself an exaggeration." The purpose of the series is not to clarify but to complicate our understanding of Latinos. Do so many individuals from different national, geographic, economic, religious, and ethnic backgrounds coalesce as an integrated whole? Is there an *unum* in the *pluribus*?

Baruch Spinoza believed that everything in the universe wants to be preserved in its present form: a tree wants to be a tree, and a dog a dog. Latinos in the United States want to be Latinos in the United States—no easy task, and therefore an intriguing one to explore. Each volume of the series contains an assortment of approximately a dozen articles, essays, and interviews never gathered together before. The authors are scholars, writers, journalists, and specialists in their respective fields. The selection is followed by a bibliography of important resources. The compilation is designed to generate debate and foster research: to complicate our knowledge. Every attempt is made to balance the ideological viewpoint of the authors. The target audience is students, specialists, and the lay reader. Thematically, the volumes will range from politics to sports, from music to cuisine. Historical periods and benchmarks such as the Mexican War, the Spanish-American War, the Zoot Suit Riots, the Bracero Program, and the Cuban Revolution, as well as controversial topics such as immigration, bilingual education, and Spanglish, will be tackled.

Democracy is only able to thrive when it engages in an open, honest transaction of information. By offering diverse, insightful collections of provocative, informed, insightful material about Hispanic life in the United States and inviting people to engage in critical thinking, The Ilan Stavans Library of Latino Civilization seeks to offer critical tools that open new vistas to appreciate the fastest growing, increasingly heterogeneous minority in the nation—to be part of the *encuentro*.

Ilan Stavans

Preface

Not all Latinos in the United States have come through the immigration door. In the mid-nineteenth century, with the conclusion of the Mexican–American War, the sale of the territories that today constitute the Southwest carried along the transfer of people from one nation to another. Others have come as refugees and are, therefore, granted a different legal status. Still, immigration—incessant, widespread, and from different geographical origins—is the main reason why Hispanics are the largest, most diverse minority in the country.

The issue is volatile because the United States oscillates between seeing itself as a permanent heaven to newcomers and resisting their invasion as a way to defend the fortress from the barbarians. The concluding lines of Emma Lazarus's 1883 sonnet, "The New Colossus," is engraved in the pedestal of the Statue of Liberty and continues to resonate.

> Give me your tired, your poor,
> Your huddled masses yearning to breathe free,
> The wretched refuse of your teeming shore.
> Send these, the homeless, tempest-tost to me,
> I lift my lamp beside the golden door!

But the United States is also about gate keeping. It alternates between embrace and rejection, and Latinos, like other immigrants, are caught in that duality.

The pieces collected in this volume are designed to simultaneously look at the historical, social, and cultural context against which immigration unfolds, as well as present a sampler of individualized narratives across economic, political, racial, and national lines. A handful of essays place the issue of Latino immigration in the context of current immigration in general, globally, and to the country in particular. To what extent is the experience of Hispanics different from that of other immigrant groups: Irish, German, Scandinavian, Jewish, Italian, and Asian? Is their ordeal closer to those of Native and African Americans?

Other essays reflect on specific dilemmas: How does immigration play out in the media? Is it vilified or encouraged? What are the various moods through which public opinion oscillates? How are Latino immigrants transforming American cities and suburbs? What is the connection of those immigrants to their respective home countries? And what is the impact of return migration on the original and host countries?

Also included here are autobiographical and poetic explorations of immigration from Cuba, Puerto Rico, Mexico, El Salvador, and elsewhere, plus vivid reportorial assessments of actual border crossing.

Unquestionably, the best way to approach American immigration is with an open mind. The United States has always been a nation of immigrants. Has the way in which it welcomes newcomers changed? Are the strategies to achieve assimilation as effective today as they have been in the past? Is globalism and the fact that immigration is redefining literally every industrialized country in the world—and, thus, all the developing countries too—forcing a reconsideration of who immigrants are and what the expectations placed on them ought to be?

PART I
CONSIDERATIONS

The Baby Bust: Who Will Do the Work? Who Will Pay the Taxes?

Rodolfo O. de la Garza

LATINO IMMIGRANTS, NATIONAL IDENTITY AND THE NATIONAL INTEREST

Immigration has been a contentious issue on the national political agenda for over a century, and the contours of the debate it has raised have remained virtually unchanged. Surprisingly, although occasionally this has included protests over the number of immigrants the nation can absorb, as was the case in recent decades when groups such as Zero Population Growth and the Sierra Club opposed immigration, the core issues of the debate have centered on whether the new immigrants could be absorbed into the nation. Would they abandon the "old ways" in favor of core American values?

These questions were first raised when the initial wave of non-Western, non-Nordic protestant European immigrants such as those from Italy and Ireland began outnumbering those from Northern Europe and England. This concern expanded to include Asians, who were not only denied the right to immigrate, but those already in the United States lost many of the rights and privileges native born citizens and legal immigrants normally enjoy.

While these same concerns now target the "new immigrants," i.e., Asians, Africans and Hispanics, they focus on Hispanics because they are so numerous, making up approximately 50 percent of contemporary immigration, and share significant cultural traits (religion and language) that enhance their ability to remain outside mainstream society. Additionally, as Samuel Huntington has recently argued (Huntington 2004), given that Mexicans make up approximately half of this group and that a significant proportion of them are undocumented, the contemporary debate specifically asks how Mexican immigration will affect the nation.

The objective of this essay is to address this issue. Specifically, it will examine the impact Latino immigrants in general and Mexican immigrants in

---

A seminar paper presented by Rodolfo O. de la Garza from Columbia University and the Tomás Rivera Policy Institute, in Washington, D.C., March 11, 2005. Used by permission of Rodolfo O. de la Garza. Courtesy of Columbia University Press.

particular are having on the nation. While it will address the cultural and economic aspects of their role, it will particularly emphasize its political dimensions because the relationship immigrants develop with the polity will shape their overall impact on the nation. Also, because Huntington's recent argument places Mexicans at the center of the current controversy, the essay will focus on key elements of his argument. I would note, however, that while Huntington is a most forceful advocate of anti-Mexican views, his perspective is not unique but rather represents the views of anti-immigrant spokesmen such as Patrick Buchanan, Congress—Tancredo of Colorado and Arthur Schlesinger (Schlesinger 1992).

IMMIGRANTS AND U.S. POPULAR CULTURE

Huntington is critical of Latino immigration because he argues that Latinos refuse to incorporate into mainstream culture and therefore they threaten the nation's historical identity which is reflective of a unifying cultural experience rooted in Protestantism and the English language. Ironically, Latinos are twice as likely as all Americans to agree with that statement (Table 1).

Nonetheless, two thirds of Latinos agree that it is very or somewhat important to "change so that they blend into the larger society" but two thirds also agree that it is very important "for Latinos to maintain their cultures" (Pew Hispanic Center 2004). Together these attitudes suggest that Hispanics see no incompatibility between having a combined cultural identity, one located within mainstream America and one built on home country sentiments and practices.

At the societal level, the impact Latin immigration has had on the nation's popular cultural impact is ubiquitous and multifaceted. Indeed the changes it brings to our daily lives have so changed the cultural landscape that they are key to explaining the current rise in anti-Latino immigrant sentiment. Among the most significant of these is that since the 1980s Latinos have become a national minority, that is, rather than being regionally isolated they now constitute substantial communities in virtually every state (Table 2).

Further illustrating this change is that there are 23 states across the country where Latinos are the largest minority group. This national presence is particularly noteworthy among Mexicans who historically were concentrated in the Southwest but now have substantial and growing settlements across the country.

Table 1
National Perspectives of American Cultural Make-Up

	All Latinos	*All Americans*
U.S. is made up of many cultures	83%	92%
U.S. has a single core Anglo-Protestant culture	10%	5%

Source: Pew Hispanic Center 2004.

Table 2
States with Largest Latino Populations, 2000

	State Population	Latino Population	% of U.S. Latino Population	Cumulative %
California	32,666,550	10,112,986	28.6%	28.6%
Texas	19,759,614	5,862,835	16.6%	45.3%
New York	18,175,301	2,624,928	7.4%	52.7%
Florida	14,915,980	2,243,441	6.4%	59.0%
Illinois	12,045,326	1,224,309	3.5%	62.5%
New Jersey	8,115,011	1,004,011	2.8%	65.4%
Arizona	4,668,631	1,033,822	2.9%	68.3%
New Mexico	1,736,931	700,289	2.0%	70.3%
Colorado	3,970,971	577,516	1.6%	71.9%
Massachusetts	6,147,132	377,016	1.1%	73.0%
Total Latino	122,201,447	35,300,000		

Table 3
Top 10 Counties of Latino Population Growth

County	State	2000 Latino	Numeric Change	% Change	% Latino
Benton	AR	13,469	12,100	891.1%	8.8%
Forsyth	NC	19,577	17,475	831.4%	6.4%
Washington	AR	12,932	11,406	747.4%	8.2%
Durham	NC	17,039	14,986	729.6%	7.6%
Whitfield	GA	18,419	16,098	693.6%	22.1%
Gwinnett	GA	64,137	55,667	657.2%	10.9%
Mecklenburg	NC	44,871	38,178	570.4%	6.5%
Wake	NC	33,985	28,589	529.8%	5.4%
Hall	GA	27,242	22,684	529.8%	19.6%
Elkhart	IN	16,300	13,368	529.8%	8.9%

They also have established major settlements in the South, the Midwest and Northwest (Table 3). In New York, 32 percent of the city's immigrants came from Latin America in 2000 (New York City Department of City Planning Population Division 2005), easily outnumbering Europeans, who historically were the most numerous. Mexicans total 122,600, outnumbered only by Dominicans with 369,200. Given that Mexico is much more distant than numerous other Latin American nations and has no historical relationship with the region, the size of this population is especially noteworthy.

The impact of these immigrants on the nation's popular culture is obvious and powerful. The most widely accepted and universal consequence is culinary. For almost a decade, Latino marketers have boasted that salsa outsells catsup. A drive across the country attests to the validity of this claim: tacos, fajitas and jalapeños are available in every town and city in the nation. Like pasta and pizzas, Mexican food has become an integral part of the American diet, and its addition to the nation's menu has improved the nation's table just as Italian food did previously. More headline grabbing has been the rise to preeminence of Latinos in the national pastime such as Pedro Martinez, Alex Rodriguez and Sammy Sosa. There is no doubt Latinos have raised the level at which American baseball is played.

Latinos have similarly impacted the nation's entertainment industries. Hispanics have their own situation comedy on a major network (*The George Lopez Show*), their own Broadway shows (John Leguzamo), and substantial roles in TV shows such as *CSI: Miami*. They also are in the ranks of the nation's most popular contemporary film and television stars (Jimmy Smits and Jennifer Lopez) and include prominent musical artists such as Gloria Estefan and Ricky Martin.

Even though Latino cultural production is altering the face and style of the nation, these changes have been welcomed by mainstream society. There are at least three possible explanations for why even the most vitriolic anti-immigrant nativists are quiet in the face of these developments. First, no one associates them with any threat (other than heartburn). Second, mainstream society so welcomes these contributions that they are beyond criticism even though there can be little doubt that the cultural practices Hispanics are introducing into the nation are changing the very core of mainstream culture. Third, immigration critics save their energies for specific cultural practices that influence the claim that undermines core American values.

IMMIGRANTS, CORE AMERICAN VALUES AND POLITICAL INCORPORATION

Contemporary anti-Hispanic immigration sentiments nonetheless also include cultural arguments. The most important of these is linguistic, i.e., Latino immigrants insist on maintaining Spanish to the exclusion of English. This leads to the allegation that because they remain linguistically separate, they are never socialized into mainstream culture but rather retain home country values. Consequently, Mexican Hispanics in general, whether they are immigrants or native born, not only will not integrate into the polity but will instead remain politically faithful to their countries of origin to the detriment of the "national interest."

Numerous sources conclusively vitiate charges that Latinos are linguistically isolated from mainstream America. The Latino National Political Survey reported that those who do not describe themselves as equally competent in both languages, 67% of native born Mexican Americans, 68% of Puerto Ricans and 68% of Cuban Americans, rate themselves as better in English than Spanish, compared to 8%, 5% and 4% of Mexican Americans, Puerto Ricans and Cuban Americans, respectively, who rate their Spanish better than their English. The foreign born, predictably, rate their Spanish much higher, but even they include few Spanish monolinguals. Indeed, 81% of Mexican immigrants report some English competence, as do 88% of island-born Puerto Ricans and 75% of Cubans (de la Garza et al. 1992, 42). The 2002 Pew Hispanic Center survey reports similar findings. While it is not surprising that 94% of the native born reported they could carry on a conversation in English very or pretty well, that 44% of the foreign born reported this level of competence is unexpected (Pew Hispanic Center 2002). In 2004, Pew found 96% of the native born indicated that they could carry on a conversation in English very or pretty well, while 38% of immigrants ranked themselves similarly (Pew Hispanic Center 2004). Buttressing this finding is the importance Latinos, especially the foreign born, attach to learning English. While 86% of non-Hispanic whites and native born Latinos agree that individuals need to learn English to succeed, 91% of the foreign born voice this view (Pew Hispanic Center 2002).

These patterns illustrate that English is the dominant language of native born Mexican Americans and other Latinos, and that Hispanic immigrants of all nationalities learn English. Indeed, Latin American immigrants "become proficient in English at a more rapid pace than immigrants from other non-English-language countries (Stevens 1994).

Even more noteworthy is how immigrants evaluate the importance of English. In 1990, approximately 40% of Mexican American, Cuban American and Puerto Rican citizens agreed that English should be the nation's official language (de la Garza et al. 1992, 97), and over 90% of each group also agreed that citizens and residents should learn English (de la Garza et al. 1992, 98). Similar results are evident from the Pew 2002 survey, which found that 91% of Latino immigrants agreed that immigrants need to learn English to succeed compared to 86% of native born Latinos and non-Hispanic whites who shared this perspective (Pew Hispanic Center 2002). Also, over 50% of Hispanics believe that immigrants must learn English to say they are part of American society (Pew Hispanic Center 2004). Their commitment to English notwithstanding, Latinos also support knowing and maintaining Spanish. Almost 95% say future generations of Hispanics should speak Spanish.

Clearly, allegations regarding anti-English attitudes and behavior among Hispanics in general and the Mexican origin native born and immigrant population in particular are not empirically grounded. Rather than threaten a core American value, their linguistic patterns are more easily seen as supporting the centrality of English to American life. Their knowledge of and commitment to Spanish thus should be seen as a resource that could serve the nation's security and foreign policy goals as well as its economic well being. As economic and political relations with Latin America expand, the presence of Latino bilinguals will insure that the U.S. government will never confront in Latin America the absence of linguistically competent officials it faced during the Iranian crisis. Also, Hispanic bilinguals constitute a pool of linguistically and culturally competent individuals who are uniquely situated to advance private and public U.S. interests. In other words, Latino bilinguals seem more likely to enhance rather than undermine the national interest.

Claims that Latino social values undercut other aspects of today's sociopolitical mainstream are equally unsupported. Latinos, especially immigrants, voice stronger support than Anglos for "family values" such as opposition to divorce, homosexuality, illegitimate children and abortion (Pew Hispanic Center 2002). They also are committed to economic individualism (de la Garza et al. 1992). Indicative of this attitude is that in California less than 2% of native born and naturalized Hispanic citizens, most of whom are Mexican, receive any public assistance even though all of them are eligible to receive such benefits (Cortina et al. 2004).

Hispanics also are more religious than Anglos. Compared to 61% of Anglos who indicate that religion is very important to their lives, 64% of the Latino native born and 71% of immigrants describe themselves this way (Pew Hispanic Center 2002) and 30 percent of all Hispanics identify as "born Again Christians" (*Washington Post*/Univision/TRPI 2004 Survey, October). However, almost three quarters (74.3%) are Catholic while only 16.7% are Protestant (*Washington Post*/Univision/TRPI 2004 Survey, October). Clearly, these patterns challenge claims that Latinos threaten the nation's core linguistic and religious culture.

Also refuting such claims is the extent to which they support the nation's core political values. There is, for example, no statistical evidence that ethnic attachments alienate Latinos from mainstream society (Dowley & Silver 2000). More noteworthy is that regardless of whether they are native or foreign born, speak English or have an intense ethnic consciousness, Mexican American citizens, including the naturalized, were at least as patriotic and supportive of core political values such as political tolerance and economic individualism as Anglos (de la Garza et al. 1996).

An additional measure of the linkage between Latino values and the "national interest" is the difference between Latino perspectives of Latin America vs. the United States. A test of two hypotheses, one explaining Hispanic perspectives as a function of cultural ties and the other arguing that Latino perspectives are shaped by socialization in the United States, found strong support for the latter and no support for the former (de la Garza et al. 1997). The study's most noteworthy finding is that, regardless of national origin, Mexican, Cuban and Puerto Rican origin citizens all were much more positively oriented toward the United States than to the region in its entirety or to any specific nation including their country of origin.

This pro-American perspective notwithstanding, there are notable differences between Latino and Anglo foreign policy views. For example, Latino elites have voiced more concern about the environment and world hunger than about military power and the security of our allies (Pachon et al. 2000). More noteworthy is that Hispanics were more likely than Anglos by 56% to 49% to agree the U.S. was responsible for the hatred that motivated the 9/11 attacks (Davis & Silver 2003). This attitude may reflect the historical Latin American view of U.S. foreign policy as arrogant and unsupportive of Latin American well being. Despite this perspective, given that 75% of Latin American immigrants agree there was no justification for the attack (TRPI 2002), it can not be argued that immigrants support anti-American terrorism.

There are fewer differences regarding Latin America. They support the government's goals of strengthening democracy and promoting international trade and investment. It is also noteworthy that the foreign policy preferences of Latino elites run counter to the preferences of Latin American states. A majority support unilateral U.S. responses to problems related to drug trafficking and massive immigration resulting from political turmoil in Mexico, and more than 40% support similar responses to human rights violations in the hemisphere (Pachon et al. 2000). Such American initiatives are anathema to Latin American states.

What is perhaps most noteworthy about Hispanic foreign policy involvement is how little there is (Dominguez 2004). Except for the Cuban American National Foundation, no Latino organization has targeted foreign policy issues (Hakim and Rosales 2000). Although this is slowly changing, as is evident in the institutionalization of the Hispanic Council on International Relations, Latinos are unlikely to engage foreign policy as home country advocates in the foreseeable future. To the contrary, these patterns suggest Latinos:

> may not form a political community with the people of their homeland. They have limited political interest in their homelands. They often think badly of those who govern the countries that they or their ancestors left. They hold different political values from the people in the homeland and do not even favor easier immigration rules for Latin Americans seeking to enter the United States. They typically lack the resources to influence U.S. foreign policy. (Dominguez 2004)

Critics like Huntington also argue that trans-nationalism encourages immigrants to retain home country ties rather than incorporate into American society. By slowing the acquisition of English and the learning of mainstream social and political values, maintaining these ties stimulates the willingness of Latino immigrants to become home-country lobbyists.

Central to this process are home town associations (HTAs) which immigrants initially established to create social spaces for others from the same community of origin to come together to reinforce old country ties. This quickly led to HTA sponsored projects such as improving local water systems or building sports arenas which were intended to improve conditions in communities of origin. Home country governments quickly moved to assist in the establishment of HTAs and by creating matching funds programs to help HTAs finance more and bigger projects (de la Garza and Hazam 2003). Perhaps the major reason officials promote these ties is that they expect stronger relations will insure emigrants will continue to remit funds to the families they left behind (Leiken 2000, 16). This flow of dollars is essential to the economic stability of Mexico, El Salvador and other countries (Cortina and de la Garza 2004).

Mexican officials, and to a lesser degree officials from Central American and Caribbean countries, are also pursuing this relationship because of the strongly held view that HTAs may be used to mobilize emigrants into pro-country of origin lobbyists. Mexican officials are circumspect about articulating this goal, but they have voiced it clearly in meetings with me personally and at meetings with Mexican American leaders (de la Garza 1997, 74). Such outreach, according to one analyst, should be seen as a part of the broader *acercamiento* characterizing contemporary U.S.-Mexico relations that includes NAFTA, increased trade and investment and expanded intergovernmental cooperation on a wide variety of issues (Leiken 2000).

To date, however, HTAs have not developed into home country lobbyists, and there is no sign they will. To the contrary, HTAs and other types of immigrant associations "are primarily concerned with facilitating immigrants' incorporation into the United States political system" (de la Garza and Hazan 2003, iii). Thus, HTAs promote naturalization, offer English courses and seminars on topics such as small business development and college counseling. The president of an HTA federation[1] explained:

> We have to say to people, "become citizens, you're not betraying your nation, you keep your roots inside of yourselves and nobody can take your roots away, no one can change our love for where we were born. But think about your kin and your grandchildren, they are the ones who need you to pave the way so that they don't have so many problems in the future, especially the ones who were born here, they're not going to live in Mexico." (Leiken 2000, 22)

Illustrative of the pattern of HTA activities is the extent to which Latino immigrants in general are linked to the home country. Despite highly publicized celebrations on Mexican Independence Day (September 15), and the festivities associated with *Cinco de Mayo*, and New York City's October 12 Dia de la Raza parade in which Latino communities of all nationalities participate, as Table 4 illustrates, few Latino immigrants regularly participate in social or cultural activities linking them to the home country.

Additionally, immigrants are not remitting in accord with governmental objectives. Specifically, they have essentially rejected governmental efforts to remit in support of economic development projects. Instead, approximately

Table 4
Hispanic Immigrant Participation in Home Country Focused Social and Cultural Activities since Immigration

	Mexicans	*Salvadorans*	*Dominicans*
Attended cultural or educational event related to home country	26.60%	23.10%	43.90%
Been a member of organization promoting cultural ties between US and home country	6.70%	5.60%	12.80%
Been a member of organization of people from community of origin	8.50%	7.80%	22.60%
Sought assistance from country of origin embassy or consulate	6%	5%	3%

Source: DeSipio, 2003.

80 percent remit exclusively to support their families. Another 31 percent send money for familial purposes and community projects such as improving local parks, athletic fields and water systems (Cortina and de la Garza 2004). Virtually none send money explicitly to support government sponsored economic development projects.

While money sent for familial purposes are examples of transnational ties, they are not indicative of the kinds of linkages with home country governments that trouble Huntington or that those governments are pursuing. That is, such remittances target or contribute to the benefit of society per se. The societal impact is indirect in that these monies alleviate extreme poverty among remitters' family members. Society also benefits when remittance recipients use these funds to acquire private medical attention. However valuable they are to specific families, thus, these funds do not qualify as indicators of immigrant political ties to the home country.

Immigrants are also disdainful of involvement with home country political issues, as Table 5 illustrates.

Further illustrating low levels of involvement with home country politics is that immigrants are substantially more likely to be concerned about U.S. issues than about issues in their country of origin (Table 6).

Table 5
Hispanic Immigrant Participation in Home Country Focused Political Activities since Immigration

	Mexico	Salvadorans	Dominicans
Followed home country politics in Spanish media	63.60%	48%	67.10%
Voted in home country	9.50%	8.50%	15.00%
Contributed money to political candidate	2.00%	2.80%	6.30%
Attended rally in U.S. for home country candidate or party	2.70%	2.30%	17.30%
Contacted by home country to participate in home country affairs	3.00%	1.80%	11.60%

Source: DeSipio, 2003.

Table 6
Focus of Political Concern: US or Home Country

	Registered Citizens	Not Registered Citizens	Non-Citizens
More concerned with U.S.	79.00%	76.00%	57.00%
Equally concerned with both	11.00%	8.00%	20.00%
More concerned with home country	6.00%	6.00%	14.00%

Source: Pew Hispanic Center, 2004.

The type of activities which HTAs emphasize combined with the limited extent to which immigrants involve themselves with home country affairs suggests that accusations claiming Latinos remain apart from U.S. society because they remain committed to their countries of origin are groundless. It is true, however, that few immigrants actively engage U.S. society (Figure 1).

This could be explained by factors such as low socioeconomic status, being undocumented and a general fear of discrimination, all of which could be ameliorated by changes in governmental policies. Thus, there is no basis for viewing immigrants as political threats because of their home country ties. Instead, it is more useful to view them as potential citizens who, under improved circumstances, would be an asset to society and the polity.

Another charge implicitly leveled by Huntington and others is that Hispanics will unite into a cohesive voting bloc that will advance its own interests at the nation's expense. As was true in 1990 (de la Garza et al. 1992) in 2004 Latinos do not behave as a political group united by ethnicity. Latinos do not see themselves as united politically (Pew Hispanic Center 2004) and they report that they will not vote for a candidate because of shared ethnicity unless the Latino and non-Latino candidate are similarly qualified (Pew Hispanic Center 2004; de la Garza et al. 1992). Analyses of their voting behavior confirm these claims (Michelson 2002).

Figure 1
U.S. Political Participation, Citizens and Legal Residents

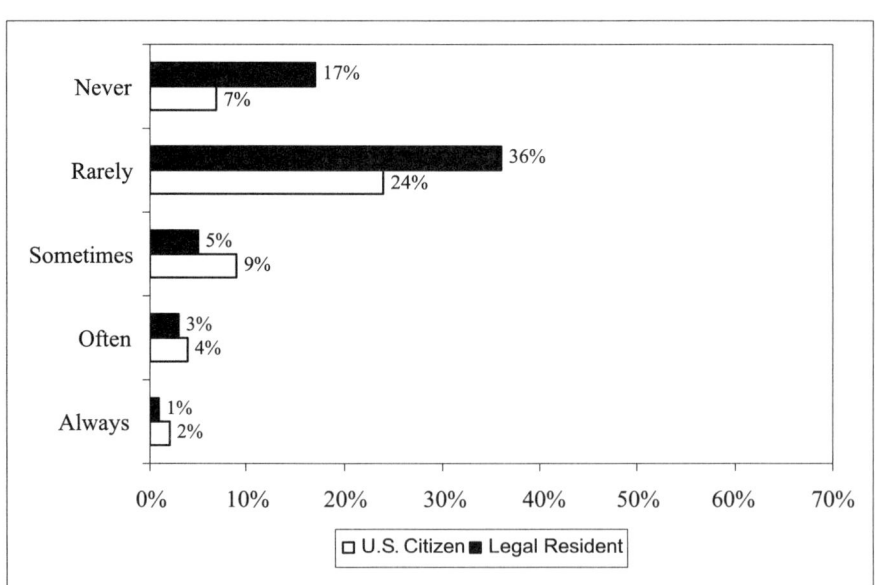

Source: TRPI 2002 Survey of Immigrant Political and Civic Activities.

IMMIGRANTS AND THE ECONOMY

The positive economic impact of immigration is well established. Public perceptions to the contrary notwithstanding, the National Research Council reports that immigrants do not displace American workers, nor do they lower wages, and that overall they contribute between $1–10 billion dollars to the economy annually (Smith and Edmonston 1997). From an economic perspective, therefore, if the nation accepted more immigrants, it would enjoy even greater benefits (Chang 2005).

Immigration provides workers for low level jobs that the native born are unwilling to take at wages that fall well below what native workers demand. They are such a vital part of the service sector that the nation's major cities would screech to a halt as parents rearrange work schedules to care for their children, restaurants can not open because of the absence of waiters, cooks and dishwashers, and cities forgo garbage collection. The general disruption that the absence of immigrants would cause is well illustrated in the recently released satirical film "A Day without Mexicans."

So much attention is given to lower end workers that the economic value Latino immigrants contribute through their roles in high end professions such as medicine is usually overlooked. Indeed, personal experience and observations suggest that the quality, cost and availability of medical services in Houston, Miami and New York would change substantially but for the presence of Latin American doctors. Furthermore, many of these professionals enrich the nation's medical services at extremely low cost because they come with medical degrees.

Latino immigrants also contribute to the economy in conventional ways. Unless employers keep them off the books, they pay taxes and contribute to social security, and there is widespread agreement that their contributions are essential to the maintenance of the social security system (Rosenbaum and Toner 2005; Greenspan 2004).

Thanks to their cultural knowledge, immigrants also benefit the nation by providing an advantage in gaining access to foreign financial and commercial markets. A key segment of this arena is the fees generated by the multi-billion remittance industry. In California alone, fees generated by remittances to Mexico total $338 million (Cortina et al. 2004). These fees generate jobs and provide profits to stockholders which could be used for additional investments. Relatedly, in addition to the role they play as domestic consumers, Hispanic immigrants enhance the nation's commercial sector by developing export markets for U.S. retailers with outlets in immigrants' countries of origin. The appliances purchased from these firms are paid for in the U.S. and picked up by relatives from outlets in the home country. Cultural knowledge also contributes to the development of ubiquitous ethnic markets that provide jobs as well as group-specific products for ethnic and non-ethnic clients.

It is argued, nonetheless, that immigrants drain resources because they consume more in social services than they pay in taxes. This claim is based on the cost of educating immigrant children or the U.S. born children of immigrants.

Even if the latter are included in the analysis, which is not normally the case, this claim is static rather than dynamic. That is, it does not take the long term tax benefits that result from educating these children. As the National Research Council reports show, when these are considered, immigrant contributions to the economy exceed the value of services they utilize.

CONCLUSION

Latino immigrants have inserted themselves into the fabric of the nation. They are influencing every facet of popular culture from music, to food, to art to sports. These influences are so ubiquitous and so established that it is no exaggeration to suggest that they have Latinized American culture in the same way that Italians and Irish, to name but two groups, did historically.

Like those immigrants, Latinos are enriching the nation as they embrace and alter its cultural core.

Latinos, however, have the potential to shape the cultural future more profoundly than did the Italians and Irish. Unlike either of those, large and growing Latino communities are nationally dispersed. This means that while St. Patrick's Day celebrations have long been concentrated in the Northeast, *Cinco de Mayo* is celebrated from Seattle to New York. Also, because of continuous immigration, Spanish will become the nation's second language. This will influence how we speak, our literature, and the legitimacy of being bilingual, an attribute the nation has historically shunned. No other immigrant group has so expanded the nation's cultural horizon.

There is also a consensus regarding Hispanic immigration's positive impact on the economy. Not only do they fill the service jobs that keep the nation running, they do so at rates that make our economy relatively competitive. Additionally, they are tax payers, real estate investors and consumers. Less recognized is their substantial contribution to the financial world via the fees they pay for remittances. Their development of ethnic enclaves enables them to contribute significantly to job creation. Finally, as highly trained professionals in medicine and other fields, they add valuable resources to the economy at bargain prices. In short, Latino immigrants are an essential part of the nation's economy.

Politically, the Latino contribution is less tangible. Like previous immigrants, the values they bring with are not transformative of the polity. Nonetheless, they so believe in the core political values of the nation that they invigorate our faith in the American dream. Nothing about their values or attitudes supports claims that they undermine the polity's foundation. To the contrary, they believe in political tolerance, democracy and the common good at levels at least as high as those of Anglos. While they differ regarding aspects of foreign policies, their disagreements are no more noteworthy than those of numerous interest groups including non-Hispanic ethnic lobbies.

Regrettably, as recent elections have shown, not all Americans cherish democratic values. To the extent that they help renew the nation's faith in itself and the values on which the nation was founded, Latinos will improve the polity.

NOTE

I would like to thank Jeronimo Cortina, Research Associate, Tomás Rivera Policy Institute, for his assistance in preparing this paper.

1. Federations are state or national level associations of local HTAs.

REFERENCES

Chang, Howard F. "Report on International Migration." Paper presented at the Columbia University Global Colloquium on International Migration and Academic Freedom, Columbia University in the City of New York, January 18–19, 2005.

Cortina, Jeronimo, and Rodolfo O. de la Garza. "Immigrant Remitting Behavior and Its Developmental Consequences for Mexico and El Salvador." Edited by Andrea Gutierrez. Los Angeles: Tomás Rivera Policy Institute, 2004.

Cortina, Jeronimo, Rodolfo de la Garza, Sandra Bejarano, and Andrew Weiner. "The Economic Impact of the Mexico-California Relationship." Los Angeles: Tomás Rivera Policy Institute, 2004.

Davis, Darren W., and Brian D. Silver. *Americans' Perceptions of the Causes of Terrorism: Why Do They Hate Us?* Department of Political Science Michigan State University, 2003 [cited August 2003]. Available from http://www.msu.edu/user/bsilver/Roots March25-Final.pdf.

de la Garza, Rodolfo O., Louis DeSipio, F. Chris Garcia, John Garcia, and Angelo Falcon. *Latino Voices: Mexican, Puerto Rican, and Cuban Perspectives on American Politics.* Boulder: Westview Press, 1992

de la Garza, Rodolfo O., Angelo Falcon, and F. Chris Garcia. "Will the Real Americans Please Stand Up: Anglo and Mexican-American Support of Core American Political Values." *American Journal of Political Science* 40, no. 2 (1996): 335–51.

de la Garza, Rodolfo O., and Myriam Hazan. "Looking Backward, Moving Forward: Mexican Organizations in the U.S. as Agents of Incorporation and Dissociation," 70. Claremont, CA: Tomás Rivera Policy Institute, 2003.

de la Garza, Rodolfo O., Jerome Hernandez, Angelo Falcon, F. Chris Garcia, and John A. Garcia. "Mexican, Puerto Rican, and Cuban Foreign Policy Perspectives: A Test of Competing Explanations." In *Pursuing Power: Latinos and the Political System,* edited by F. Chris Garcia, 401–26. Notre Dame, Ind.: University of Notre Dame Press, 1997.

DeSipio, Louis, Harry Pachon, Rodolfo de la Garza, and Jongho Lee. "Immigrant Politics at Home and Abroad: How Latino Immigrants Engage the Politics of Their Home Communities and the United States." Los Angeles, CA: Tomás Rivera Policy Institute, 2003.

Dominguez, Jorge. "Latinos and U.S. Foreign Policy." Paper Commissioned by The Tomás Rivera Policy Institute, 2004.

Dowley, Kathleen M., and Brian D. Silver. "Subnational and National Loyalty: Cross-National Comparisons." *International Journal of Public Opinion Research* 12 (2000): 357–71.

Greenspan, Alan. "Remarks by Chairman Alan Greenspan." Paper presented at the Symposium sponsored by the Federal Reserve Bank of Kansas City, Jackson Hole, August 27, 2004.

Hakim, Peter, and Carlos A. Rosales. "The Latino Foreign Policy Lobby." In *Latinos and U.S. Foreign Policy: Representing the "Homeland"?* edited by Rodolfo O. de la Garza and Harry Pachon, 133–36. Lanham, Md.; Oxford: Rowman & Littlefield Publishers, 2000.

Huntington, Samuel P. *Who Are We? The Challenges to America's National Identity.* New York: Simon & Schuster, 2004.

Leiken, Robert S. "The Melting Border: Mexico and Mexican Communities in the United States." Washington, DC: Center for Equal Opportunity, 2000.

Michelson, Melissa R. "Competing Vote Cues and the Authenticity of Representation: Latino Support for Anglo Democrats and Latino Republicans." Paper presented at the Annual Conference of Midwest Political Science Association, Chicago, Il, April 25–28, 2002.

New York City Department of City Planning Population Division. "The Newest New Yorkers." New York: New York City Government, 2005.

Pachon, Harry, Rodolfo O. de la Garza, and Adrian Pantoja. "Foreign Policy Perspectives of Hispanic Elites." In *Latinos and U.S. Foreign Policy: Representing the "Homeland"?* edited by Rodolfo O. de la Garza and Harry Pachon, 21–42. Lanham, Md.; Oxford: Rowman & Littlefield Publishers, 2000.

Pew Hispanic Center. "2002 National Survey of Latinos." The Pew Hispanic Center/Kaiser Family Foundation, 2002.

Pew Hispanic Center. "2004 National Survey of Latinos: Politics and Civic Participation." The Pew Hispanic Center/Kaiser Family Foundation, 2004.

Rosenbaum, David E., and Robin Toner. "To Social Security Debate, Add Variable: Immigration." *The New York Times,* Wednesday, February 16, 2005, A18.

Schlesinger, Arthur Meier. *The Disuniting of America.* New York: Norton, 1992.

Smith, James P., and Barry Edmonston, eds. *The New Americans: Economic, Demographic, and Fiscal Effects of Immigration, Panel on the Demographic and Economic Impacts of Immigration.* Washington: National Research Council, 1997.

Stevens, Gillian. "Immigration, Emigration, Language Acquisition, and the English Language Proficiency of Immigrants in the U.S." In *Immigration and Ethnicity: The Integration of America's Newest Arrivals,* edited by Barry Edmonston and Jeffrey Passel, 163–86. Washington, DC: The Urban Institute Press, 1994.

Tomás Rivera Policy Institute. "Survey of Immigrant Political and Civic Activities." 2002.

Tomás Rivera Policy Institute. "*Washington Post*/Univision/TRPI Pre-Election Survey of Latino Registered Voters October 2004." 2004.

Proposition 187: Misrepresenting Immigrants and Immigration

Otto Santa Ana

The textbooks say the United States is a nation of immigrants. However, while schoolchildren are steeped in the pageantry of American history, they seldom learn to appreciate the depth of its reprehensible acts and persistent inequities. A case in point is the history of Mexican Americans. For most, it is news that in 1846, when President James Polk initiated the U.S.–Mexican War, between 75,000 and 100,000 Mexicans were already living in the Southwest,[1] including my father's family.

The virulent racism with which nineteenth-century white Americans elevated themselves above all other people also infected relations with Mexicans, leading to the view that the Southwest was rightfully granted to white America, and that its Mexican residents were a contemptible mongrel breed.[2] Today's Americans generally are not cognizant that the U.S.–Mexican War ended with the Treaty of Guadalupe Hidalgo, which guaranteed language, property, and citizenship rights to the Spanish-speaking residents of this territory.[3] Moreover, from its establishment in 1848 and on through the twentieth century, the new border between Mexico and the United States was an arbitrary and largely vain restraint on the historic and prehistoric free movement of people north and south.[4] Thus it is particularly painful to have witnessed the continuing mistreatment of Mexicans and Mexican Americans in the twentieth century.

In spite of its overwhelmingly immigrant origin and its self-satisfied adulation of the immigrants' contribution to its strength and wealth, the United States maintains a Janus-faced attitude of self-interest toward immigrants. When the country is in the growth part of the economic cycle, cheap labor is at a premium. During these times, U.S. commerce promotes the virtues of America and its "American Dream" of unbounded opportunity for the hardest worker, no matter who and from what circumstances. When native-born Americans scorn essential labor, workers from other countries are recruited for the lowest-paid and least desirable work. The immigrants come in great

---

From *Brown Tide Rising: Metaphors of Latinos in Contemporary American Public Discourse* by Otto Santa Ana, Copyright © 2002. By permission of the University of Texas Press.

numbers, do the work, dream the Dream, and honor their end of the bargain. For example, from 1880 to 1920, with a population much less than 100 million, the United States accepted 24 million immigrants.[5]

However, as the economic cycle wanes, Janus's second face is manifest toward immigrants and their children. Then the immigrant is regaled as a menace. Evidence for this attitude abounds in American history. For example, between 1921 and 1924 Congress set up a restrictive immigration quota system which disfavored immigrants from Eastern and Southern Europe as well as Asia and Latin America.[6] These attitudes have also turned punitive. Between 1929 and 1935 authorities mobilized the U.S. military to force the repatriation of 500,000 Mexican immigrants and their U.S.-born children,[7] including my mother.

A post–World War II economic upswing in California did not waver for forty-five years. During that time immigrants were recruited by business and industry to power an unparalleled period of economic growth. Middle-class families also employed immigrants to do the gardening, to clean their homes, and to tend their children. With immigrant labor, the middle class achieved a higher standard of living than they otherwise could afford. Today it is rare for middle-class women in Los Angeles to do their own nails, or for suburban homeowners to cut their own lawns on Saturday morning.

However, with the end of the Cold War in 1989, the expansion period of California's military-based economy also came to a close. Over 830,000 jobs were lost between 1990 and 1993, primarily in the defense sector. A ripple effect from the defense industry layoffs and cut-downs was felt throughout the economy. The economic recession led as well to reductions in state and local governmental incomes and created budgetary shortfalls.[8]

The demographic profile of California has also changed in the last decades, becoming decidedly less "Teutonic"[9] and more multiethnic. While there was a general increase of the proportion of foreign-born residents in the United States from 5 percent in 1970 to 8 percent in 1990, these figures (the highest since 1930) belie a skewed distribution of immigrant residence. Sikhs, Mexicans, and Armenians are not settling in Idaho. Seventy-five percent of foreign-born residents settle in seven states, with California at the top of the list. Nearly 25 percent of all documented immigrants settled in California during the decade of the 1980s. And overall, California's foreign-born population was about 22 percent of the population in the 1990s; in Los Angeles County it was 33 percent. Los Angeles Unified School District officially listed more than seventy-five mother tongues spoken in its kindergartens. While a plethora of cultures is represented, 85 percent of documented immigration during the 1980s was from Asia and Latin America. Adding to an already large population of Mexican-origin citizens, the continued browning of California is inevitable. Latinos now make up over 30 percent of the population of the state. They are projected to become a majority by 2040.[10] In Los Angeles the tendency is more pronounced, since Latinos are projected to be the majority by 2007. For Californians brought up with the unspoken belief that American society means a preeminently Anglo-American culture, these demographic changes have been unnerving.

The first nativist reaction to this sense of a changing social order in the 1990s was Proposition 187. This initiative was overwhelmingly passed by the

California electorate even though its provisions had been denounced throughout the campaign as unconstitutional. Indeed, it was enjoined by the courts within hours of its enactment. While the laws of the land already dictated sanctions against employers utilizing the labor of undocumented immigrant workers, and the federal government provided for a policing body, the Border Patrol, to apprehend and deport such immigrants, Proposition 187 was designed to supersede and radicalize federal law. It would have denied to undocumented immigrants a range of public benefits, including education and nonemergency health care. It would also have made school administrators, health care workers, social service personnel, police, and other state employees responsible for determining the residence status of any "apparently illegal alien" (to use the controversial phrasing of the referendum) among their clients and for notifying the Immigration and Naturalization Service of suspected undocumented immigrants for deportation.

This article presents the findings of an empirical analysis of the public discourse metaphors in California during the Proposition 187 period. Over one hundred *Los Angeles Times* articles were published on Proposition 187, as indexed by the commercial distributor of a CD-ROM version of the newspaper. All of these were included in this study. Two issues stood out for the voters and general public: immigration, namely, the demographic process; and immigrants themselves. Consequently, the public discourse on these semantic domains was examined in terms of metaphor use, and will be presented as follows.

In Section 1, the metaphors for IMMIGRATION are described. One dominant metaphor will be discussed more fully than, and separately from, other less prevalent metaphors. Its ontology will be specified, namely, the semantic notions that are imposed on the concept IMMIGRATION by means of the dominant semantic source domain. In Section 2, the context for these immigration metaphors will be presented. This pattern of metaphors, when used, invokes a narrative of the relationship of immigration to the nation. A rendition of the narrative will be presented.

The metaphorization of IMMIGRANT in public discourse is presented in Section 3, beginning with a discussion of the dominant metaphor, its ontology, and associated narrative, followed by Section 4, which lays out the patterning of other metaphors for immigrants in public discourse. In order to provide further support for the study, in Section 5 a formidable test is carried out to probe whether or not these metaphors are as demeaning and unique as the findings suggest. Section 6 provides a comparison of the present findings to other studies of the representations of Latinos during the Proposition 187 campaign, while Section 7 discusses the wider implications of these metaphors.

SECTION 1: IMMIGRATION AS DANGEROUS WATERS

One of the two key notions debated during the campaigns for and against Proposition 187 was the demographic process of the movement of people, IMMIGRATION. As a concept at the heart of the political contest, this notion

Table 7
IMMIGRATION Metaphors Published during the Proposition 187 Campaign

Source Domain	Type	Totals	Percentages
DANGEROUS WATERS, e.g., *floods, tide*	dominant	113	58.2
WAR, e.g., *invasion, takeover*	secondary	45	23.2
ANIMAL, e.g., *curbing illegal immigration*		17	8.8
BODY, e.g., *disease, burden*		6	3.1
various metaphors, e.g., AIR, WEED, CRIMINAL, MACHINE, FIRE, *etc.*	occasional	13	6.7
	TOTAL	194	100

Source: 116 *Los Angeles Times* articles published June 1992–December 1994. The list accounts for immigration metaphors, i.e., the demographic process. It excludes metaphors that target immigrants as people.

was constantly being referred to in the public discourse of the period, and was frequently metaphorized. This metaphorization reveals the worldview that is promulgated in public discourse. In this section the metaphors that construct and reinforce commonly held views of immigration will be displayed. Although there is overlap of the discourse on immigration and on immigrants, discussion of the people themselves will be undertaken in Section 3.

As will be noted in Table 7, there are dominant, secondary, and occasional metaphors. These are three informal groupings of semantic source domains found in the data, combining all instances of closely related semantic domains under a single heading. The dominant metaphor class is composed of scores of textual instances of metaphor with a similar semantic source domain that occur relatively frequently and appear in a great variety of forms. In the *Los Angeles Times* data sampled, the dominant metaphor comprises the greatest proportion of all instances of metaphors characterizing immigration. The demographic process of immigration to the United States is conceptualized in terms of dangerous moving water. Before launching into a full examination of the dominant public discourse metaphor for immigration, DANGEROUS WATERS, secondary metaphors and those which occur on occasion in our Proposition 187 database will be presented.

SECONDARY METAPHORS

For the moment, discussion of the dominant metaphor will be deferred. Instances of secondary source domains appear much less frequently, and with less variety of expression, than the dominant metaphor used to characterize immigration. One such metaphor for immigrants is IMMIGRATION AS INVASION.

Still, these secondary metaphors appear with appreciable frequency. Over 20 percent of IMMIGRATION metaphors have a martial source domain:

1. Some believe that Wilson, by filing a lawsuit against the federal government and arguing that illegal immigration is tantamount to a **foreign invasion,** has made a whipping boy of migrants. (September 27, 1994, A3)
2. "People are saying, 'I don't like this **Third World takeover,'"** said Guy Weddington McCreary, a North Hollywood Chamber of Commerce member favoring the initiative. "It is literally an **invasion** and very upsetting." (September 17, 1994, B3)
3. **"invasion"** of illegal immigrants is causing economic hardship and eroding lifestyles of U.S. citizens and authorized immigrants (October 30, 1994, A1)
4. Oft-voiced fears that California was under **"invasion"** spawned a loose network of community-based groups. (November 9, 1994, A1)
5. "I don't want us to look like that country. If we continue this **alien invasion,** we will be like Mexico." (October 11, 1996, A3)
6. "This is a **state of siege** in California," says an observer from Washington, immigration expert Demetrios Papademetriou of the Carnegie Endowment for International Peace. (September 6, 1993, A1)

The features structuring the semantic domain of INVASION are a subset of the domain of WAR. An invasion is an organized attack by armed forces with the objective of taking over a region or country. One paradigmatic invasion is the Japanese Empire's 1937 invasion of China. This invasion included the infamous "Rape of Nanking," the Chinese capital city, in which 300,000 civilians were raped, murdered, or butchered in one year. This was an offensive action to dominate a neighboring country. Another is the key counteroffensive of World War II, the 1948 D-Day invasion of France by the Allied forces under Eisenhower, which had as its objective the liberation of occupied France. These organized actions are rightly considered acts of war. The war metaphor used during the Proposition 187 campaign stresses a violent aggression against America. This metaphor patently ignores the nation's entire immigration experience, which always has been the search for employment and freedom by unarmed and peaceful individuals. The objective of immigrants is not conquest and spoils, but rather industry and enterprise, and the hope of a better life for their children. IMMIGRATION AS INVASION was the least obscure anti-immigrant metaphor in general use, because of its bold disregard of the evidence. Consequently, it was frequently printed in scare quotes and was explicitly rejected at least once in the *Los Angeles Times* database by the advocates for immigrants:

7. "That is not an **armed invasion** coming across." (September 19, 1993, A1)

These metaphors demonstrate the level of anger focused on immigrants by a significant segment of the citizenry; however, much can be made of these blatant anti-immigrant metaphors. Without further discussion we will concentrate on less overt, all the more insidious, metaphors.

Other secondary metaphors in general use indicate other metaphorically structured worldviews or commonplace understandings of immigration, including IMMIGRATION AS DISEASE or AS BURDEN:

8. The report—which...linked illegal immigration to a **host of society's ills**—has been branded by Latino and Asian leaders as insensitive and one-sided. (June 29, 1993, B1)[11]
9. Not stopping or controlling the flow of illegal immigrants because it isn't a magical solution to all of our societal **ills** is not a valid reason for allowing it to continue unchecked. (June 17, 1994, B6)

As is the case with all metaphors, some of the presuppositions of this metaphor have been explicitly drawn out and others remain available for reference.[12] For example, the societal affliction, within the medical model, can be made well with societal remedies.

10. Hernandez also suggested that Umberg's motivation isn't so much to **cure** illegal immigration as it is to make a name for himself. (August 31, 1993, B1)

This metaphor was also contested by the advocates for immigrants during the Proposition 187 campaign:

11. If illegal immigration was a **disease,** Prop. 187 was the **wrong medicine.** (October 26, 1994, A3)

Occasional Metaphors

Occasional metaphors are expressed only once or a few times. They do not seem to be associated with other more commonly used semantic source domains. All the occasional metaphors in the *Los Angeles Times* database are single or rare instances of a source domain.

12. The membership of the Sierra Club is in the midst of an emotional debate about whether to take a public stand on the hot button topic of the day. "It's not as simple as **clean air,** or like pollution, where less is better," said Executive Director Carl Pope. (September 6, 1993, A1)
13. Another confirmation that immigration from Latin America **powered the engine of change** is that 36 percent of North Hollywood households now speak Spanish, up from 19 percent only 10 years earlier. (June 14, 1992, B3)
14. And more than half the respondents said legal immigration, too, should be **pared back.** (September 19, 1993, A1)
15. Most who choose to "ride the snake," however, are **drawn by the same sirens of economic opportunity** that attracted their Cantonese compatriots to California's "Gold Mountain" more than a century ago. (June 13, 1993, Magazine p. 12)

16. "[the task of the] Border Patrol is so great that the addition of even those officers puts them in the position of trying to **fight a forest fire with a squirt gun**," [Governor Pete] Wilson said. (August 12, 1993, A1)

Some of these metaphors may be more difficult to grasp than others. In excerpt 12 the objective of Carl Pope is to move people's views away from a simplistic view of immigration, whereas in excerpt 13 immigration is the fuel for the engine of change.

Dominant Metaphor

While 7 percent of all metaphors are individual characterizations which resist consolidation into a single semantic domain, the majority of textual instances of metaphors on immigration are based in only one semantic domain. The major metaphor for the process of the movement of substantial numbers of human beings to the United States is characterized as IMMIGRATION AS DANGEROUS WATERS. Perhaps it should be restated that to characterize the movement of people as moving water might seem quite natural, but such a formulation of movement of people is not the only possible image that can be employed, as can be noted among the secondary and occasional metaphors. Moreover, strongly negative connotations associated with immigration in particular had decidedly negative implications for the target population. A few instances are listed below:

17. **awash under a brown tide** (October 2, 1994, A3)
18. Like **waves on a beach,** these **human flows** are literally remaking the face of America. (October 14, 1993, A1)
19. **a sea of brown faces** marching through Downtown would only antagonize many voters (October 17, 1994, A1)
20. In April, Gov. Pete Wilson sued the federal government to recover costs associated with illegal immigrants, claiming that they are sapping the state budget, taking jobs from legal residents and **swamping** hospital emergency rooms. (June 12, 1994, A3)
21. **the human surge** (July 5, 1992, A3)
22. **the inexorable flow** (September 22, 1993, A1)

The dangerous waters of immigration come in many forms, *rough seas, treacherous tides, surges*.[13] The DANGEROUS WATERS metaphors do not refer to any aspect of the humanity of the immigrants, except to allude to ethnicity and race. In contrast to such nonhuman metaphors for immigrants, U.S. society is often referred to in human terms. This provides an ironic contrast when these metaphors appear in tandem, as in excerpt 18, which likens the United States to a person who is defaced by an ocean of immigrants.

Within IMMIGRATION AS DANGEROUS WATERS there are clear subcategories. The first is volume, which emphasizes the relative numbers of immigrants. Individuals are lost in the mass sense of these volume terms. The negative connotation is highlighted in the excerpts that contain strong adjectives such as *relentless* and *overwhelming*.

23. the foreigners who have **flooded** into the country (November 10, 1992, World Report p. 1, col. 2)
24. "I thought that it was a waste of time, frankly," [California Governor] Wilson said of [U.S. Senator Robert] Byrd's line of questioning. "What we ought to be doing is focusing on the fact that federal failure continues to provide this **massive flow of illegal immigrants** into my state and the other states." (July 23, 1994, A3)
25. **the relentless flow of immigrants** (May 30, 1993, A5)
26. **an overwhelming flood** of asylum-seekers have put the country in an angry funk (October 1, 1992, A1)

Note that immigration waters are seen to be dangerous, as when coupling an exacerbating adjective to a neutral noun, as with *inexorable flow*. The second subcategory of DANGEROUS WATERS is movement, which emphasizes the direction of waters, primarily northward as from Mexico to the United States. With regard to the destination of the migration, the nation is conceived as a basin or some kind of container and the migration taken to be an inward-flowing stream, in terms such as *influx*.

27. Residents of the San Fernando Valley are increasingly outraged about illegal immigration—if not immigration generally—in the face of economic hard times, growing congestion, widespread crime and a **dramatic influx of Latinos.** (August 1, 1993, A1)
28. **the tide and flow of illegal immigration** (October 26, 1994, A27)
29. Glenn Spencer...says his interest in the subject was sparked about two years ago when he began noticing that an **influx of minorities had flooded the city.** He compiled research and launched a newsletter that he circulated among his neighbors. Ultimately, he formed Valley Citizens Together, but the group changed its name after residents from other parts of Los Angeles wanted to get involved.... When asked what motivates him, Spencer points to the photos of his two blond, blue-eyed grandchildren on the mantel in his orderly living room. "What I'd like to achieve is a little better world for my grandchildren," he said. "I don't want my grandchildren to live in chaos. Isn't that enough?" (November 15, 1994, A1)[14]
30. **the flood of legal and illegal immigrants streaming** into the country (September 7, 1993, A3)

The terms used to characterize the immigration do not describe beneficial and enriching flows, but *dramatic influxes* and *floods* that endanger the country. The third subcategory is the control of dangerous waters. Here the intent to reduce the immigration of undocumented workers pursues a correspondence with the dangerous waters metaphor by describing means by which the waters can be held back, or *stemmed*, which means "to make headway against an adverse tide."

31. an attempt to **stem illegal immigration** (December 22, 1994, B1)

32. the opportunistic criminal element that exploits our **porous borders** (November 27, 1992, A3)
33. On the other hand, [Clinton] warned, if the government is unable to "show some more discipline" in its control of illegal immigration, "I'm afraid the genie out of the bottle will be passion to **shut off legal immigration.**" (August 13, 1993, A1)
34. [The] Executive Director of the Federation for American Immigration Reform...said Clinton's approach is akin to "**trying to dam the Mississippi with toothpicks.**" (September 7, 1993, A1)

Ontology of Immigration as Dangerous Waters

The metaphor labeled IMMIGRATION AS DANGEROUS WATERS is a tightly structured semantic relationship. It is a coupling and mapping of the semantic ontology of DANGEROUS WATERS onto the domain of IMMIGRATION. It establishes semantic associations between the two meaning domains, taking the well-developed framework of everyday knowledge of floods and tides and imposing it on an entirely human activity. In schematic form, the mapping, to wit the ontology of immigration to the United States as dangerous waters, is a four-point relationship as follows:

- Immigration corresponds to moving waters.
- America is a landmass or other entity such as a house that is subject to flooding.
- Greater immigration corresponds to an increased threat to America.
- America's vulnerability to flooding corresponds to its susceptibility to change.

Some of the pertinent everyday understandings of this source metaphor, moving water, will be explicitly elaborated in order to present the elements of the source domain that are reinforced with each repetition of the metaphor. These semantic associations obscure or pass over some aspects of the target domain as they highlight others. In the absence of alternative metaphoric imagery, such highlighted features of the source domain, DANGEROUS WATERS, are taken as natural features of the target domain, IMMIGRATION.

Moving water is a fluid. Above all other characteristics, fluids are normally understood and measured in terms of volume and mass, not units. They are most often named with mass nouns, such as *water, milk,* or *beer.*[15] Greater amounts of a fluid are registered in terms of volume, not larger numbers of individuals. The everyday use of such noncount words reflects a motile energy. Water moves, and when placed under pressure cannot be compressed, but forces its way or is channeled in some direction. This dynamism implies kinetic and hydraulic power, and control of the movement of water also requires power. There are naturally occurring masses of waters, geophysical bodies such as streams, rivers, ponds, lakes, and oceans, as well as formations created by humans such as channels and reservoirs. With most naturally occurring and all human-made formations, human power and control are involved. The control of water varies from total mastery, such as when people shut off a kitchen faucet, to partial control, as in a hydroelectric dam. Greater volume and movement of water imply greater need for safeguards and controls, and more powerful human agency to control the water (which of course is not a human force). Insufficient human control of the kinetic energy pent up in volumes of water can lead to flooding and other ravages.

The main effect of invoking the DANGEROUS WATERS semantic domain to characterize the IMMIGRATION domain is to transform aggregates of individuals into an undifferentiated mass quantity. Immigrants are not merely described in terms of a mass noun; they are transfigured. The demographic process, immigration, is also vested with potential kinetic energy that is released in its movement, just as when water is commonly discussed. This misleading association is established by the metaphor. Further, salient features of the human immigration process are omitted with this metaphor. At its most simplistic yet still acceptable association, the potency of workers is in their labor, which is just one of a number of aspects of immigration entirely passed over by the IMMIGRATION AS DANGEROUS WATERS metaphor.

For investigators working within cognitive metaphor theory, metaphors have an "inherent logic."[16] In the case of IMMIGRATION AS DANGEROUS WATERS, three weighty presuppositions will be pointed out. These associations are inherited from WATER, the semantic source domain, but are entirely inappropriate characterizations of the demographic process of immigration. Since people conventionally talk about immigration using this metaphor, the presuppositions are often taken as given and overlooked. Since the power of metaphor increases with repetition of such implicit, but unnatural, associations, it is important to point them out. First, by way of the IMMIGRATION AS DANGEROUS WATERS metaphor, aggregates of human beings are reduced to or remade into an undifferentiated quantity that is not human. Second, as this mass moves from one contained space to another, some sort of kinetic energy is released. The contained space referred to is California, the United States, Los Angeles, or other polities. Recall that political entities are not inherently a contained finite space. Third, such movements are inherently powerful, and if not controlled, they are dangerous.

In excerpts 17–34, provided above, the vocabulary of dynamic bodies of water and their movement includes: *tide, sea, flood, influx, flow, waves, drowning, dams, porous, stem,* and *shut off,* to which we can add multiple instances of *swell/ing, absorb, funnel, surge/ing, pour/ing, stream/ing, swamp, pool,* and *safety valve,* among other water terms from the Los Angeles Times database.

IMPLICATIONS OF THE METAPHOR

The implications of this metaphor are extensive. Treating immigration as dangerous waters conceals the individuality of the immigrants' lives and their humanity. In their place a frightening scenario of uncontrolled movements of water can be played out with *devastating floods* and *inundating surges* of brown faces.

The impending flood is taken to be washing away something basic to America. What the anti-immigration advocates initially claimed is that immigrants were an economic threat to the United States and California. However, no presuppositions or entailments built into the DANGEROUS WATERS metaphor imply economics. Consequently the impact of the metaphor does not center on commonsense understandings of the U.S. economy. The threat constructed by DANGEROUS WATERS is cultural.

To make this point it may be useful to compare the implied associations of the frequently invoked *flood* metaphor to other metaphors that have unmistakable economic implications. Compare a metaphor that was often found in the database, *immigration as a burden*. Such metaphors clearly refer to the economic state as human body. If the threat felt by the public was principally a matter of economics, as is often taken to be the case by pundits, one would expect that the dominant metaphor in the public discourse on immigration would reinforce a fiscal message. Yet nearly 60 percent of the metaphors in the public discourse on immigration were DANGEROUS WATERS, while less than 5 percent were BURDEN metaphors. By this measure, although the 1990–1993 recession was the catalyst that initiated the xenophobic animus of the decade, the public discourse metaphors of the time did not have a fiscal focus.

Again, immigrants supply the cheap labor to maintain personal living standards that were higher than otherwise attainable for the average Californian, while at the same time sustaining labor-intensive industries, such as garment manufacturing and certain agribusiness concerns, in an increasingly postindustrial state economy. Moreover, there were counterindications to Governor Wilson's warnings. He repeatedly stated during his reelection campaign that California faced economic disaster, based primarily on $3 billion in purported costs incurred yearly by the state due to immigration. Wilson's claims proved grossly overstated. Five years later, Wilson supervised the largest budgetary surplus in California history, over $4.4 billion.[17] Neither the deficit nor the surplus was due in large part to immigrant labor.

Instead of budgetary issues, the principal signal that DANGEROUS WATERS expresses is cultural alarm. The fear is that the *rising brown tide* will wash away Anglo-American cultural dominance. The panic expressed in DANGEROUS WATERS metaphors reflecting the perceived threat to Anglo-American hegemony is also articulated by the overtly anti-immigrant IMMIGRATION AS INVASION metaphor. Together, DANGEROUS WATERS and INVASION account for over 80 percent of all metaphors expressed in public discourse on immigration. Hence the relative absence of anomaly in the ready references to the American "complexion," as in excerpt 18, *these human flows are remaking the face of America*, and to the Californian economic body in excerpt 35, below:

> 35. Councilwoman Joyce C. Nicholson said illegal immigration is a serious problem and "the state of California is **drowning** in it." (September 17, 1994, B2)

In this excerpt, while the explicit complaint is economic, the metaphor invokes the state as a person drowning in a body of water representing immigration. During the anti-immigrant period, it was considered above-board to critique immigration on economic terms. However, the most frequent metaphors appearing in public discourse did not refer to fiscal arguments. As seen in this excerpt, there is more implied than a metaphorical reference to state finances. Thus in this excerpt the Los Angeles councilwoman openly called for economic relief, while metaphorically warning her constituency about the cultural threat that immigration seemingly posed. It was common to talk explicitly about the economy, all the while invoking the ostensible danger to Anglo-American cultural hegemony by the use of the DANGEROUS WATERS metaphor.[18]

Since only a trickle of water can be enough to signal an impending flood, warnings about *rising brown tides* are apt metaphors to inspire fear. All other considerations aside, the hardworking, family-oriented immigrant who believes in the American Dream was concealed with the DANGEROUS WATERS metaphor. This allowed California voters to remain comfortable in their daily interactions with the individual immigrant worker, part of an important workforce in the economy, while feeling justified in supporting the referendum and voting to end the only-apparent menace to the social order.

NARRATIVE OF IMMIGRATION AS DANGEROUS WATERS

A narrative of the dominant metaphor can also be constructed in which its principal presuppositions and social context are made explicit.[19] This metaphor narrative of immigration to the United States is based on the preceding ontological mapping, which, in cognitive semantic terms, established associations between the semantic domains of DANGEROUS WATERS and IMMIGRATION, as well as with the NATION AS HOUSE metaphor we will discuss presently.

> A flood of immigrants is flowing into the land or house of America. In controlled quantities, America can either channel and absorb the influx unchanged. Because of the enormous volume of these floodwaters, America will be inundated with a sea of people unlike Anglo-Americans. Anglo-America will be engulfed and dispossessed.

The narrative of immigration to the United States is invoked, and its ideological content reinforced, with each repetition of the metaphor. This constitutes the pattern of social inference on—that is to say, the prevalent way to think about—immigration.

NATION AS HOUSE

Metaphors do not make sense in isolation. This is the case for poetic metaphor.[20] This is also the case with conventional metaphors that give structure to and reinforce the generally held worldview of U.S. society. These immigration metaphors are comprehensible, as are all metaphors, because they are woven layer upon layer in webs of semantic associations, starting with foundational metaphors that give structure to higher-level ones.[21] This web of associations and presuppositions constitutes the basis for a semantically congruent understanding of the world.

Truly original metaphors, such as IMMIGRATION AS TURTLE FOOD or AS RAINFOREST, fail to make sense because few if any conventional semantic associations can be pressed into service to edify the target domain, IMMIGRATION. Moreover, since these novel metaphors are not woven into the total web of customary metaphoric associations, the link between the source and target semantic domains seems abnormal. The technical semantic term is *anomalous*. Its etymological meaning, "abnormal," highlights the contingent (non-natural) and conventionalized (learned and reinforced to the point of being naturalized) character of everyday semantic mappings.

Thus the IMMIGRATION AS DANGEROUS WATERS, AS INVASION, and AS BAD WEATHER metaphors, in order to be comprehensible in public discourse on immigration, must be associated with some compatible metaphor for the nation. We turn now to one of these metaphors, NATION AS HOUSE, one of the two most productive metaphors for the United States, in order to demonstrate its arbitrary and contingent, non-natural associations. NATION AS HOUSE is also used to refer to other political entities, such as the state of California. It is invoked in many of the preceding excerpts that have been provided. A few more of these include:

36. With recent immigration reforms proposed by President Clinton, the governor and other political leaders, the issue has moved to the **nation's front burner** and it looms as an explosive topic for debate in the 1994 elections. (August 22, 1993, A1)
37. The fantasy of Proposition 187 supporters seems to be that once California is **cleansed** of its illegal menace, welfare recipients can be coerced into the fields. (October 2, 1994, A3)
38. "I understand the principles that our country was **built on,** but **our house is pretty raggedy** and we need to take care of our own first." (August 20, 1993, A1)

In brief, the NATION AS HOUSE metaphor was used or invoked with regularity in the Proposition 187 campaign with respect to the threats posed by IMMIGRATION AS DANGEROUS WATERS. Many linguistic expressions characterize immigrants in terms of chaos, destruction, and other perils to the NATION AS HOUSE.

39. "That's like saying, 'I've got this **great house, but it's on fire, it's built on a fault and the bank is moving in to repossess it.'**" (June 16, 1993, A1)
40. a growing body of evidence that Canada, long a **haven** for the world's oppressed, is banking its lamp unto the nations. (June 18, 1992, A1)
41. When U.S. Atty. Gen. Janet Reno toured Nogales this month to announce a 30 percent increase of Border Patrol forces in Arizona—she described the state as the "**side door**" to California. (January 30, 1995, A1)
42. "[Wilson] **cut a hole in the fence** to allow millions of illegal immigrants in, and now he wants **to patch that hole** because that's what the polls tell him to do." (September 16, 1994, A1)

43. "What are you going to do to **close our borders tight** to illegal aliens and drug-runners?" (June 10, 1993, J1)
44. "**Put up a Berlin Wall!**" cried Vines, an African-American who denies that racism has anything to do with his get-tough stand. He says that any fool can see it: Immigration is bringing this country down. (August 30, 1993, A1)
45. "Lots of folks say we have to **shut the door** now. Others disagree pretty strongly.... And so maybe we shouldn't be so quick to **shut the door**." (October 3, 1993, E1)

The frequency and diversity of (metaphoric) threats to the NATION AS HOUSE, as indicated in Table 7, demonstrate that this immigration metaphor was customarily used to impugn the motivation and character of immigrants to the United States.

The metaphor NATION AS HOUSE came into prominent use in the late fifteenth century and was apt to characterize the emerging European nationhood at a time when the majority of the population did not travel and long-distance communication was dependent on animal transportation. The use of a fixed dwelling place as a metaphoric source for the American political entity is increasingly challenged by the early-twenty-first-century system of rapid global transportation, instant worldwide televisual communication, broadening cross-national regional integration, and an increasingly globalized economy.

However, the inadequacy of NATION AS HOUSE as a metaphor for the United States did not distract from or diminish the impact of the rampant use of the IMMIGRATION AS DANGEROUS WATERS metaphor during the Proposition 187 period. DANGEROUS WATERS divests immigrant workers and their families of their humanity, to become at best a natural resource to be controlled and exploited, and at worst to be feared for the potential damage that *floods* and *rising seas* of brown faces can visit on the nation. Geological metaphors invoke certain unwarranted associations about movements of human beings. In the context of a political campaign, the dehumanizing presupposition of the metaphor was fully exploited, transfiguring people into fear-inspiring floods and dangerous tides.

SECTION 2: IMMIGRANT AS ANIMAL

We turn now from metaphors about demographics to the metaphors about the immigrants themselves. An empirical study of metaphor use in the public discourse on immigrants will furnish a principled analysis of how immigrants, as a group, were conceptualized in the United States of the 1990s. In the public discourse presented in the *Los Angeles Times*, immigrants were characterized with decided aversion. This antipathy was articulated metaphorically in several different ways, as illustrated below:

46. For some, the reaction of Valley residents is a natural outgrowth of **onerous burdens**—including budget-busting social service, educa-

tion and criminal-justice costs—**thrust upon** Southern California by the nation's porous immigration laws. (August 1, 1993, A1)
47. An Orange County Grand Jury called for a nationwide, three-year moratorium on all immigration to the United States in an attempt to ease the **drain** on government programs. (June 17, 1993, B1)
48. The problem [of immigrant clients] is significant, because it has **placed added strain** on the state's public hospitals and has cost programs such as Medi-Cal many millions of dollars. (September 1, 1993, A1)
49. "We now have a **runaway situation** of undocumented aliens coming into this country. We have to stop it...." (June 10, 1993, J1)

As mentioned above, one often-commented-upon aspect of the political debate centered on the fiscal costs associated with an apparent increase of immigrants, particularly undocumented immigrants, in Southern California. The cause of anger and outrage, Proposition 187 supporters repeatedly claimed, was the economic expense incurred by American society due to undocumented immigrants. Excessive fiscal costs with minimal returns were cited by California's governor as an abuse borne by the California taxpayer. When the governor's claims were countered with alternative economic analyses, however, the public debate did not focus on the comparative validity of the contending reports.[22] Had the public discussion emphasized economic analysis, then one could argue that economics was the basis for the outrage. In terms of metaphors, there was some focusing of the political debate over immigration costs, as expressed in excerpts 46–48. But as discussed above, in terms of the metaphoric record, California's economic condition was a lesser consideration. The principal characterization of immigrants in public discourse, as a group of people or as individuals, does not primarily focus on their net contribution or cost to California and the country (see Table 8).

The table accounts for the metaphors for immigrants, as people, and excludes tropes metaphorizing immigration, the demographic process. NB: *Tonk* "immigrant," an INS slang term, mimics the sound of an aluminum baton striking.

Dominant Metaphor

The dominant immigrant metaphor used in the *Los Angeles Times* was IMMIGRANT AS ANIMAL. Immigrants were seen to be animals to be lured, pitted, or baited, whether the instance was intended to promote a pro-immigrant or an anti-immigrant point of view:

50. [Governor] Wilson said he believed public benefits are a **lure** to immigrants and his intent was to discourage illegal immigration by denying them access to health care, education and welfare programs. (August 22, 1993, A1)
51. "We're not going to play into those games of **pitting workers against each other.**" (November 3, 1994, D1)

Table 8
IMMIGRANT Metaphors Published during the Proposition 187 Campaign

Source Domain	Type	Totals	Percentages
ANIMAL, e.g., *hunted*	dominant	70	31.8
WAR, e.g., *invader, soldier*	secondary	43	19.5
WATER, e.g., *wave, tsunami*		38	17.3
DISREPUTABLE PERSON, e.g., *marauder, felon*		15	6.8
BODY, e.g., *burden, parasite*		12	5.5
COMMODITY, e.g., *resource, traffic*		10	4.5
ALIEN, e.g., *illegal alien*		9	4.1
OBJECT, e.g., *tonk, menace*		7	3.2
WEED		5	2.3
BIBLICAL, e.g., *angel*		5	2.3
e.g., *instrument, runner*	occasional	6	2.7
	TOTAL	220	100

Source: 107 *Los Angeles Times* articles published June 1992–December 1994. The table accounts for the metaphors for immigrants, as people, and excludes tropes metaphorizing immigration, the demographic process. NB: *Tonk* "immigrant," an INS slang term, mimics the sound of an aluminum baton striking.

52. Once the electorate's **appetite** has been **whet** with the **red meat** of deportation as a viable policy option, the slope toward more aggressive ways of implementing that policy is likely to get slippery. (June 4, 1995, M2)

Immigrants were seen as animals that can be attacked, and hunted:

53. Beaten-down agents, given only enough resources to catch a third of their **quarry,** sense the objective in this campaign is something less than total victory. (July 5, 1992, A3)
54. the I-5 [freeway], where the agents now must **quit the chase** (July 5, 1992, A3)

Immigrants were seen as animals to be eaten, by U.S. industry, by the Immigration and Naturalization Service or its Border Patrol agents, and by the anti-immigrant Proposition 187 supporters:

55. The truth is, employers **hungering** for really cheap labor **hunt out** the foreign workers. (June 9, 1992, D3)
56. "187 backers **devour the weak and helpless**" (September 6, 1994, B4)

This can also be noted in excerpt 52. At times immigrants were considered, as in the following case, rabbits:

57. The rapid increase comes at a time when many state and federal officials are calling for beefed-up border patrols to **ferret out** illegal immigrants. (November 30, 1993, A1)

As it happens, ferrets prey on rabbits and other small animals. More often, immigrants were characterized as pack animals:

58. the specter...has **spurred** an exodus (August 31, 1992, A1)
59. Those who want to sharply **curb** illegal immigration include conservatives, liberals and most unions. [*curb* "a mouthpiece used to control animals"] (June 9, 1992, D3)

The connotations of IMMIGRANT AS ANIMAL should be abundantly clear. In Western European culture a purported natural hierarchy has been articulated since the time of Thomas Aquinas to justify social inequity. In its full extension, it subordinates other living creatures to human beings, and ranks the inherent quality of humans from base to noble. In its elaborated form, it has been called the "Great Chain of Being."[23] Lakoff and Turner provided an extended discussion of the pervasiveness of the Great Chain of Being metaphor in Western European thinking.[24] This "moral ordering"[25] has justified the social inequality in Europe for two millennia and deprecated people of color in the United States for centuries. Stephen Jay Gould quotes Gunnar Myrdal on Americans' complacent use of biological determinism to maintain social advantage over people of color:

> "Under their long hegemony, there has been a tendency to assume biological causation without question, and to accept social explanations only under the duress of a siege of irresistible evidence."...Or as Condorcet said more succinctly a long time ago: they "make nature herself an accomplice in the crime of political inequity."[26]

More recently Gould has stated that the notion of "progress" in evolution, human or otherwise, is incongruous. Gould does not equivocate:

> There is no progress in evolution. The fact of evolutionary change through time doesn't represent progress as we know it. Progress is not inevitable. Much of evolution is downward in terms of morphological complexity, rather than upward. We're not marching toward some greater thing. The actual history of life is awfully damn curious in the light of our usual expectation that there's some predictable drive toward a generally increasing complexity in time. If that's so, life certainly took its time about it: five-sixths of the history of life is the story of single-celled creatures only. I would like to propose that the modal complexity of life has never changed and it never will, that right from the beginning

of life's history it has been what it is; and that our view of complexity is shaped by our warped decision to focus on only one small aspect of life's history.[27]

Progress has bankrupted its scientific credentials, according to Gould. In good faith, it cannot be used to hierarchize living things, much less to demean people via social determinism. Gould's repudiation will undoubtedly surprise many readers. As an evolutionary biologist, he represents a strong current of contemporary thinking about evolution. Still, this view flies in the face of the commonplace understanding of human evolution, in spite of the increasing number of popular accounts that dispute it.[28]

Ontology of Immigrant as Animal

Again, a metaphor is a tightly structured conceptual correspondence mapping the structure of the semantic source domain, ANIMAL, onto a very different target domain, IMMIGRANT. The formal ontological mapping of the metaphor labeled IMMIGRANT AS ANIMAL follows:

- Immigrants correspond to citizens as animals correspond to humans.

The correspondence allows speakers to use the same frame of reference to reason about immigrants that is commonly employed to reason about animals. In this manner speakers and listeners inadvertently apply to immigrants their knowledge base of what animals are. The power of such metaphoric mappings is robust and productive, since the mapping is conceptual and is not limited to a finite set of linguistic phrases. Many metaphoric mappings are more or less conventional and unchanging.[29] As a political metaphor which is debated and negotiated, this mapping is a less fixed part of our conceptual system.[30] However, as frequently and as exclusively as the mapping is used in daily discourse, the dominant ANIMAL metaphor persists as the major productive way to conceptualize immigrants. Its effects are profound.

It is not hard to document contemporary examples of white racism directed at Latinos premised on the tenets of biological evolutionary progress, particularly by people in positions of power. The remarks of a California senator will illustrate. While presiding over a 1993 meeting of the Special Committee on U.S./Mexico Border Issues, W. A. Craven disputed the right to public education of children of undocumented immigrants, even after these children provide proof of residency. On the official record he stated: "It seems rather strange that we go out of our way to take care of the rights of these individuals who are perhaps on the lower scale of our humanity." Offended, Latino professors and staff at California State University San Marcos wrote letters insisting on a retraction, or at least a clarification, of the senator's comments. None was forthcoming. Instead, the local media excoriated the Latino faculty, while ranking CSUSM administrators assumed their benefactor's patronymic by publicly defending the senator. That same year the administration building at CSUSM was fittingly named Craven Hall.[31]

The ontology of evolutionary progress presupposes an inherent preeminence of one species over another and a superiority of one group over others. The Darwinian imperative of survival of the fittest within the human species has long been viewed as self-evident. This stance recapitulated the social relations of the Great Chain of Being. In the nineteenth century a biological decree replaced the divine apology for injustice. Not surprisingly, many of the same prerogatives of the superior were maintained, such as institutional advantages in juridical, educational, financial, and political spheres. And the same vanities persisted, namely, the presumptions of greater strength, beauty, intelligence, sophistication, and benevolence. With the decline in the twentieth century of racism's biological justification, the immigrant's purported cultural deficits and an associated ideology of Anglo-American cultural superiority became the basis for continuing racism.[32] As a premise for bias, Anglo-American cultural nationalism permits prejudice against individuals who, by all human standards, have merit equal to the citizen. Only by the arbitrary ascription of birthplace, the immigrant is deemed less than the citizen.

When characterized as animals, immigrants are portrayed as less than human, which sets up unmistakable divisions of expectations. Actions that are natural for both humans and animals are lexically distinguished:

60. This woman said she was upset about something else: why the offspring of women who "come across the border and **drop their babies**" are granted American citizenship. (June 10, 1993, J1)

Thus in excerpt 60 the different verbs *give birth* and *drop* distinguish identical human and nonhuman actions. Note the terms found in the *Los Angeles Times* texts used to characterize the immigrant, such as *hungered over, preyed upon, hunted out, targeted, herded, devoured; a menace, animal, dog, rat, rabbit, coyote,* and, of course, *scapegoat.*

Further, other irrevocable divisions ensue. Civil rights and human rights only pertain to humans. The value of life is highest for humans. Slavery has been outlawed for humans but still is permitted for animals, although it is not called slavery. Note that animals are owned, and the same terminology is used for animals as was used for slaves. Animals are said to be wild by nature. At times animals can be domesticated, but due to the biological hierarchy based on progress, they can never be human. When animals are wild, which is to say, uncontrolled by humans, they may be appropriately feared by humans, and are justifiable targets for human hunters. Certain animals become valuable to humans only when domesticated, either as beasts of burden or as sources of food for humans.

The inherent logic of the IMMIGRANT AS ANIMAL metaphor thus includes a biological, or at least birthplace-based, hierarchy, on which purported inborn inferiority is based. On the biological hierarchy, an unequal value set is based, with higher forms being more valued and granted by fiat greater rights and privileges than lower orders of life. Superiors, again naturally, rule over their inferiors, as in the biblical edict in Genesis that humankind has dominion over the animals and the rest of the Earth, and will rule over them. One critical presupposition of the dichotomy assigns moral, ethical, and judicial considerations to and for humans; these considerations are not invoked to constrain human actions over the less-than-human.

The discourse principle that governs commonly used patterns of inference is metaphor, as a part of the conceptual system shared in large part by speakers of the English language and encoded in part in the ways Americans use the English language. Metaphor permits a shared understanding of the semantic domain of immigrants in terms of the semantic domain of animals. Following Lakoff's formula, these patterns of inferences are presented in terms of the following narrative of the immigrant versus the citizen:[33]

> On the hierarchy of living things, immigrants are animals. Citizens, in contrast, are humans. This hierarchy of life subordinates immigrants to citizens. Human beings are vested with birthright privileges, such as "human rights" and "dignity." Animals have no such privileges and are not equal to humans in the estimation of social institutions. Animals can never become humans by legislation or fiat. Their inferiority is inherent. Humans have full control over animals, from ownership to use as a food source. Animals are either domesticated, that is to say, owned by humans, or are wild and consequently are outside of the dominion of human society, and can be hunted.

The *Los Angeles Times* documents many statements that demonstrate that immigrants were aware of the widespread racist attitude and behavior that they encounter in the United States. Two will be repeated. In the first excerpt, a Guatemalan mother of three expressed shock that state and federal legislators, one of whom will be quoted below, denied assistance to undocumented immigrants following a major California earthquake:

> 61. Illegal and legal immigrants "are both human beings...regardless of what papers they carry....We all felt the earthquake the same," added Dora Ramirez, a tent city resident who said she is undocumented. (February 2, 1994, A14)

The second is the description of treatment that a Los Angeles soccer fan said police officers meted out at a Rose Bowl game, including beating him, dragging him down stairs, uttering racist slurs, and knocking him out:

> 62. "Like an **animal** was the way I was treated," Aguilar said. "It was racist." (May 3, 1996, B5)

The public discourse about immigrants, then, is not an incidental correlation of words, but a lived reality for immigrants and Latinos in this society. Still, for many the metaphor may be a sobering finding. Its implications will be discussed in a later section of this chapter. In the following section the other metaphoric mappings will be described, although not in the detail of the ANIMAL metaphor. This will be followed by a section in which a counterargument to the force of this major finding is tested. A set of alternative framings of the public discourse on Proposition 187 will be considered in the penultimate section of the chapter. After these considerations, commentary on the implications can be made.

SECTION 3: SECONDARY METAPHORS

The metaphor labeled IMMIGRANT AS ANIMAL is not the only mapping used in the *Los Angeles Times*. Below are a few nonanimal metaphors for immigrants. A widely varied mapping, which is tentatively labeled IMMIGRANTS AS DISREPUTABLE PEOPLE, includes all classes of people who do not merit respect:

63. "I recently had some tourists say that the problem with today's immigrants is that they're so **bizarre** and unpredictable," says O'Donnell. (October 3, 1993, E1)
64. A middle-aged woman tells of the "**marauders**" who take over the streets at night. (September 6, 1993, A1)

Another metaphor that is used is IMMIGRANT AS WEED:

65. take children [of immigrants] and their dream hostage in a crude scheme to **uproot** their parents (September 27, 1994, B7)
66. And while 33 percent said they believed **the new crop** of immigrants have inferior job skills and education than did their predecessors (September 19, 1993, A1)
67. **spring up** among us a generation of ignorant and troubled children who, lacking our common language and political and social ideals, will evolve into a huge, parallel underclass (August 1, 1993, A1)
68. "We see it as our responsibility to **weed out** illegal aliens." (May 16, 1992, A30)

In excerpt 66 the term *crop* associates immigrants not with productivity and wealth but with inferior attributes. These and other secondary mappings degrade the immigrant.

SECTION 4: TESTING IMMIGRANTS AS ANIMALS

It could be argued that animal metaphors are used to discuss all kinds of people in many situations in daily discourse: "You dog!," "I smell a rat," "Don't be so catty," and so forth. Accordingly, the argument of the skeptic would be that animal metaphors are not used to any greater degree to characterize immigrants than, for example, businesspeople or sports figures. Certainly, following the skeptic's line of thinking, businesspeople are often characterized in negative and unflattering terms. "It's a dog-eat-dog world" is a hackneyed portrayal of the business milieu. Likewise, sports figures are no longer revered as they might have been in a nostalgic past. They are now portrayed as selfish and at times brutish athletes. If the use of animal metaphors to characterize businesspeople and sports figures is similar to the patterns used to characterize immigrants, so the skeptic's argument goes, then the abnegation of immigrants with animal metaphors is not special and should not be overemphasized.[34]

In order to test the skeptic's hypothesis, all the metaphors that characterized sports figures in a month of the *Los Angeles Times* sports section were catalogued.[35] An equivalent amount of text was catalogued, in terms of word count, in the business section of the *Los Angeles Times* from the same period. The discourse about these kinds of people was selected since U.S. newspapers commonly have separate sections devoted to sports and business, which permits straightforward comparison. The skeptic would predict that the animal metaphor is commonly used for sports figures and businesspeople. Consequently the skeptic would state that the IMMIGRANT AS ANIMAL mapping is only part of a broader target domain, and does not single out immigrants.

The writing in sports is much more playful, with more creative use of description than the writing on immigration. Remarkably, no metaphors about sports figures in this sample have animal source domains:

69. "Heather is our defensive **catalyst** and Katie is our offensive **catalyst**." (November 30, 1995, C6)
70. Tyson gets his **tune-up** (November 25, 1995, C7)
71. Holmes has been a **godsend** (November 25, 1995, C10)
72. Franson is a **blue-collar big** man (November 24, 1995, C6)

As for the business section, there is a great deal more written on a typical day on business topics than on sports in the *Los Angeles Times*.[36] In contrast to metaphor use on immigration and immigrant topics, a relatively limited use of metaphor in the business section was noted. Newspaper descriptions of businesspeople tend to follow a formula. They usually are limited to a title, or a title with a limiting clause:

73. Blue Cross Chairman Leonard Schaeffer (November 30, 1995, D2)
74. Analyst Harold Vogel with Cowen & Co. (November 30, 1995, D2)
75. Barry Diller, the Home Shopping Network chairman who is trying to build a TV network from scratch (November 30, 1995, D2)

Most of the metaphors about businesspeople did not have an animal source domain:

76. cost-**cutter** Sanford I. Weill (November 30, 1995, D1)

However, in the data sample, two metaphors about businesspeople appeared that had animal source domains:

77. "The market is going crazy, the foreigners are the ones that appear most **bullish**," a trader said. (November 30, 1995, D4)

78. "I'm looking forward to **squishing** Rupert like a **bug**," Turner said. (November 30, 1995, D2)

In the latter excerpts, there are special circumstances to note. Both instances are direct quotes taken from individuals, rather than the business writer's text. In the lead sentence of the article, as written by the newswriter, a second instance of the bug metaphor is rephrased to direct the metaphor away from the businessperson, and toward the business enterprise.

79. Ted Turner said Wednesday he will **squash** "like a **bug**" an all-news TV network media magnate Rupert Murdoch hopes to launch to compete with Turner's 24-hour Cable News Network. (November 30, 1995, D2)

Thus the quote in excerpt 78 which attributes the animal metaphor to a businessperson was clearly reapportioned in excerpt 79, the lead sentence of the *Times* article, namely, the part of the story that would most likely be read. From this limited sample it might be concluded that businesspeople use animal metaphors in reference to colleagues and competitors. At the same time it would indicate that *Los Angeles Times* business writers may deemphasize ruder business discourse, presumably to uphold the dignity of commerce.

Business-news writers tend not to use metaphor to characterize businesspeople, but contrastingly, they often cast nonhuman elements of the business world in anthropomorphic metaphors:

80. "This market is like **an old soldier** that just doesn't give up." (November 30, 1995, D3)
81. Stocks **sprinted** higher Wednesday.... Broad market indexes **broke records** as well. (November 30, 1995, D3)
82. Bank mergers are **vulnerable** to protests filed under the... Act. (November 30, 1995, D2)

Note *crazy* in excerpt 77 as well. Since only two expressions of animal metaphor appeared in a substantial sample of articles on businesspeople, the skeptic's hypothesis was not confirmed. However, the idea was further explored.

A second sampling of articles was gathered on two individuals of particular notoriety in sports and business. The distribution of animal metaphors in these newspaper sections was tallied. Again the skeptic would predict that animal metaphors are used to characterize businesspeople and sports figures no more or less than they are used to characterize immigrants. Note, however, that the skeptic's original claim had to be significantly weakened. The skeptic's second hypothesis is much less sweeping. Now notoriety, rather than normalcy, marks the individuals whose metaphors will be studied. In the second test, Mike Tyson was selected as a boxer who has been as praised for ferocity in the ring as he has been rebuked for his criminality outside of the ring. A financier, Charles Keating, was chosen to represent unscrupulous businesspeople. Keating was convicted in 1993 of bilking small investors out of millions of dollars through his institution, Lincoln Savings and Loan. As an infamous white-collar criminal, Keating is much more likely to be characterized with animal metaphors than the average businessperson. A number of articles on each person were drawn from the *Los Angeles Times* archives using the computerized topic selection function to select a set of articles that would provide approximately similar numbers of words.[37]

Animal metaphors were indeed used for Tyson. However, the boxer is portrayed as a particular kind of animal. In this sample he was characterized as a predatory carnivore, as illustrated by:

83. "...into the **lion's** den and take the meat out of the **lion's** mouth" (July 21, 1989, C1)
84. a man who keeps the **tiger** at bay with a long, strong left jab (July 21, 1989 C1)

This sports figure is metaphorically characterized as an animal at the top of the proverbial food chain. These "noble" animals are used as emblems for nations. The lion and tiger, for example, respectively symbolize Great Britain and India. The sports writers sampled in 1989 always wrote respectfully about Tyson. His sports prowess was never deprecated, and for these skills he was respected. It was expected that Tyson would be denigrated with animal metaphors, because of his profession, criminality, antipathies, and race. This expectation was not met. Nevertheless, it should not be concluded that the animal metaphors used to describe Tyson are similar to those used to describe the immigrants, since the animals linked to immigrants are not symbolically noble creatures, but beasts of burden or "lower" creatures.

The foregoing metaphor analysis was made using news reports published prior to Tyson's 1997 fight with Evander Holyfield. In that fight Tyson was disqualified for repeatedly biting Holyfield's ear, which was followed by a spate of sports commentaries which capitalized on TYSON AS CARNIVORE metaphors.

As for the other ill-famed news figure, the case of the felonious businessman is unequivocal. In the sample of news reports catalogued, Keating was never characterized as an animal:

85. **Midas-touch** businessman (April 8, 1990, D3)
86. **the villain, the man in the black hat** (April 8, 1990, D3)

No animal metaphors were used in reference to Keating. The metaphors used by the newswriters tend to focus on his successes, rather than his failings. His political and legal enemies, not the *Times* business writers, call him a *crook* and a *scam artist*. Contrary to the representation of immigrants in the same newspaper, there is no denigration of the man as a human being in the texts sampled.

It should be noted that these *Times* texts were published before 1996, when a judge overthrew Keating's conviction. "That means Keating is no longer a criminal in the eyes of the law—but he is a deadbeat. He still faces roughly

$5.2 billion in civil judgments against him stemming from Lincoln's collapse. All his identifiable property, including his home, was long ago auctioned off by the government."[38]

Although the samples of articles on Tyson and Keating are limited, these infamous individuals are not characterized in metaphors as inferiors. In the larger samples of articles on sports figures no animal metaphors were located. For businesspeople, two animal metaphors were found. Both of these excerpts were direct quotes attributable to businesspeople, rather than text written by the *Times* writers. These results provide evidence that animal metaphors are not commonly used in newsprint to describe these types of citizens, as the skeptic predicted, although there was some reason to expect such characterizations. Consequently there is stronger support for the original finding, lamentably, that the ANIMAL domain is uniquely associated with immigrants. Animal metaphors are not generally used in the *Los Angeles Times* to characterize other types of people, even infamous individuals.

SECTION 5: OTHER ANALYSES OF IMMIGRANT REPRESENTATIONS DURING THE PROPOSITION 187 CAMPAIGN

Analysts with diverse disciplinary backgrounds have proposed alternative accounts of what amounts to the metaphoric framing of the political events surrounding Proposition 187. From the present theoretical position, which emphasizes the metaphoric understanding of social events, a comparison of their views is warranted. Hugh Mehan argues that the proponents of Proposition 187 utilized an IMMIGRANT AS ENEMY discourse strategy.[39] By discourse strategy,[40] Mehan refers to generally unconscious linguistic means to frame a particular view of the world. The discourse strategy framework is generally consistent with the framework used in this book. Mehan uses the ENEMY metaphor as the cover term for the anti-immigrant discourse strategy which includes the use of deixis to split American society into the in-group, us, and the Other.[41] The term deixis refers to the use of words such as *that, this, them, those, here,* and *there,* among others, for purposes of "pointing out" things in the world. As illustrated below, deixis reinforces the differences that are entailed in the dominant metaphor IMMIGRANT AS ANIMAL, i.e., the immigrant is an animal and hence not like us:[42]

87. "**They** create problems for jobs....If **they** can go to school and get health care **we're** allowing **them** to be here....**We** can't even take care of **our own** and **we're** letting more in. **They** should be taking care of **themselves** and not draining **our** pocketbooks." (August 22, 1993, A1)

88. "There are so many more of **them,** so many more of **them** in **our** schools. **Their** parents won't speak **our** language, and **they** don't seem to try to improve **their** lifestyles. There are exceptions, but most of **them** don't." (June 26, 1993, B3)

A second part of the discourse strategy first discerned by Mehan is the difference in the rhetorical style of the proponents of Proposition 187, who use compelling anecdotes rather than scientific discourse to articulate their economic arguments to the electorate. Reliance on anecdotes is associated with what Mehan considers a third part of the discourse strategy, the studied disregard of traditional authorities who were opposed to Proposition 187, including several prominent right-wing politicians, a conservative former U.S. cabinet member, the president of the country, an ecumenical set of clergy, and diverse public health, law enforcement, and educational officials. According to Mehan, the fourth element of their discourse strategy was a penurious appeal to self-interest, rather than to the greater public good and human rights. The listed discourse strategy features were all noted in abundance in this independent study of the public discourse of the time period. Mehan's cover term is, of course, copiously instantiated in the IMMIGRANT AS SOLDIER metaphor. In the present work, a good deal of confirmation of Mehan's analysis was located, as noted in Table 8.

Mehan notes three other studies of Proposition 187 that are complementary to his own. Carola and Marcelo Suárez-Orozco state that Proposition 187 is a "catharsis...that does not necessarily cure the underlying pathology." The pathogen in their analysis is not the immigrant, but the California public's anxiety that has arisen with a seemingly unending series of natural disasters, rage at the videotaped police brutality committed against African American Rodney King, as well as the so-called Los Angeles riots that followed the verdict acquitting the police of wrongdoing. This public uneasiness has been channeled into the re-creation of the Other, the immigrant, to "contain overwhelming anxieties and focus their rage," in particular in the void left by the collapsed "Evil Empire" of the communist Soviet Union.[43] Mehan does not accept the psychocultural analysis of Suárez-Orozco and Suárez-Orozco, which for him ignores "the elite's use, indeed cynical manipulation, of the immigrant-as-enemy construct in public discourse."[44] In spite of Mehan's critique, one can also readily locate reflections of the Suárez-Orozco analysis in the public discourse sampled in the *Los Angeles Times*. Indeed the IMMIGRANT AS DISEASE and IMMIGRANT AS CRIMINAL are quite salient metaphors, as noted in Table 8.

The third commentator, Kitty Calavita, asks why the present period is "focused almost single-mindedly on IMMIGRANTS AS A TAX BURDEN, a focus that is unusual, if not unique, in the history of U.S. nativism."[45] Calavita's answer focuses on economics, and her analysis is framed in terms of ideology:

> With the [federal] deficit seemingly out of control, increased economic uncertainty for all but the most affluent, and the safety net shrinking, frustrated and anxious voters are predisposed to place the blame on excessive government spending and the poor, who are seen as the major cause of such spending. Immigrants are one among several targets consistent with this balanced-budget ideology and the scapegoating of the marginalized "other" that it spawns.... Those who are not even citizens—indeed, are not legal residents—are the ideal target of blame, more undeserving even than the traditional "undeserving poor."[46]

She cites "balanced-budget conservatism" as the framework of political values underlying California's Proposition 187. This is Plotkin and Scheureman's term for the general ideological response displayed in U.S. politics to the ongoing crisis of Fordism (reduced industrial profitability of U.S. capitalism since the Seventies). At a time when wages have been cut so much that 14 million full-time workers earn less than the official poverty level, when nonpermanent workers now comprise 30 percent of the entire U.S. workforce, and when the social safety net is being cut, Calavita notes that there has been an ideological assault on the public sector, not the economic sector. The public's attention was not drawn to the massive industrial and capital restructuring "designed to make the workers pay,"[47] rather, its outrage was redirected toward the federal deficit and rising taxes. Antigovernment rhetorical attacks and contempt and hostility expressed toward the poor were hallmarks of the budget-balancing conservative ideology of the 1990s. In contrast to Mehan's ENEMY metaphor, Calavita focuses on the IMMIGRANT AS BURDEN. Again there is a great deal of support for Calavita's analysis in the present *Los Angeles Times* public discourse sampling. Her metaphor of choice is linked to the NATION AS BODY metaphor rather than the NATION AS HOUSE metaphor.

George Lakoff, whose theoretical research over the last fifteen years brought metaphor to scholarly prominence, also used metaphor analysis to study the nature of politics in American society.[48] Based on personal observations of American political life and backed by text examples he generated or sampled on occasion from public discourse sources as he conducted cognitive linguistics research on metaphor, Lakoff claims that the major division in U.S. politics between liberals and conservatives is systematically based on dichotomous models of what ideal families should be. He claims both conservatives and liberals base their different political judgments on distinct forms of a NATION AS FAMILY metaphor. Within this analysis he addresses the U.S. politics of immigration. Consequently, evidence of this division should be found in public discourse expressed with differential use of metaphors.

On the one hand, the conservative view of politics is based on what Lakoff calls the Strict Father model of the family. For the conservatives, immigrants are first and foremost lawbreakers who should be punished. That is why they are called "illegal." Lakoff, speaking from the point of view of conservatives, avows:

> They are not citizens, hence they are not children in *our* family. To be expected to provide food, housing, and health care for illegal immigrants is like being expected to feed, house, and care for other children in the neighborhood who are coming into our house without permission. They weren't invited, they have no business being here, and we have no responsibility to take care of them.[49]

Numerous statements can be cited in the *Los Angeles Times* that corroborate the conservative point of view when referring to actual children, including the following statement by California's governor:

> 89. "We cannot educate every child from here to Tierra del Fuego." (September 16, 1994, A1)

On the other hand, the liberal view of politics is based on the Nurturing Family model in Lakoff's analysis. The NATION AS FAMILY metaphor that maps the politics of liberals characterizes immigrants as powerless people with no immoral intent. Consequently within the metaphor they are seen as:

> innocent children needing nurturance.... Through the NATION AS FAMILY metaphor, they are seen as children who have been...brought into the national household and who contribute in a vital way to that national household. You don't throw such children out onto the street. It would be immoral.[50]

Again there are quite clear statements in the *Los Angeles Times* that corroborate the liberal point of view, particularly when addressing the actual children of immigrants:

> 90. How dare we deny education to the children of women who clean our home and raise our children? How dare we deny medical care to those who harvest our crops, clip our lawns and golf courses, bus our dishes, wash our cars and every night leave spotless the very office towers whose top executives support the governor behind this mean proposal? (September 27, 1994, B7)

For Lakoff, metaphoric references to children are an entailment, IMMIGRANT AS CHILD, that emerges from within the mapping of family value to political value in NATION AS FAMILY. In the public discourse on immigrants generated during the Proposition 187 period, one would expect to find an empirical reflection of the NATION AS FAMILY and IMMIGRANT AS CHILD. However, only two instances of metaphors in the *Los Angeles Times* sample make reference to immigrants as children. Both were reported at a press conference called by a California legislator to announce the passage of his bill which denied emergency earthquake relief to undocumented immigrants:

> 91. For Rohrabacher, of Huntington Beach, the legislative victory gave flight to his more visceral kind of rhetoric. "This will have a real impact on federal agencies' ability to put out a flyer, saying (to illegal immigrants), 'Come on in and get the money.' **We're all part of the same family,** of all racial backgrounds. When you're in an emergency situation, **what kind of person takes limited emergency resources from his own family and gives it to a stranger?** We cannot afford to supply benefits for illegals without hurting our citizens and legal residents." (February 3, 1994, A1)

This inhumane legislative action was commented on by an immigrant quoted in excerpt 61 above. Representative Dana Rohrabacher's explicit reference to the nation as family, however, may well be interpreted as sarcastic. (Note his reflexive reference to race.) Few other IMMIGRANT AS CHILD metaphors appeared in the *Los Angeles Times* dataset.

It is understandable why Lakoff would expect Americans to speak about immigrants as children.[51] Such a metaphor is a more benevolent representation of the immigrant.[52] Unfortunately, the dominant ANIMAL metaphor evidenced in the *Los Angeles Times* of the 1990s did not grant human status to immigrants; it debased them. In the hierarchy of living things held by Americans, as expressed in metaphor, immigrants are not the children of citizens. They metamorphosed into lower-life forms.

The lack of empirical confirmation in the *Times* of family or child metaphors does not repudiate Lakoff's major assertion that morality is embodied in the commonly used metaphors of political discourse. This is a key empirical finding of the present book.

These four analyses of the anti-immigrant sentiment and its political expression in Proposition 187 were each confirmed in the present sample of the metaphors of public discourse. However, each is only a partial analysis of the public discourse sampled in this chapter. Beginning with the cognitive theorist, Lakoff aims to capture the big picture. As the researcher attending most closely to the material discourse, Mehan focuses on the IMMIGRANT AS ENEMY, while Suárez-Orozco and Suárez-Orozco draw a psychoanalytic portrait centering on the IMMIGRANT AS DISEASE and AS CRIMINAL. Calavita brings economics to the forefront with the IMMIGRANT AS BURDEN metaphor.

Their respective interpretations follow from the proclivities of their respective disciplines. Their findings are consequently particularly germane to the disciplines from which the analysts operate, and yet, with the exception of Mehan, each is conspicuously bounded. The range of each of their separate analyses is encompassed in Table 8, which catalogues the range of structuring metaphors about immigrants. Still and all, one omission is common to the four analyses. The most frequent and virulent metaphor was not noted by these investigators. Turning now to the implications of the IMMIGRANT AS ANIMAL metaphor, one must ask what it is that makes this metaphor invisible to the scrutiny of social scientists.

SECTION 6: INTERPRETATION OF THE DOMINANT METAPHOR

The conceptual correspondence IMMIGRANT AS ANIMAL is racist. It deprecates immigrants as it separates noncitizens and citizens, since it assigns the former nonhuman standing. This finding confirms previous research that also investigated racism and metaphor. Toine van Teeffelen, in a study of political metaphor in popular literature, states:

> in its metaphoric meaning racism compares and contrasts the domains of the self and the other.... When applied skillfully, metaphors can have a strong impact due to their "literary" quality and visual concreteness. This rhetorical thrust allows them to emphasize particular elements and linkages, and simultaneously to de-emphasize others. Since they organize the understanding of cause and effect, symptom and essence, and especially praise and blame, metaphors can be employed to serve

political aims or interests. When thus used as ideological devices, they privilege, and when turning into common sense, naturalize particular accounts of reality.[53]

The charge of racism can be made on the basis of standard definitions. From a political economics perspective, for example, Robert Miles defines racism as actions that postulate natural divisions among people which are in fact not natural. This false assignment of individuals to groups, on the basis of such so-called natural traits, categorizes people into a false hierarchy. In this way of thinking, racism attributes meaning to

> human beings in such a way to create a system of categorization, and [attributes] additional (negatively evaluated) characteristics to the people sorted into those categories. This process of signification is therefore the basis for the creation of a hierarchy of groups, and for establishing criteria by which to include and exclude groups of people in the process of allocating resources and services.[54]

Certain essentialist criticisms can be made about this kind of definition. Nevertheless the reach of the definition should be clear. Note that this definition presumes that the criteria used by racists characterize the Other merely as an inferior human being, and not the equivalent of horses, rabbits, ferrets, and dogs.

Moreover, the metaphoric mapping IMMIGRANT AS ANIMAL is an element of racist discourse. The present finding thus reaffirms the research of van Dijk in which he demonstrated that racist discourse is replete with animal themes.[55] A definition of racist discourse which does not invoke intrinsic properties follows:

> Racist discourse, in our view, should be seen as discourse (of whatever content) which has the effect of establishing, sustaining and reinforcing oppressive power relations.... Racist discourse... justifies, sustains and legitimates those practices which maintain... power and dominance.[56]

Sustaining a discourse practice is the root power of metaphor. Following Foucault, such discourse practices uphold social practice, as they embody unreflected and naturalized ideological assumptions about their subject space. The entirely contingent background understandings about social spaces, beliefs, relationships, and identities of our lives are established in daily interactions which we only rarely question. The discourse practices are so frequently and casually used that they become automatic and invisible to our everyday view.

Correspondingly, metaphor, arguably the crucial unit of discursive practice, most effectively influences people when it does not draw attention to itself; when, without the slightest mindfulness on the part of the interlocutors, it invokes and rearticulates the cognitive structure of a source semantic domain to its target semantic domain. Notice that when a truly original metaphor is used, the reader/listener of the fresh turn of phrase is prompted by its novelty to evaluate the metaphor for its appropriateness, creativity, and utility. The mindful reader/listener can choose to reject the linkage. However, if the metaphor does not draw attention to itself, then the reader/listener is most likely to remain unaware that a conventional and contingent semantic link has been reinforced. Moreover, the semantic and cultural presuppositions of the conceptual correspondence are also automatically strengthened. IMMIGRANT AS ANIMAL is a metaphoric mapping that reproduces a view, with semantic associations, and most importantly political and social consequences, to denigrate human beings. Its dominant use sustains a covertly racist worldview.

As for explicitly legitimating a racist discourse, "there can be little doubt that of all forms of printed text, those of the mass media are most pervasive, if not most influential, when judged by the power criteria of recipient scope."[57] While the *Los Angeles Times* newswriters are not overtly racist, their continued use of the metaphor, like that of any other American English speaker, contributes to demeaning and dehumanizing the immigrant worker. Given the *Los Angeles Times*'s privileged role as a major vehicle for political discourse in California, IMMIGRATION AS DANGEROUS WATERS and IMMIGRANT AS ANIMAL are continually reinforced when these dominant metaphors are part of the *Times*'s entrenched discourse practice.

On the other hand, in defense of the newspaper, contemporary cognitive theory claims that prosaic metaphor constructs the fundamental worldview of everyday life. Rather than explicitly legitimating racist practices and power relationships, in these political contexts the newspaper merely reflects the basic, embodied values of the dominant social order. This discursive practice transfigures people—into threatening floods or domestic beasts—as it subjugates their humanity. Since "media practices usually remain within the boundaries of a flexible, but dominant consensus, even when there is room for occasional dissent and criticism... fundamental norms, values, and power arrangements are seldom explicitly challenged in the dominant news media."[58] Thus the foundational racism of U.S. society is mirrored in the discursive practice of the *Los Angeles Times*.

First, by way of the use of IMMIGRATION AS DANGEROUS WATERS, the individuality and humanity of the immigrants are replaced with a frightening scenario of *inundating surges of brown faces*. While the ostensible point of Pete Wilson's anti-immigrant campaign was to recoup government costs associated with essential services for undocumented workers and their children, the force of the DANGEROUS WATERS metaphor was not directed toward fiscal deficits. Rather, Wilson capitalized on the sense of increasing loss of sociocultural preeminence among his core constituency, as the *rising brown tides* ostensibly reshaped the Anglo-American hegemonic order.

Second, the IMMIGRANT AS ANIMAL metaphor is unquestionably racist. This racism is constructed in public discourse via the use of the metaphor. This is different from the racist language with which the public is familiar. Racist language is commonly understood to be the blatant invectives and slurs that were common in the United States over most of its history, when it was an openly racist society. These expletives are no longer tolerated in most polite settings. They are no longer common currency in political discourse. Hence, as Frank Reeves noted, such discourse has been "sanitized." However, epistemological racism continues to be expressed via the dominant metaphors most commonly used in the public discourse on immigrants and immigration.

Lastly, the public discourse which distinguishes citizen from immigrant repudiates one celebrated principle of American society. The nation's most distinguished claim is the Great Experiment, which was given expression in the Constitution. Sadly, the experiment has always been compromised insofar as all the people in the country are not included. As Frederick Douglass hammered home with ringing eloquence, their exclusion debases the nation's noble design:

> Its language is "We the people"; not we the white people, not even we the citizens, not we the privileged class, not we the high, not we the low, but we the people; not we the horses, sheep and swine, and wheelbarrows, but we the people, we the human inhabitants; and if Negroes are people, they are included in the benefits for which the Constitution of America was ordained and established.[59]

When Douglass wrote, African Americans were not citizens but had the legal status of domesticated animals. Today's immigrants are spoken about as if they were animals, and via these words actions are taken that disregard their humanity. The principles of the country are debased as long as this current dominant metaphor of public discourse is sustained.

The discursive construction of racism may currently be unobtrusive, but once noted, it is far from subtle. Immigrants are not referred to, in a patronizing but humane manner, as children. While there were other metaphoric mappings evident in the database, such as IMMIGRANT AS WEED, all but one of these were pejorative. The absence of productive dominant metaphors for immigrants and immigration supports the thesis that the U.S. public discourse on immigrants is racist. The metaphoric element of discursive racism is particularly insidious, since the metaphors remain invisible. These metaphors are manifestations of deeply held concepts of *what* (not who) immigrants are. Such a worldview precludes the view that they are vested by birth with the same human rights as citizens, and that they should be shown due respect for the difficult and ill-paid work they provide for U.S. society.

NOTES

1. Gutiérrez 1995, p. 13.
2. Gutiérrez quotes such nineteenth-century viewpoints as that of South Carolina's well-known Senator John C. Calhoun, who objected to embracing in the United States a large number of Mexicans. For Calhoun, Mexicans consist of "impure races, not as good as the Cherokees or Choctaws" (1995, p. 16).
3. Griswold del Castillo 1990.

4. Vélez-Ibáñez 1997, in Chapter 1, "Without Borders, the Original Vision."
5. Brownstein and Simon 1993.
6. Higham 1955.
7. Hoffman 1974, p. 126.
8. Davis 1995.
9. "Teutonic" was the nineteenth-century term for the preferred "race" of European immigrant, with "Alpine" and "Mediterranean" successively lower on the scale of purity (Higham 1955, p. 155).
10. Brownstein and Simon 1993.
11. Two kinds of ellipsis are used in the excerpts throughout the book: a wide-spaced version signals the abridgement originally found in the *Times* texts; narrow-spaced ellipses mark my own truncation.
12. Presuppositions are semantic associations accompanying a proposition, or semantic domain. The sentence *"Michael's wife is named Martha"* logically presupposes that *"Michael is married."* Likewise, they are consequences of a semantic association, such as between the source and target semantic domains of a metaphor. In semantics, logical presupposition is narrowly defined. In everyday discourse, a wider range of semantic associations is commonly inferred.
13. Each italicized metaphor appearing in the body of this book, like the sequentially numbered excerpts, is drawn from the *Los Angeles Times* database. Any exceptions are expressly described as fabrications.
14. In the excerpts throughout the book, additional metaphors can be noted which will not be discussed in the body of the book, such as in excerpts 1, *whipping boy,* 3, *erode,* 4, *spawn,* 20, *sap,* and 29, *chaos*. Mixing metaphors in nonliterary genres and everyday talk is rarely noticed. There is little sense of confusion of thought, or of anomalous passages. In the excerpts from the *Times,* there is ready mixing of metaphors that are associated with the distinctive NATION AS HOUSE and NATION AS BODY metaphors.
15. The exception to noncount measures occurs with the use of quantifiers followed by *of,* such as *two teaspoons of vinegar,* in which case the intrinsic liquid nature of fluids becomes secondary to the extrinsic calibration.
16. Lakoff 1987, pp. 141–144; Johnson 1987, pp. 113–119.
17. *Los Angeles Times,* July 6, 1998, B4.
18. On another note, the use of the term *literal,* in excerpts 2 and 18, demonstrates tacit recognition on the part of the writer of the force of metaphor. Since *face of the nation* in excerpt 18 is a metaphor, there is nothing literal to be understood by the term *literally.* In such cases the adverb can only function as an intensifier, meaning "very," or "intensely." Its use is intended to heighten the expressed severity of the effect of cultural change caused by non-European immigration.
19. Lakoff 1993.
20. Lakoff and Turner 1989.
21. As discussed by Gibbs 1994.
22. At the time of the political debate, the studies that contended that immigrants were a net loss to the economy included the 1992 Parker and Rea studies, a San Diego County survey, and the 1993 Huddle studies. Those which indicated that the immigrants were a net gain to the economy included the 1992 Los Angeles County study, a 1993 Urban Institute study, and a 1991 Federal Reserve Bank study. See G. Miller 1993; Simon 1993; A. Miller 1993a, 1993b; Lee 1993. Also see Vérnez and McCarthy 1996 for a

meta-analysis of these contending reports and Hinojosa and Schey 1995 for a nontechnical critique of those same studies.

23. Lovejoy 1936.
24. Lakoff and Turner 1989, pp. 170–189.
25. Lakoff 1996, p. 81.
26. Gould 1981, p. 21.
27. Gould 1995, p. 52.
28. For a recent example, see McKie's *Dawn of Man. The Story of Human Evolution*, a book written to accompany a BBC television series (2000, p. 38).
29. Lakoff 1993, pp. 208–209; Lakoff and Turner 1989, p. 55.
30. Chilton and Ilyin 1993.
31. González, Ríos, Maldonado, and Clark 1995.
32. Wetherell and Potter 1992; Valencia 1997.
33. Lakoff 1993.
34. I want to thank my colleague Guillermo Hernández for his commentary which led to this section.
35. In the November 1995 sample, eighteen sports articles, totaling 13,000 words, were reviewed.
36. One day (November 30, 1995) yielded thirty-one business articles, totaling 14,500 words.
37. Seven articles on Tyson were sampled (July–November 1989, totaling 5,750 words). Five articles on Keating were sampled (April–May 1990, n = 5,710 words).
38. Zagorin 1997.
39. Mehan 1997.
40. Gumperz 1982.
41. Said 1978.
42. D. Johnson 1994.
43. Suárez-Orozco and Suárez-Orozco 1995, p. 193.
44. Mehan 1997, p. 267.
45. Calavita 1996, p. 285. I emphasize the metaphor with SMALL CAPITALS.
46. Ibid., p. 296.
47. Piven and Cloward 1993, quoted in Calavita 1996, p. 294.
48. Lakoff 1996.
49. Ibid., pp. 187–188, Lakoff's emphasis.
50. Ibid., pp. 188–189.
51. However, FAMILY may not be a serviceable metaphor for the twenty-first-century nation. This metaphor suggests blood links among compatriots which are stronger bonds than those suggested by the NATION AS HOUSE, or even the NATION AS BODY. Although rarely used these days, the metaphor was used in reference to the United States in earlier centuries. One example will illustrate its problematic implications. In his second State of the Union address, Abraham Lincoln invoked a biblical allusion to the permanence of land:

> A nation may be said to consist of its territory, its people and its laws. The territory is the only part which is of certain durability. "One generation passeth away, and another generation cometh, but the earth abideth forever." It is of first importance to duly consider and estimate this everlasting part. That portion of

the earth's surface which is owned and inhabited by the people of the United States is well adapted to be the home of one national family, and it is not adapted for two or more.... Our national strife springs not from our permanent part; not from the land we inhabit; not from our national homestead.... Our strife pertains to ourselves.... In this view, I recommend the adoption of the following resolution and articles amendatory to the Constitution of the United States. (Basler 1953, pp. 528–530, emphasis added)

Although the nation was in the midst of the Civil War, Lincoln was not referring to Yankee and Rebel. Zarefsky (1999), among others, argues that the families contending for the nation were slaves and Whites. "Slavery...endangered the nation; no one doubted that. Lincoln [in this speech] presented his vision for disentangling the nation from its corrosive foe" (Paludan 1994, p. 163). To preserve the Union, Lincoln suggested in this speech a system of "compensated emancipation," coupled with colonization, to preserve the republic for Whites alone. The government would requisition the slaves from their owners, then these African Americans would be cast out of their homeland to foreign colonies.

The shared ancestry notion that is invoked by the NATION AS FAMILY metaphor places greater weight on lineage than can be sustained in a nation of immigrants, unless one line of descent is privileged over all others.

My colleague Richard Anderson (personal communication) contested this account of Lincoln's address and articulated another view about the NATION AS FAMILY metaphor. Anderson's view is acknowledged by Paludan, who states that "recent historians have downplayed Lincoln's proposal," citing James McPherson, who describes compensatory emancipation as "a peace measure to abolish the institution everywhere by constitutional means" (Ibid., p. 165).

On the second count, Anderson's heartening view on the value of the family metaphor deserves mention: "If we can use a term like 'brethren' to describe persons of another race than our own, then family metaphors need not be racially exclusionary metaphors. Because we perceive the United States as divided by race, there is a tendency among all racial groups to describe themselves as families to the exclusion of other races, but if we were to describe the American family, we might well preempt the use of family metaphors by particular racial groups. This might even contribute to changing the way Americans perceive each other."

52. There are other semantic associations of the NATION AS FAMILY metaphor to consider. Anderson 1999, in a comparative study of Soviet Russia and electoral Russia political discourses, demonstrates that Communist Party leaders employed family metaphors to place themselves "above" an infantilized citizenry, while post-empire Russian political leaders employ fewer vertical and hierarchical metaphors to describe their relationship to the electorate.

53. van Teeffelen 1994, pp. 384–386.
54. Miles 1989 quoted in Wetherell and Potter 1992, pp. 15–16.
55. van Dijk 1987, 1991.
56. Wetherell and Potter 1992, p. 70.
57. van Dijk 1989, p. 42.
58. Ibid., p. 43.
59. From "The Constitution of the United States: Is It Pro-Slavery or Anti-Slavery?" in Foner 1950, p. 477.

REFERENCES

Anderson, Richard D., Jr. 2001. "Metaphors of Dictatorship and Democracy: Change in the Russian Political Lexicon and the Transformation of Russian Politics." *Slavic Review* 60 (2): 312–335.

Basler, Roy P., ed. 1953. *The Collected Works of Abraham Lincoln,* vol. 5. New Brunswick, N.J.: Rutgers University Press.

Brownstein, Ronald, and Richard Simon. 1993. "Hospitality Turns to Hostility. California Has a Long History of Welcoming Newcomers for Their Cheap Labor—Until Times Turn Rough." *Los Angeles Times,* November 14, p. A1.

Calavita, Kitty. 1996. "The New Politics of Immigration: 'Balanced-Budget Conservatism' and the Symbolism of Proposition 187." *Social Problems* 43 (1): 284–305.

Chilton, Paul A., and Mikhail Ilyin. 1993. "Metaphor in Political Discourse: The Case of the 'Common European House.'" *Discourse and Society* 4 (1): 7–31.

Davis, Mike. 1995. "The Social Origins of the Referendum." NACLA *Report on the Americas* 29 (3): 24–28.

Foner, Philip S. 1950. *The Life and Writings of Frederick Douglass, Pre–Civil War Decade 1850–1860.* New York: International Publishers.

González, Gerardo M., Francisco A. Ríos, Lionel A. Maldonado, and Stella T. Clark. 1995. "What's in a Name? Conflict at a University for the 21st Century." In *The Leaning Ivory Tower: Latino Professors in American Universities,* ed. Raymond V. Padilla and Rudolfo Chávez Chávez, pp. 165–188. Albany: State University of New York Press.

Gould, Stephen J. 1981. *The Mismeasure of Man.* New York: W. W. Norton & Co.

Gould, Stephen J. 1995. "The Pattern of Life's History." In *The Third Culture,* ed. John Brockman, pp. 52–73. New York: Simon & Schuster.

Griswold del Castillo, Richard. 1990. *The Treaty of Guadalupe Hidalgo: A Legacy of Conflict.* Norman: University of Oklahoma Press.

Gumperz, John. 1982. *Discourse Strategies.* Cambridge: Cambridge University Press.

Gutiérrez, David G. 1995. *Walls and Mirrors: Mexican Americans, Mexican Immigrants, and the Politics of Ethnicity.* Berkeley: University of California Press.

Higham, John. 1955. *Strangers in the Land: Patterns of American Nativism, 1860–1925.* New Brunswick, N.J.: Rutgers University Press.

Hoffman, Abraham. 1974. *Unwanted Mexican Americans in the Great Depression: Repatriation Pressures, 1929–1939.* Tucson: University of Arizona Press.

Johnson, Donna M. 1994. "Who Is We?: Constructing Communities in U.S.–Mexico Border Discourse." *Discourse and Society* 5 (2): 207–231.

Johnson, Mark. 1987. *The Body in the Mind: The Bodily Basis of Meaning, Imagination, and Reason.* Chicago: University of Chicago Press.

Lakoff, George. 1987. *Women, Fire and Dangerous Things: What Categories Reveal about the Mind.* Chicago: University of Chicago Press.

Lakoff, George. 1993. "The Contemporary Theory of Metaphor." In *Metaphor and Thought,* 2d ed., ed. Andrew Ortony, pp. 202–251. Cambridge: Cambridge University Press.

Lakoff, George. 1996. *Moral Politics: What Conservatives Know That Liberals Don't.* Chicago: University of Chicago Press.

Lakoff, George, and Mark Turner. 1989. *More than Cool Reason: A Field Guide to Poetic Metaphor.* Chicago: University of Chicago Press.

Los Angeles Times. June 1992–June 1998. *CD-News.* New Canzan, Conn.: News Bank, Inc.

Lovejoy, Arthur O. 1936. *The Great Chain of Being: A Study of the History of an Idea.* Cambridge, Mass.: Harvard University Press.

McKie, Robin. 2000. *Dawn of Man. The Story of Human Evolution.* New York: Dorling Kindersley Publishing.

Mehan, Hugh. 1997. "The Discourse of the Illegal Immigration Debate: A Case Study on the Politics of Representation." *Discourse and Society* 8 (1): 249–320.

Paludan, Phillip Shaw. 1994. *The Presidency of Abraham Lincoln.* Lawrence: University Press of Kansas.

Said, Edward. 1978. *Orientalism.* New York: Routledge and Kegan Paul.

Suárez-Orozco, Carola, and Marcelo Suárez-Orozco. 1995. *Transformations: Immigration, Family Life, and Achievement Motivation among Latino Adolescents.* Stanford, Calif.: Stanford University Press.

van Dijk, Teun A. 1987. *Communicating Racism: Ethnic Prejudice in Thought and Talk.* Newbury Park, Calif.: Sage Publications.

van Dijk, Teun A. 1989. "Structures of Discourse and Structures of Power." *Communications Yearbook,* vol. 2, pp. 18–59.

van Teeffelen, Toine. 1994. "Racism and Metaphor: The Palestinian-Israeli Conflict in Popular Literature." *Discourse and Society* 5 (3): 381–405.

Vélez-Ibánez, Carlos G. 1997. *Border Visions: Mexican Cultures of the Southwest United States.* Tucson: University of Arizona Press.

Wetherell, Margaret, and Jonathan Potter. 1992. *Mapping the Language of Racism: Discourse and the Legitimation of Exploitation.* New York: Columbia University Press.

Zagorin, Adam. 1997. "Charlie's an Angel?" *Time,* February 3, p. 36.

Zarefsky, David. 1999. "Lecture 22: Moving toward Emancipation." *Abraham Lincoln in His Own Words.* Springfield, Vao: The Teaching Company.

Face the Nation: Race, Immigration, and the Rise of Nativism in Late-Twentieth-Century America

George J. Sánchez

On April 30, 1992, Americans across the nation sat transfixed by a television event that grew to symbolize the sorry state of race relations in late-twentieth-century urban America. The image of Reginald Denny, a white truck driver, being pulled from his cab at the corner of Florence and Normandie Avenues in South Central Los Angeles, beaten and spat upon by a group of young African-American males, quickly became a counterimage of the inhumane beating of black motorist Rodney King a year earlier. These two events of racial conflict, both captured on videotape, dominated representations of the Los Angeles riots in a city haunted by poverty, racism and police brutality. So focused have all Americans become of a bipolar racial dynamic in this country, usually framed in white/black terms, that we lost an opportunity to dissect one of the most important and complex events of our time. As the perceptive playwright and artist Anna Deveare Smith has observed, "We tend to think of race as us and them—us or them being black or white depending on one's own color." Indeed, the Los Angeles riots provide stark, critical evidence of the rise of a racialized nativism directed at recent immigrants and the American born who racially represent those newcomers, one of the most important social movements of our era.

A closer look at the victims of violence at the corner of Florence and Normandie reveals the way in which the Los Angeles riots were fundamentally an anti-immigrant spectacle at its very beginning. Most people outside of Los Angeles are surprised to hear that Reginald Denny was not the only person injured on that corner. Mesmerized by video images of a single beating of one white man, it is difficult to imagine that at least 30 other individuals were beaten at that same spot, most pulled from their cars, some requiring extensive hospitalization. Most importantly for my purposes, only one other victim of the violence at that corner besides Denny was white—and he was,

---

First published in *International Migration Review* 31 (Winter 1977): 1009–1030. Reprinted from "Face the Nation: Race, Immigration, and the Rise of Nativism in Late-Twentieth-Century America" George J. Sánchez, in *American Immigration and Ethnicity*, by David A. Gerber and Alan M. Kraut, editors, pp. 131–145. Reproduced with permission of Palgrave Macmillan.

like Denny, a truckdriver passing through the region. All others were people of color, including a Mexican couple and their one-year-old child, hit with rocks and bottles; a Japanese-American man, stripped, beaten and kicked after being mistaken for Korean; a Vietnamese manicurist, left stunned and bloodied after being robbed; and a Latino family with five-year-old twin girls, who each suffered shattered glass wounds in the face and upper body. All of these acts of violence occurred before Reginald Denny appeared.

Indeed, the first victims at Florence and Normandie were Latino residents who lived in the neighborhood. Marisa Bejar was driving her car through the intersection at 5:45 PM when a metal-covered phone book sailed through her car window, opening up a wound that took thirteen stitches to close. Her husband, Francisco Aragon, was hit on the forehead with a piece of wood, while their seven-month-old infant suffered minor scratches when a large metal sign was hurled through the rear window. Minutes later, when Manuel Vaca drove his 1973 Buick into the intersection, Antonine Miller and Damian Williams threw rocks through the windshield, causing Vaca to stop the car. Six men pulled Vaca, his wife and his brother from their car, then beat and robbed them. As Anthony Brown remembered, he kicked at Vaca "because he was Mexican and everybody else was doin' it." Sylvia Castro, a fourth-generation Mexican American and prominent activist in South Central, was shocked when bricks and bottles shattered her car window. Having worked closely with gang members in the area, she was able to escape with only a bloodied nose by speeding way.

Later, after Denny's assault was recorded and broadcast worldwide, several shocked black residents of the area risked their lives to save other victims. James Henry left his porch to pull Raul Aguilar, an immigrant from Belize, to safety after he had been beaten into a coma and a car had run over his legs. Donald Jones, an off-duty fireman, protected Sai-Choi Choi after several men beat and robbed him. Gregory Alan-Williams pulled a badly wounded Takao Hirata from the bloody intersection. Another savior at that corner was 59-year-old Reverend Bennie Newton, pastor of the Light of Love Church. He rescued the life of Fidel Lopez, a twenty-year resident of Los Angeles from Guatemala. Lopez, driving to his home one block from the intersection, was pulled from his car and later required 29 stitches in his forehead for a wound received by a blow with an auto stereo, 17 stitches to his ear, which someone had tried to slice off, and 12 stitches under his chin. Laying unconscious in the street from the beating, Lopez had motor oil poured down his throat and his face and genitals spraypainted blue. His life was saved when Newton began praying over his prostrate body with a bible in the air.

Over the four days of the Los Angeles riots, the dynamics of racial and class tensions, rage against the police, and antiforeign sentiment came together in violent, unpredictable fashion. From that corner of Florence and Normandie, the mayhem spread to engulf the city, creating the worst modern race riot in American history. Fifty-two lives were lost and 2,383 people were injured. About $1 billion of damage was done to residences and businesses, and over 14,000 arrests were made. In the first three days of rioting, over 4,000 fires were set and 1,800 people were treated for gunshot wounds. The destruction occurred throughout the Los Angeles basin, and the participants and victims were indeed multiethnic. But at its core, the Los Angeles riots provide stark evidence of the way in which immigrants provided the perfect scapegoat for American populations frustrated with developments in their society.

The decisions made by angry, young African Americans at that corner as they chose whom to hurt speak volumes to anyone interested in the intertwining of issues of race and immigration in late-twentieth-century America. For some, the decision was not about who was white, but about who was not black. For others it centered around how Latinos and Asians had "invaded the territory" of South Central, one which they claimed as their own turf, despite the fact that South Central Los Angeles had a majority Latino population in 1992. Others shouted (as heard on various videotapes) to "let the Mexicans go," but "show the Koreans who rules." Although the violence began as a response to a verdict passed by an almost all-white jury against an almost all-white set of police officers, quickly other people of color—those deemed foreign or foreign looking—were engaged in the deadly exchange. The meaning of racial and national identities was consistently at issue at the corner of Florence and Normandie, with serious and sometimes bloody outcomes for all participants.

Since May 1992, more clearly visible evidence has appeared which allows most social commentators to identify our current historical moment as one experiencing a particularly sharp rise in American nativism. Two years after the Los Angeles riots, California voters would resurrect their longstanding history as leaders in anti-immigrant efforts since the days of Chinese Exclusion by passing Proposition 187, a state initiative intended to punish illegal immigrants by restricting their access to schools, medical care, and other social services. This would be accomplished by deputizing social service providers as immigration inspectors, including teachers, social workers and doctors, and forcing them to identify to local law enforcement officials students and clients who had entered the country illegally. Here was legislation that tied issues of crime and immigration into a tidy package and allowed voters to voice nativist fears in the anonymous sanctity of the voting booth, a populist solution long well known in California. Polls showed that this piece of legislation won wide-spread approval across a range of ethnic groups, including 67 percent of whites (who formed 80% of the total electorate) and 50 percent of both Asian Americans and African Americans, with only 23 percent of Latinos voting in favor.

One feature of the campaign in favor of Proposition 187 was the prominent role played by California Governor Pete Wilson, a "moderate" Republican who had lost favor with the California electorate when his term coincided with the worst economic performance in the state since the Great Depression. His support of anti-immigrant positions was a centerpiece of his political comeback in California, where he won reelection from rival Kathleen Brown in November 1994 after coming from as much as 20 percentage points behind. This was not, of course, the first time politicians had found nonvoting immigrants to be the perfect scapegoat for an attempt at political resurrection. Indeed, at the height of the Great Depression in 1930, Herbert Hoover's Labor Secretary, William Doak, had promised to rid the country of "four hundred thousand illegal aliens" who he believed were taking jobs away from American citizens, thereby causing the great economic calamity of the period.

Indeed, Pete Wilson and Herbert Hoover have more in common than their tortured political paths through economic downturns. Both had previously been ardent supporters of the easing of immigration restrictions before the convenience of immigrant scapegoating in the political process became evident. During World War I, when Hoover had been Food Administrator for the U.S. government, he had personally encouraged President Woodrow Wilson to exempt Mexican immigrants from the provisions of the 1917 Immigration Act in order to allow them to engage in much needed agricultural labor and wartime production. In 1985, during the height of the congressional debates over the Immigration Reform and Control Act, then-Senator Pete Wilson was the key player in securing an exemption for California agricultural growers, enabling them to continue using undocumented workers long after more stringent enforcement was already in place in urban areas. Pete Wilson's ill-fated presidential campaign in 1995–96 cannot obscure the fact that his career remains the epitome of opportunistic politics, taking full advantage of America's longstanding fears of immigrants and foreigners when such a strategy can bring success at the polls.

During the past year, we also have witnessed the publication and media hype of a book which can easily be characterized as our era's equivalent to *The Passing of a Great Race,* the 1916 classic by [nativist writer] Madison Grant. Grant's contemporary counterpart is Peter Brimelow, senior editor at *Forbes* and *National Review.* His *Alien Nation: Common Sense about America's Immigration Disaster* (1995) unabashedly claims that recent immigration is likely "to transform—and ultimately, perhaps, even to destroy...the American nation." Within the first ten pages of the book, recent immigrants are blamed for rising crime rates, the health care crisis, lowering overall educational standards, and causing Americans to feel alienated from each other. Unlike other nativists, Brimelow wants to be clear to offer an overtly racial argument: "Race and ethnicity are destiny in American politics" declares Brimelow repeatedly, so all Americans should be concerned about restricting immigration of people who are colored differently than they.

Signs, therefore, point to a resurgence of a nativism unparalleled in this country since the 1920s. From attacks on immigrants in urban unrest to legislative action attacking immigration policies to academic and media discussions resonating the familiar intellectualized examinations of racialized dissonance of the past, today's nativism is as virulent as any that has gone before. Yet this era's nativism, like this era's immigration, has unique characteristics which differentiate it from that which appeared in the early twentieth century at the height of European immigration to the United States. Traditional hostility towards new immigrants has taken on a new meaning when those immigrants are racially identifiable and fit established racial categories in the American psyche. With the increase of immigration from Asia and Latin America, a new American racism has emerged which has no political boundaries or ethnic categorizations. From the left and right of the political spectrum, and from both white and black individuals, this new racism continually threatens to explode in contemporary American society.

One point worth making is that while nativist discourse is often decidedly linked to racial discourse, they are not one and the same, and they often lead in different directions. Part of the problem in separating racism from nativism is the fact that our collective understanding of what constitutes racism has become murkier since the 1960s. Having long abandoned biological categories of race and definitions of racism which rely fundamentally on individual prejudice, most academic discourse on racism in the social sciences remains unclear and undeveloped.

One shining exception to the academic murkiness I have been describing is the work of sociologists Michael Omi and Howard Winant, who define racism as a historically situated project which "creates or reproduces structures of domination based on essentialist categories of race." Not only would this definition allow us to convincingly label Brimelow's project racist but, for the purposes of this exploration, it would allow us to differentiate and complicate our present notions of nativism. To be able to do this is critical because historically there have always been proponents of open immigration who can be characterized as racist. For example, many of the employers of Mexican migrant labor during the 1920s voraciously fought against immigration restriction on the basis that Mexicans were biologically suited for stoop labor. W. H. Knox of the Arizona Cotton Growers' Association belittled nativists' fears of a Mexican takeover of the United States in 1926 by invoking racist constructions of Mexicans to the House of Representatives:

> Have you ever heard, in the history of the United States, or in the history of the human race, of the white race being overrun by a class of people of the mentality of the Mexicans? I never have. We took this country from Mexico. Mexico did not take it from us. To assume that there is any danger of any likelihood of the Mexican coming in here and colonizing this country and taking it away from us, to my mind, is absurd.

It is not difficult to find other instances, including in the contemporary period, of antirestrictionists espousing racist views of those immigrants they want to entice to come into the country.

Moreover, it should be clearly stated that not all restrictionist positions are fundamentally based on racial assumptions. The late Barbara Jordan, Chair of the United States Commission on Immigration Reform and former Congresswoman from Texas, while presiding over two reports which emphatically favor reduced entry of legal immigrants and the toughening of measures to curb illegal immigration, nevertheless offers a picture of immigration restriction which simultaneously evokes a renewed faith in American diversity. Jordan wrote:

> Legitimate concern about weaknesses in our immigration policy should not, however, obfuscate what remains the essential point: the United States has been and should continue to be a nation of immigrants.... The United States has united immigrants and their descendants around a commitment to democratic ideals and constitutional principles. People

from an extraordinary range of ethnic and religious backgrounds have embraced these ideals.... We are more than a melting pot; we are a kaleidoscope, where every turn of history refracts new light on the old promise.

Indeed, the active role of black public figures in contemporary discussions of immigration policy suggest that African Americans will play an increased role in contributing to a more exclusionary definition of American citizenship than has hitherto prevailed. Barbara Jordan was chosen by President Clinton as head of a federal advisory commission charged with proposing new measures to curtail illegal immigration, not just because of her expertise as a former member of the House, but also because of her race. Jordan's very presence on such a commission allowed her blackness to deflect potential charges of racism directed at the stringent provisions of the policy recommendations. In this new climate, it is obvious that all Americans can get caught in the white–black paradigm of race relations, a model that relies on opposites, opposites which too often substitute for the complexity and diversity of social and ethnic relations in the late-twentieth-century United States.

To understand the vexing dilemma of these issues, we must remember that two seemingly contradictory directions mark recent scholarship on race in the United States. On one hand, social scientists throughout the twentieth century have worked hard to challenge the biologistic paradigm which explained racial inferiority as part of a natural order. Despite recent exceptions like *The Bell Curve,* most scientific studies reject the notion that race should be equated with particular hereditary characteristics. Instead, social scientists have increasingly explored how race is a social construction, shaped by particular social conditions and historical moments to reflect notions of difference among human groups. Many academics have subsumed race under other categories deemed more critical to understanding social stratification, such as class or ethnicity. Yet racial theorists increasingly point out that race has its own particular role in modern society that cannot simply be buried as a byproduct of other social phenomena. Omi and Winant offer a definition of race which takes into account the instability of a social construction, yet does not see race as merely an illusion: "race is a concept which signifies and symbolizes social conflicts and interests by referring to different types of human bodies."

Indeed, the other major development in academic discussions is that "race matters" in understanding all forms of social conflicts in the modern world including those which do not, on the surface, appear to be racially inspired. [The] eruption of ethnic tensions in the wake of the collapse of the Soviet Union has forced non-American scholars to reassess their previous dismissal of these conflicts as holdovers from a premodern age, likely to disappear in our new postmodern world. In the United States, while this work has shaped a critical reconsideration of the drift toward discounting racial tension as simply a byproduct of class antagonism or cultural conflict, it also has largely remained limited to a discussion of the problematic relationship between African Americans and the majority white population. Even when other racial minorities are discussed, a binary relationship with the Anglo majority remains the central focus of these academic studies. The academic discussions of multiculturalism, in other words, have yet to produce a wide array of scholarship which effectively theorizes the fundamental multiracial character of either contemporary or historical U.S. society.

Although many philosophers and theorists have stressed that "race matters" in understanding American society, race in the national imagination has usually been reserved to describe boundaries between whites and blacks. Indeed, the 1990s has produced many important works by noted social commentators that continue to utilize a strict white/black racial dichotomy. Andrew Hacker (1992), author of *Two Nations: Black and White, Separate, Hostile, Unequal,* justifies his title and emphasis by claiming that Asians and Hispanics "find themselves sitting as spectators, while the two prominent players (Blacks and Whites) try to work out how or whether they can coexist with one another." While including voices of Asian Americans and Latinos in his collection of oral histories about "race," Studs Terkel subtitles his 1992 book, *How Blacks and Whites Think and Feel about the American Obsession.*

Asian Americans and Latinos, despite their active presence in American society in the mid-nineteenth century, are depicted as only the latest of immigrant groups to America, and they are described as engaging in patterns which more clearly represent early-twentieth-century European immigrant groups than separate racial populations. [Andrew] Hacker, for example, rather than using the actual history of Asian groups or Latinos in the United States, argues that "second and subsequent generations of Hispanics and Asians are merging into the "white" category, partly through intermarriage and also by personal achievement and adaptation. No more important figure than Nobel Prize winner Toni Morrison has made this claim recently in the newsmagazine, *Time.* In a special issue dedicated to immigration [published in 1993], Morrison writes:

> All immigrants fight for jobs and space, and who is there to fight but those who have both? As in the fishing ground struggle between Texas and Vietnamese shrimpers, they displace what and whom they can. Although U.S. history is awash in labor battles, political fights and property wars among all religious and ethnic groups, their struggles are persistently framed as struggles between recent arrivals and blacks. In race talk the move into mainstream America always means buying into the notion of American blacks as the real aliens. Whatever the ethnicity or nationality of the immigrant, his nemesis is understood to be African American.

This perspective, for all its insight into the crucial place of African Americans in American history, ignores the long history of racial discrimination aimed specifically at Asian Americans and Latinos in the United States. National scholars have a responsibility to study the whole nation and its history, but too often East Coast social commentators present a very thin knowledge of U.S. history more than a few miles away from the eastern seaboard. Both "Asians" and "Latinos" have been decidedly constructed as races in American history, long before the decade of the 1960s, and today both these subgroups have become lightning rods for discussions of race, equality, and the meaning of citizenship in contemporary America.

Even more importantly, a new perspective is needed in order to encourage us to rethink the meaning of multiracial communities in American history. Rather than simply being "communities in transition" to neighborhoods of racial exclusivity, these areas of cultural exchange and conflict can come to represent the norm in American racial and ethnic life, at least in the western half of the nation, not the exception. Indeed, refocusing on the persistence of these mixed communities allows urban scholars to compare the diversity of ethnic communities in the late twentieth century to the seemingly transitional ethnic communities of the early twentieth century. For Los Angeles and other large metropolitan areas, this perspective is crucial. Watts, for example, in the heart of South Central Los Angeles, had a majority Mexican population until the late 1920s, when African Americans from the American south began to migrate in large numbers to the city. Likewise, Boyle Heights in east Los Angeles was the center of the L.A. Jewish community in the 1920s, as well as home to a large Japanese American population stretching east from Little Tokyo and a sizable Mexican American group.

More recently, post–World War II racially restrictive policies of segregation have been replaced by a return to class-based zoning. This change, coupled with extensive post–1965 immigration, has created new communities of racial interaction in most urban centers in the United States. Most of these, however, include few white Americans. Yet, multiracial communities as diverse as Uptown and Edgewater in Chicago, Mt. Pleasant in Washington, DC, and Sunset Park and Jackson Heights in New York City have begun to focus attention on this seemingly new phenomenon. This interesting constellation of multicultural enclaves has produced some rather noteworthy, but not altogether new, racial dynamics. Much residential community interaction between blacks, Latinos and Asian Americans has occurred in urban centers in the American West over the past one hundred years, but never before in such a visible—that is, national—fashion. The histories of these past multiracial communities in the West, therefore, is as important a model for ethnic community as the homogeneous *barrio* depicted in so many works of Chicano history, or the standard portrait of a completely African American ghetto.

One result of homogeneous depictions of ethnic communities can be seen in the immediate media coverage of "communities" involved in the L.A. uprising. The erasure of Latino participation in the Los Angeles riots as both full-fledged victims and victimizers is troubling to those concerned about contemporary discussions of race in American life. In the 1980s, Los Angeles County added 1.4 million residents, and nearly 1.3 million—or 93 percent—were Latino. Even though Latinos made up the majority of residents in South Central Los Angeles and 45 percent of the residential population of Koreatown by 1990, both communities were defined in such a way that Latinos were considered "outsiders" in community politics and media formulations. Latinos were the single largest ethnic group arrested during the period of the riots, not only for curfew violations and undocumented status, but also as looters of their local Korean merchants. Estimates also indicate that between

30 to 40 percent of stores that were lost were Chicano or Latino owned. Moreover, during the three days of rioting, the Immigration and Naturalization Service took advantage of those arrested for curfew violations to deport over 2,000 Latino aliens. Yet the wider media and most academic accounts of the events of 1992 in Los Angeles have largely ignored the Latino role because it disturbs strongly held beliefs in notions of community, belonging, and race in this country. It is the constant depiction of Latinos as "newcomers" and "foreigners" that provides insight into the particular form of racialization which surrounds this group in American society.

It is time to consider what factors are at work during our current age which inform and promote our own brand of American nativism. Let me suggest three different antiforeign sentiments which mark the racialized nativism of the end of the twentieth century. The first is an extreme antipathy towards non-English languages and a fear that linguistic difference will undermine the American nation. Despite the fact that English has become the premier international language of commerce and communication, fueled by forces as widespread as multinational corporations, the Internet, popular culture and returning migrants, Americans themselves consistently worry that immigrants refuse to learn English and intend to undermine the preeminence of that language within American borders. Captured by statewide "English Only" proposals, which began in California but spread quickly across the nation, this fear seems to emanate from Americans' own linguistic shortcomings and their feeling of alienation from the discourse—be it personal, on the job, or on the radio—that monolingualism creates.

A second fear is one directly tied into issues of multiculturalism and affirmative action. Like papist conspiracy theories, this fear involves the uneasy belief that racialized immigrants take advantage of, in the words of [journalist] Michael Lind, "a country in which racial preference entitlements and multicultural ideology encourage them to retain their distinct racial and ethnic identities." Going beyond the denial of white privilege in contemporary U.S. society, this sentiment directly believes that contrived, misguided, and sometimes secretive government policies have tilted against white people in the 1990s. Though tied to a general antipathy towards people of color, the place of immigrants and those perceived as racially connected to Latino and Asian immigrants heighten the nature of some of these fears. Even some proaffirmative action activists bemoan the extension of programs to nonblacks, having equated the history of U.S. racism as that directed against only one racial group incorrectly defined as wholly non-immigrant. These programs, then, are deemed to be un-American, not only because they contradict America's supposed commitment to equality of opportunity, but also because they are literally favoring "non-Americans" in their results. While invoking the name of the CORE national director in the early 1960s, Lind writes:

> One wonders what James Farmer, the patron saint of quotas, would have said, if he had been told, in 1960, that by boycotting Northern corporations until they hired fixed numbers of black Americans, he was inspiring a system whose major beneficiaries would ultimately be, not

only well-to-do white women, but immigrants and the descendants of immigrants who, at the time of his struggles, were living in Mexico, Cuba, Salvador, Honduras, and Guatemala.

A third antiforeign sentiment has emerged in the 1990s, embodied in California's Proposition 187, which is quite unique and has not been seen since the Great Depression. Current anti-immigrant rhetoric focuses on the drain of public resources by immigrants, both legal and illegal, particularly their utilization of welfare, education and health care services. Unlike nativist calls which center around immigrants taking jobs from citizens, this sentiment feeds into stereotypes of nonworking loafers, particularly targeting women who supposedly come to the United States to give birth and sustain their families from the "generous" welfare state. Even when presented with evidence that immigrants are less likely to seek out government assistance than citizens, today's nativists scoff at the data and the researchers, like 187 proponent Harold Ezell, who retorted to one study showing immigrant underutilization of government-sponsored medical programs by saying, "He's obviously never been to any of the emergency rooms in Orange County to see who's using them—it's non-English speaking young people with babies." The notion that immigrants are now coming to the United States to take advantage of welfare, health and education benefits has led directly to federal legislation which allows states to ban such assistance to even legal immigrants, and this has enabled Governor Wilson to mandate such cut-offs in California.

Although cultural antipathies are often at work in producing fear of newcomers, more often than not economic fears of competition have also played a critical role. Nativism has always cut across political lines, finding adherents on both the right and left. In the 1920s, the American Federation of Labor played a critical role in encouraging immigration restriction by raising the spectre of newcomers' threat to the economic security of the American workingman. Samuel Gompers, president of the AFL, who supported voluntary and relatively unencumbered immigration as late as 1892, became a virulent nativist by the 1920s. Today's nativists similarly stretch across the political spectrum, from right-wingers like Pat Buchanan, to political "moderates" like Pete Wilson, to self-proclaimed liberals like Michael Lind.

What binds these individuals together is a profound sense of the decline of the American nation. With the rise of nativism since 1965, we are once again witnessing a defensive nationalism in the wake of profound economic restructuring. In place of a period of modernization which pushed the U.S. agricultural economy towards widespread industrial production, we are now witnessing rapid deindustrialization, the rise of a service and high tech economy, and the worldwide movement of capital which undercuts the ability of American unions to protect U.S. jobs. This economic transformation, coupled with antagonistic government policies, has certainly undermined central cities in the United States and made for fertile ground for nativist sentiments.

Indeed, underlying much of the frustration of the Los Angeles riot participants was the collapse of the inner-city economy, the negative flipside of the new "Pacific Rim" global economy. Los Angeles had lost 150,000 manufacturing jobs in the previous three years, and each of these jobs was estimated to take another three associated jobs with it. The new jobs which were created were disproportionately low-wage and dead-end forms of employment; in fact, 40 percent of all jobs created in Los Angeles from 1979 to 1989 paid less than $15,000 a year. Most of these jobs were taken by recent immigrants to the area, leaving African Americans few viable options for secure employment. The average earnings of employed black men fell 24 percent from 1973 to 1989, and unemployment swelled to record levels in the inner city. Middle-income Los Angeles was rapidly disappearing, leaving little opportunity for anyone to move up the economic ladder. This inequality was also highly racialized; the median household net worth for Anglos in the city in 1991 was $31,904, while only $1,353 for non-Anglos.

Clearly, one obvious target for the frustration in the [rioters] was the Korean merchants in South Central, who had replaced the Jews who left in large numbers after the 1965 Watts Riots. In 1990, 145,000 Koreans lived in Los Angeles County, a 142 percent increase over the previous decade and a phenomenal growth from only 9,000 in 1970. Unable to transfer their education and skills to the U.S. labor market, many Korean immigrants had pooled their funds to start small businesses in ethnic communities throughout the city. Koreans now saw their businesses burn to the ground and suffer widespread looting. These small merchants had filled a vacuum created by discrimination against African-American entrepreneurs and the abandonment of the by large retail businesses.

Yet much of the damage to Korean businesses occurred in Koreatown itself, where one third of that community's businesses were located. This community was unique in that it did not represent an area of ethnic succession, well known in the East, where one identifiable ethnic group was slowly being replaced by another, with the resulting tensions that succession produces. Here two recent immigrant populations met in unequal fashion, both reflecting cultures which had long been part of the L.A. racial makeup, but neither with particular historical roots to this area before 1965. Unlike other Asian enclaves in southern California, the residential population of Koreatown was overwhelmingly Latino, and it was this ethnic group which was primarily engaged in the looting of these stores. In fact, 43 percent of those arrested during the riots were Latino, while only 34 percent were African Americans, contradicting the notion that the Los Angeles riots were a simple black-Korean conflict. Economic frustrations fueled this looting and mayhem of the Los Angeles riots, even though a different racialized nativism set the events of late April 1992 in motion.

It is clear that we are in a period of economic transformation which can and should be compared to the period of industrialization that occurred a century ago and that has provided the social context for the rise of nativism in the United States that occurred in both periods. Yet today's economic transformation is intimately tied to an economic globalization propelled by multinational corporations and an age where capital and information flow relatively freely across national borders. From 1890 to the 1920s, the industrial transformation which changed the American economy and fueled international migration led to a breaking down of local community control towards a national interdependency which propelled Americans to "search for order" in new and varied ways. Not only did bureaucracy and science rise to provide this national order, but so did immigration restriction and scientific racism emerge to provide ideological comfort to Americans in search of a glue to keep together a nation undergoing fundamental social and economic change.

Many Americans have been shielded since World War II from the convulsions of the international economic order by the enormous strength of the U.S. economy, and liberal policies of inclusion have been crafted which assume the continuation of this extraordinary growth. Most important in coming to terms with the complexities of race, immigration and nativism in the late twentieth century is a perspective which can deal with the multiple meanings of race and equality in American society in an age of liberal political retrenchment and widespread economic restructuring. During the Reagan/Bush administrations and the current era of Republican ascendancy in Congress, hard-fought victories in racial and economic policy were and are continually threatened with extinction. In addition, supposedly "race-neutral" policies, such as tax reform and subsidies to the private sector, have disproportionally and adversely affected racial minorities.

Yet increasingly we must account for the fact that at least the Reagan/Bush era did not see a reversal of government spending despite all the rhetoric, but instead witnessed its redirection towards wealthy and corporate interests and away from long-term investment in education, infrastructure and safety nets for the poor. This "trickle-down" theory of social advancement has become the biggest failure of the 1980s, and it has left in its wake a sizable, disgruntled white electorate, one disaffected with politics that clamors for "change" at every turn. This group helped give the White House to the Democrats in 1992, handed large numbers of votes to Ross Perot, and offered the Republican Party a majority in both houses of Congress for the first time in thirty years in 1994. In this setting, one in which expectations of newfound prosperity grow with every change of political power, a scapegoat must be found amidst the citizenry that can be blamed for delaying the promised economic security. For many Americans in our era, the poor, especially the black poor, have served this role of scapegoat; increasingly, however, that role is being transferred to or combined with the blaming of the immigrant.

While the industrial economy was being sent through convulsions over the past thirty years, Americans produced largely cultural explanations for structural social problems. The demonization of black families, for example, served for white Americans as a plausible justification for the economic backwardness of African Americans, despite affirmative action and civil rights. Instead of focusing on the ravages of deindustrialization in both black and white communities, white Americans increasingly revived traditional stereotypes of black laziness. While these racialized beliefs were no longer acceptable public discourse in the post–civil rights era, researchers who take anonymous polls can still ferret out extensive negative race stereotyping rampant in the white community.

Indeed, it seems to me that cultural beliefs in innate difference have worked together with structural forces of inequality to frame (and hide) discussions of white privilege. Literary scholar Eric Lott has argued that attitudes towards blackness are shaped by white self-examination and insecurity, rather than by the realities of African American life. Indeed, contemporary white perceptions of blacks probably tell us more about the dangers of being "white" in this era than about strongly held beliefs regarding black inferiority. In fact, it is the language of liberal individualism that keeps many whites from seeking structural explanations for racial inequality. However, liberalism has always been a two-edged sword. When economic conditions become tenuous for whites, meritocratic rhetoric about the rewards of hard work and self-reliance also generates individual anxiety and a fear of personal victimization. Whites who are faced with economic failure or insecurity in spite of their racial privilege become a sure breeding ground for the scapegoating of racial others. This classic projection further obscures the need to acknowledge or understand the structural and economic sources of one's own oppression.

Closer analysis of the workings of liberal language deepens our understanding of the relationship between liberal racial attitudes and the structural causes of inequality. For example, liberal individualism, as a dominant value in American society, has an impact on the actions of individuals of all races. Indeed, a look at liberalism's impact on blacks and other racial minorities, including recent immigrants to the United States, would reveal that routine, systematic and unyielding discrimination does not necessarily lead to collective protest. More often than not, it produces a sense of individual victimization and anger. The Los Angeles riots demonstrated that injustice can provoke African American rage, not only against white authority, but against "racialized others," most notably Asians and Latinos living among blacks in newly "reintegrated" communities.

Today, the United States finds itself increasingly having to compete economically with nations from all over the world, including Third World nations trying to gain a stronger foothold in the international exchange of goods and services. At the same time, American corporations seem to have themselves become internationalized, more interested in gaining profit than in maintaining an economic nationalism rooted in American hegemony. It is not difficult to understand how immigrants from these developing nations can be seen as both drains on our national economy and symbols of countries who threaten American economic hegemony and the dream of a multicultural future in the post–Cold War era. These conditions have produced increasing calls for a "liberal nationalism" in the United States from the left side of the political spectrum, which often has gone hand-in-hand with calls for severe restrictions on immigration to the United States. In an analysis intended to aid working-class Americans, particularly American blacks, Michael Lind writes, "The most promising way to quickly raise wages at the bottom of the income ladder in the United States is to restrict immigration." Though always claiming that these efforts should not be characterized as nativist, the defensiveness of these renewed calls for nationalism and protectionism on the backs of recent and future immigrants point towards the eruption of a "liberal nativism" in American political discourse.

[In] the United States, the history of white on black racism blinds Americans from recognizing any other forms of interracial tensions. Racism against Asians and Latin Americans is dismissed as either "natural byproducts" of immigrant assimilation or as extensions of the white–black dichotomy. Moreover, when African Americans perform acts of racism, they are quickly ignored or recast except as a threat to a white-dominated society.

As the participants in the violence at Florence and Normandie indicate, interracial understanding and an inclusive sense of "community" is not simply formed by living in close proximity to those from other racial/ethnic groups. Rather, what is disturbing about the Los Angeles riots is the insistence that "community" reflects a single racial group. The irony of black protesters stopping construction projects in South Central Los Angeles on the basis that no one from the "community" was employed, even when Latino workers were their neighbors, seemed to be lost on everyone concerned. Moreover, these strategies of protest usually encouraged African American entrepreneurs who had left the residential neighborhood to return to invest and to hire (but not to live), with the untested assumption that they would be more likely to hire other blacks.

Indeed, to equate "community" with a particular racialized "identity" seems more to naturalize a recent geography of local communities which can easily forget the multiracial histories of the past. In Los Angeles, commentators rarely discuss the longstanding Asian and Latino communities which have been part of the region's history since the city's founding, relying instead on depictions of these racial groups as almost wholly recent immigrants. Ironically, African Americans become the perfect choice to project this historical amnesia and defend the sanctity of national boundaries, since their presence alone deflects any charge that anti-immigrant policies are racist. Since race in this nation has been constructed as a white/black affair, the continuation of this bipolar approach becomes critical to the ideology of an ordered American nation. In the United States, no less than in Germany or Japan, the power embedded in certain notions of territory must be critiqued and analyzed for the grounds upon which certain peoples and histories are privileged. Indeed, racialized immigrants have become the stepping stools for claims of American citizenship in the late twentieth century.

How have the immigrants themselves responded to these recent attacks? One response has been a marked increase in political involvement among all immigrants in U.S. politics, on the local and national levels. Within communities of immigrants from various nations in Asia, political involvement has usually emerged within racialized organizations, increasingly "pan-ethnic" in orientation. Although immigrants from Latin America have seemed to lag in their commitment to a pan-Latino consciousness, recent anti-immigrant efforts in California seem to have produced a decided turn towards political strategies and identities which go beyond national origins. Immigrant citizens and American-born ethnics in these communities have also heightened their own political involvement to fight for the rights of immigrants with the acknowledgement that their own racial construction often hangs in the balance. Surprisingly, this acknowledgement of common ties has even stretched beyond party affiliation. In California, Republican Bill Davila, the high-profile spokesperson and former CEO of Vons supermarkets, took out a full-page advertisement in 1994 asking voters to reject Proposition 187, even though he supported Pete Wilson's reelection campaign, calling the measure a "divisive, unproductive initiative...turning neighbor against neighbor."

Ironically, one of the most concrete expressions of this new political consciousness is the upsurge in the rates of naturalization among legal immigrants across the nation. The INS office in Los Angeles began receiving as many as 2,000 applications a day for naturalization after passage of Proposition 187, and offices around the country experienced similar increases. An all-time high was reached in 1995, with over 1 million immigrants becoming new American citizens. With the legalization of previously undocumented immigrants by the 1986 IRCA law, more long-term immigrant residents of the United States see the protection of citizenship in this time of immigrant-bashing and reduced benefits as a way to protect themselves and their families.

While on the surface these developments of political incorporation seem to reflect patterns of Americanization among earlier European immigrant groups to the United States, this is a decidedly ambivalent Americanism borne of racial tension and antiforeign sentiment. One 1994 statewide poll in California found that 25 percent of immigrants in the state personally feared discrimination and violence directed at them by virtue of looking foreign. As sociologist Rubén Rumbaut has put it, "the moral of the story is we reap what we sow. When you welcome people to a community, you encourage them to feel they matter and that they have a stake here. But if you sow hate, you'll reap the products of hate."

Do Home-Country Political Ties Limit Latino Immigrant Pursuit of U.S. Civic Engagement and Citizenship?

Louis DeSipio

Over the past decade, the number of immigrants naturalizing in the United States has surged. According to the Immigration and Naturalization Service (INS) and the Bureau of Citizenship and Immigration Services, naturalizations grew from an average of 146,000 annually in the 1970s, to 221,000 annually in the 1980s, to 562,000 annually in the 1990s. In the years since 1996—the beginning of the contemporary surge—the number of immigrants naturalizing annually averages 650,000.

The origins of this steady increase in naturalization are several. While there are particular shocks and enhanced incentives that appear periodically (Portes and Stepik 1993, DeSipio 1996a), the underlying cause of the contemporary growth in naturalization is the combination of high interest among immigrants in pursuing U.S. citizenship and steady growth in the long-term immigrant population (Pachon and DeSipio 1994, NALEO Educational Fund 2004). These long-term immigrants have been shown consistently to be more likely to naturalize than are more recent immigrants, particularly among Latinos, who make the largest pool of immigrants to permanent residence.[1] The increase in immigration beginning with the 1965 amendments to the immigration law ensures that there now are large numbers of immigrants with the twelve to fifteen years of legal residence that often precedes naturalization among Latinos (U.S. Immigration and Naturalization Service 2003: Tables M and 54, and INS *Statistical Yearbooks*, previous years).

The rapid increase in the number of immigrants naturalizing should not obscure the fact that there is also an increase in the number of immigrants eligible to naturalize who have not. Data on the emigration and deaths of the legal permanent residents is not maintained, so it is not possible to provide an exact number of citizenship-eligible immigrants. A recent estimate of 2000 census data conducted by the Urban Institute's Jeffrey Passel for the NALEO Educational Fund estimated that there were 7.7 million legal permanent

---

Lee, Taeku, S. Karthick Ramakrishnan, and Ricardo Ramirez, eds. *Transforming Politics, Transforming America: The Political and Civic Incorporation of Immigrants in the United States*, pp. 106–126. © 2006. University of Virginia Press. Reproduced by permission of the University of Virginia Press.

residents in the United States eighteen years of age or above with sufficient residence (generally, five years) to be eligible to naturalize. Of these, 4.2 million were Latinos (NALEO Educational Fund 2004). Legal permanent residents under eighteen years of age can naturalize only as part of their parents' naturalization.

This large pool of immigrants, including a significant share of longer-term immigrants, raises a recurring question for the polity. Will these immigrants join the polity and participate as equals with the U.S. born? The United States has faced this question before, but the cyclical nature of large-scale immigration makes it particularly pressing now. The roots of much contemporary immigration can be traced to the 1965 changes to immigration law. The dramatic effects of that law on the numbers of immigrants were not felt until the 1980s. So, we are now in the era of a mature immigration, where there are large numbers of recently naturalized citizens, many long-term permanent resident immigrants, and an even larger pool of short-term immigrants, many of whom are undocumented. This variety offers an analytical opportunity, exploited here, but also a pressing policy challenge.

In this essay, I want to revisit two existing scholarly literatures on the civic engagement of immigrants and on what differentiates immigrants who naturalize from those who do not. I want to see if the findings of this existing scholarship remain when a newly emerging characteristic in the contemporary immigrant experience is added to the story. Specifically, I want to analyze the impact of transnational political engagements and comparative evaluations of political opportunities in the United States and the country of origin on civic, residential, and political attachment to the United States.

This essay has three parts. First, I briefly review the existing scholarship on immigrant civic engagement and immigrant naturalization propensity and indicate why "transnational" politics might alter traditional patterns of U.S. immigrant political adaptation. Second, I discuss a new data source—the Tomás Rivera Policy Institute (TRPI) 2002 Immigrant Political Participation Survey[2]—that allows me to test the impact of several sets of immigrant characteristics that have been shown to shape immigrant civic engagement and naturalization propensity (demographic, attitudinal and familial, and immigration and settlement), but that also includes a rich battery of questions relating to home-country political engagement and attitudes toward the individual-level political opportunities in each country. Finally, I test three models of immigrant civic and political attachment to the United States.

IMMIGRANT CIVIC AND POLITICAL ENGAGEMENT

The degree to which immigrants engage U.S. politics has long been a topic of scholarly and public policy debate. Fear of permanent immigrant nonincorporation is often balanced in the popular mind by equally ungrounded fears that immigrants will dominate U.S. politics and change its core values (Huntington 2004a, 2004b, as contemporary examples). The reality, of course, has been somewhere between these poles historically and continues to be today. In this essay, I examine three measures of immigrant civic, residential, and political engagement in U.S. politics. Specifically, I assess community organizational involvement among Latino immigrants, long-term residential intentions, and naturalization behaviors. Community organizational activities are open to all immigrants and provide the opportunity to participate in civic life at the local level. All immigrants can plan long-term residence in the United States, but immigrant legal status may significantly shape those plans, particularly for those without legal status. Naturalization, conversely, is open only to legal permanent residents who meet statutory eligibility requirements (for most, five years of legal residence).

Immigrants from Mexico and other parts of the Americas have long participated in the activities of organizations meeting collective needs. The rebirth of Mexican American politics in the late nineteenth century and the first manifestations of Caribbean immigrant politics in this same era took the form of locally driven organizations formed to meet collective needs (Arellano 2000; Gutiérrez 1995, chapter 1; Sánchez Korrol 1994, chapter 5). Some of the major evolutions in twentieth century Latino politics were driven by new organizational formulations.[3]

Despite the critical role that organizations have played in the establishment and evolution of Latino politics in the twentieth century, organizational politics has diminished in importance for the broader field of Latino politics since the 1975 extension of Voting Rights Act (VRA) coverage to Latino communities (DeSipio 2004). The politics of U.S.-citizen Latinos has increasingly focused on electoral politics and community-based organizations often serve as foundations for candidacies and campaigns. The relative decline in the importance of organizational life to politics, of course, is not a characteristic unique to the Latino community (Skocpol 2003), but the decline is more dramatic in the Latino U.S.-citizen population, because organizations played a relatively more important role in the era before the VRA reduced the manipulation and exclusion of Latino voters.

For immigrant Latinos, who are largely precluded from direct participation in electoral politics, organizations retain their more traditional role as a centerpiece of community politics. Despite the importance of organizations to Latino immigrant politics, the majority of immigrants do not participate in organizations (a characteristic also true of U.S.-born Latinos) (de la Garza, with Lu 1999). The dynamics of which among Latino immigrants participates in organizations and who does not is relatively understudied. Sidney Verba, Kay Lehman Schlozman, and Henry Brady (1995, chapter 8; Burns, Schlozman, and Verba 2001, chapter 11) find that Latino immigrants are generally less likely than U.S.-born Latinos as well as whites and blacks to be organizationally involved.

Immigration has steadily increased in the 1980s and 1990s as has naturalization, so there is consistently a higher share of recent Latino immigrants relative to longer-term, nonnaturalized immigrants. A few characteristics of the Latino immigrant population are worth noting. First, Latinos generally, and Latino immigrants specifically, are younger and have lower levels of education and income than non-Hispanic whites. Also, the longer the length of residence in the United States, the higher the likelihood of community organizational participation among Latino immigrants (DeSipio et al. 1998).

Not all permanent residents naturalize. What distinguishes those who do from those who don't? As previously indicated, the single most important predictor of naturalization among immigrants is length of residence: immigrants who reside in the United States longer are more likely to naturalize than those with shorter periods of residence. This is true today and was true of turn-of-the-century immigrants (Gavit 1922; U.S. Immigration and Naturalization Service 2003, table 54). Speed of naturalization, however, varies by nationality and by region of origin. In the contemporary era, Asian immigrants naturalize the fastest and immigrants from the Americas naturalize the slowest. Traditionally, the nationalities with the longest wait between immigration and naturalization are nationals of the two countries that border the United States, Mexico and Canada.

At the individual level, several factors explain diverse rates of naturalization, among them demographic characteristics, attitudinal and associational variables, immigration and settlement characteristics, and inconsistent bureaucratic treatment. Of these, demographic characteristics of immigrants are the most studied and have been shown to have the most reliable and most sizeable impact on naturalization. Income, white-collar employment, professional status, home ownership, years of schooling, and English-language abilities increase the likelihood of naturalization (Barkan and Khokolov 1980, Portes and Mozo 1985, Jasso and Rosenzweig 1990, Yang 1994, DeSipio 1996b, Johnson et al. 1999). The married are more likely to naturalize than the unmarried, and women more likely than men. Immigrants who arrived as young children are more likely to naturalize than are those who arrived as teenagers or adults, controlling for length of residence.

Attitudinal and associational variables have also been shown to shape the likelihood that an immigrant will naturalize. Roots in the United States, attitude toward life in the United States, and social identification as an American each has been shown to have a positive impact on the likelihood of naturalization (García 1981, Portes and Curtis 1987). Immigrants who associate mostly with noncitizens are less likely to naturalize (DeSipio 1996b). Michael Jones-Correa (1998) finds that an "ideology of return [to the home country]" discourages naturalization. Finally, permanent residents who state an intention to stay in the United States are more likely to express an interest in pursuing naturalization and in successfully naturalizing (DeSipio 1996b).

Immigration and settlement experiences also shape naturalization propensity. Immigrants who entered as refugees, skilled workers, or for political reasons are more likely to naturalize (Jasso and Rosenzweig 1990, Portes and Mozo 1985). The higher the sending country's GNP, the lower the likelihood of naturalization (Yang 1994). National-origin differences persist after controlling for other factors shown to influence naturalization. Guillermina Jasso and Mark Rosenzweig (1990) find that immigrants from Mexico are less likely than average to naturalize than nationals of other large immigrant-sending countries. Controlling for sociodemographic, associational, and immigration-related factors, Louis DeSipio (1996b) finds that among Latinos, Cubans and Dominicans are more likely than Mexicans to begin the naturalization process and, once they began the process, to become U.S. citizens. Hans Johnson and colleagues (1999) examine how local governments can influence immigrant naturalization propensity.

The administration of the U.S. naturalization program (now part of the Department of Homeland Security—DHS) is the final factor shown to influence naturalization. Naturalization has traditionally been decentralized, which results in differential treatment of applicants from one INS district office to another (DeSipio and Pachon 1992). INS has recently proposed reforms that will minimize the variation in applicant treatment between naturalization offices (DeSipio, Pachon, and Moellmer 2001), but the legacy of this differential treatment will likely continue to cause confusion among some immigrants and, perhaps, discourage pursuit of naturalization. Potential naturalizees are further confused by repeated changes in the fees associated with naturalization (currently $390).

Incentives to naturalize and resources to assist immigrants seeking to naturalize also change. In the mid-1990s, for example, many immigrants felt besieged and feared losing the rights that had traditionally been extended to permanent residents (DeSipio 1996a). California passed Proposition 187, which denied state education and social service benefits to undocumented immigrants, and Congress passed the 1996 Welfare Reform bill, which eliminated permanent resident eligibility for federal social welfare benefits such as Supplemental Security Income and Aid to Families with Dependent Children. Congress also made it easier to deport permanent residents who committed crimes in the United States. Administrative changes at the Immigration and Naturalization Service (INS) also encouraged permanent residents to pursue naturalization. Permanent residents with green cards more than ten years old had to replace their cards for the first time in the agency's history. INS also repeatedly raised the fee for naturalization in this period. Finally, Latino and immigrant organizations increased the resources available to assist immigrants to pursue U.S. citizenship. Univision and other Spanish-language media promoted the importance of naturalization to Latino audiences.

It is not possible to disaggregate the impact of changes on an individual Latino's propensity to naturalize (DeSipio and Pachon 2002), but the cumulative effect of these pressures and the growing pool of citizenship-eligible immigrants was to move the largest number of immigrants in American immigration history to apply for naturalization.

Over the past decade, scholars of the U.S. immigrant experience have increasingly analyzed the degree to which immigrants, and in some cases their U.S.-born children, engage the politics of their sending communities and countries. This emerging scholarship of immigrant political transnationalism has made important, if sometimes overstated, contributions to our understandings of the mechanisms of immigrant participation in home-community and home-country society and of politics and of immigrant settlement in the United States. For the most part, the case studies of active political transnationalism examine a specific immigrant-sending community (e.g., Levitt 2001) or a specific form of transnational behavior across multiple immigrant-ethnic populations, for example, migrant remittances (de la Garza and Lowell 2002). Some transnational scholarship theorizes about the opportunities for the creation of sustained transnational connections between immigrants and their sending communities (Glick Schiller, Basch, and Blanc-Szanton 1992; Smith and Guarnizo 1998).

The new scholarship of transnational politics has also explored the administrative structures and political implications of sending-country efforts to extend nationality or citizenship to emigrants abroad (de la Garza and Velasco 1997, González-Gutiérrez 1999, de la Garza and Pachon 2000, Jones-Correa 2001b). Scholars have also begun to explore whether transnational political attachments extend into the second generation (Fouron and Glick Schiller 2001, Levitt and Waters 2002). Finally, political theorists have also begun to explore the impact of new transnational political formation among émigrés on traditional conceptions of citizenship (Guarnizo 1997b, Ong 1999). As more émigrés and, perhaps, their children begin to maintain political ties in both the United States and their country of origin/ancestry, traditional country-bound notions of citizenship may have to be recast (Soysal 1994, Bosniak 2001).[4]

This burst of scholarship and the underlying phenomenon that it documents highlights what might be a weakness in existing study of civic engagement and naturalization propensities among immigrants in the United States. While certainly not a new phenomenon, the volume of contemporary immigration and the relative ease of international communication and transportation make it much easier for immigrants to be transnational. The transnational scholarship shows that some subset of immigrants—approximately 20 percent of Latino immigrants and few in the second generation, by my estimate—engage the civic and political life of their sending communities or countries after emigration (DeSipio et al. 2003). Yet, this scholarship does not, for the most part, ask about the consequences of transnational engagement for civic engagement in immigrant-receiving societies, in residential plans of immigrants, or in naturalization.

Transnationalism raises questions about what we know about immigrant civic engagement and immigrant naturalization propensity. One possibility (hypothesis one) is that transnational engagement in the civic and political life of the sending country reduces the likelihood that immigrants will become involved in U.S. civic life or seek naturalization. If the transnational engagement allows a space for immigrants to achieve their political goals in their countries of origin and reduces the bonds that have developed in the past between immigrants and the United States, then immigrants who are transnationally engaged will be less likely to manifest civic or political attachment to the United States, controlling for other factors. A second possibility (hypothesis two) is that the transnational engagement offers a resource for immigrants who have engaged in transnational activities and that they can translate the skills, networks, and interests that they have developed to U.S. civic life and to naturalization.

This hypothesis—that the transnationally engaged will be more likely to be civically engaged in the United States and to naturalize—builds on two notions. The first piece is that political learning is transferable, so skills and interests developed in transnational politics can be applied to U.S. politics (and visa versa). The second is that some people are more likely than others to become engaged in civic and political life. For immigrants, these interests are more likely to first manifest themselves in home-country focused community and civic activities because those are more pressing and more attainable. The interests of these more civically/politically engaged immigrants, however, soon shift to their communities in the United States. Clearly, the null hypothesis is that transnational behavior is irrelevant to immigrant civic engagement or naturalization. If this is the case, then the measures of transnational behavior will not prove significant, and traditional predictors of civic and political engagement will assume their traditional roles.

In the analysis that follows, I test three models of civic and political engagement in the United States among contemporary Latino immigrants. The first model measures Latino immigrant propensity to participate in U.S. civic organizations. The second looks at long-term residential intentions. Finally, the third analyzes naturalization among Latino legal permanent residents eligible for naturalization. These models include factors shown to influence the likelihood of organizational participation and naturalization. I add to these predictors two measures of transnational political behaviors and two measures of attitudes toward political opportunities in the sending country and in the United States.

DATA

The analysis is based on the results of a telephone survey with 1,602 Latino immigrants conducted by the Tomás Rivera Policy Institute in July and August 2002. To ensure that we could analyze between Latino national-origin groups, TRPI targeted the survey to four nationality groups—three of the four largest Latino immigrant populations (Mexicans, Dominicans, and Salvadorans)[5] as well as Puerto Ricans. Although Puerto Ricans are not immigrants because of the Jones Act, TRPI hypothesized that they experience a political adaptation as migrants that parallels most experiences of immigrants. Puerto Ricans have, for the most part, been neglected in the scholarship on transnational politics. That said, they are U.S. citizens by birth and, consequently, are excluded from my analysis of U.S. naturalization propensity.[6]

The survey includes at least 400 respondents from each national origin group. In households with more than one eligible adult, TRPI randomly selected the respondent (using the "most recent birthday" method) to reduce bias in sample. Respondents were given the opportunity to respond in either English or Spanish, and all interviewers were fully bilingual. Approximately 94 percent of respondents answered the questionnaire in Spanish. On average, surveys took seventeen minutes to complete once the screening was completed.[7]

Characteristics of respondents' families, as well as the respondents' demographic immigration characteristics appear in the DeSipio and colleagues 2003 study. A quick review of these data indicates that the respondents to the TRPI Immigrant Political Participation Survey are broadly representative of the immigrant populations from these four nations. The share of naturalized respondents among those either reporting citizenship or legal permanent resident status also closely resembles the Latino legal immigrant population as a whole.

U.S. CIVIC AND RESIDENTIAL ATTACHMENT AMONG CONTEMPORARY LATINO MIGRANTS

I test the relationship between transnational political engagement and U.S. residential and civic attachments using multivariate models of this engagement. The first model tests for the predictors of engagement in at least one of seven U.S. civic organizations (a church, a labor union, a parent-teacher organization, a sports club, a fraternal order, a hometown association, or any other club). Approximately 28 percent of respondents reported *no* memberships in any of these organizations. This is a straightforward test of participation in organizations that immigrants can participate in regardless of legal status and that are reliable predictors of other forms of political activity. The second model tests for the predictors of intent to make a permanent home of the United States. Overall, approximately 61 percent of respondents reported that they did plan to make a permanent home of the United States. Although this is probably an underestimate of the actual long-term residential patterns of these migrants, it offers an indication of where immigrants see their long-term future and captures a nascent sense of connection between immigrants and the United States, regardless of immigration status. Finally, the third model focuses on predictors of naturalization. Since naturalization is limited to permanent residents with five years of legal residence, I exclude respondents without legal status and permanent resident respondents with fewer than five years of permanent residence from this model. I also exclude Puerto Ricans. This diminishes the sample somewhat to 710. In the TRPI Immigrant Participation Survey, approximately 28 percent of residents from Mexico, the Dominican Republic, and El Salvador reported that they were not permanent residents or naturalized U.S. citizens. Of the remainder, 62 percent were permanent residents and 38 percent had naturalized.

The models I tested included three components: respondent demographics, respondent immigration and settlement characteristics, and respondent transnational political engagement and evaluations of political opportunities in the United States and the sending country.

As I have indicated, demographic characteristics have long been known to influence naturalization and civic engagement. I include four demographic traits in this model: age,[8] education, household income, and gender. Based on the available scholarship, I anticipate that older, more-educated, and higher-income respondents are more likely to be civically engaged in the United States and to be naturalized. I would also expect these demographic characteristics to be positive predictors of intending to reside permanently in the United States, though there is no scholarship on this question to substantiate this expectation. Latina immigrants have been shown to be more likely to be engaged in community organizations and to pursue naturalization (Alvarez 1987, DeSipio 1996b, Pardo 1998).

I also control for the impact of several immigration and settlement-related characteristics: length of residence in the United States, respondent immigrant legal status, location of the respondent's immediate family, experience of discrimination in the United States, and country of origin. Based on the previous scholarship, I anticipate that migrants who have resided in the United States for longer periods will be more likely to be engaged in U.S. civic activity, more likely to anticipate spending their lives in the United States, and much more likely to be naturalized. Those with legal status or who had naturalized would also be more likely to be civically engaged. Respondents whose immediate families are in the United States or are divided between the United States and the country of origin will be more likely to engage U.S. civic activities and be naturalized than are those whose family members are primarily abroad. Finally, based on some previous research in immigrant responses to discrimination in the United States (DeSipio 2002), I anticipate that respondents who perceive greater levels of discrimination in U.S. society will be more likely to be engaged in U.S. civic activities and to have naturalized. Discrimination here is a learned response that measures understanding of U.S. political institutions. I also include country of origin as a control, but have no prediction as to the effects.

Finally, I include four measures of transnational political engagement: (1) participation in organizations facilitating transnational engagement in the past year, (2) participation in home-country elections or election-related activities in the period since migration, (3) attitudes toward where the respondent's political voice would be more likely to be heard, and (4) perceived levels of influence in the home country and the United States.

If transnational engagement facilitates incorporation in the United States, I would anticipate that these factors would have a generally positive effect on the dependent variables, controlling for the other factors. If, however, transnationalism encourages greater distance from the United States, the variables would be signed negatively.

Organizations, meetings, and sending-country government offices offer a connection between immigrants and their countries of origin. Overall, approximately 70 percent of immigrants/migrants from the four nations under study have engaged in transnational organizational activity in the year before the survey. Dominicans and Puerto Ricans were the most likely to have engaged in these transnational activities and Salvadorans the least likely. Just 60 percent of Salvadorans had participated in transnational organizational activity in the year before the survey.

With the exception of following politics in the news, very few Latino immigrants engaged in transnational electoral or partisan activities. No more than one in nine, for example, had voted in home-country elections. Few had contributed money to candidates or parties in the home country, attended a rally in the United States for a home-country party, or had been contacted by a representative of the home country to become engaged in home-country political or cultural affairs. Overall, just 19 percent had participated in some electoral behavior in the country of origin since migration. Puerto Rican migrants and Dominican immigrants were the most likely to have participated in home-country electoral behaviors, and Mexicans and Salvadorans were the least likely. Nearly 30 percent of Dominican immigrants had been electorally active in the Dominican Republic since immigration to the United States.

The final two variables in the model test respondents' perceptions of political opportunities in the United States and in the country of origin. The first is a question of how much influence the respondent perceives that she or he has on home-country politics. I report it as a three-point scale from "none" to "a great deal." I include this as a control to make sure that the reported transnational behaviors do not oversignify a sense of influence. In other words, it is possible that immigrants who are engaged at home are doing so for family or social reasons and do not perceive their activities to be politically influential. Few respondents believe that they have no influence (less than 10 percent for each nationality group); the majority of each nationality group reports that they have "some" influence on the home nation. Between 24 percent (Puerto Ricans) and 36 percent (Salvadorans) perceive that they have "a great deal of influence."

The final transnational variable asks respondents where they perceive they have more influence—the home country, the United States, or both equally. Nearly 50 percent of respondents report that they have more influence in the United States. Dominicans are the most likely of the four nationality groups under study to report that they have more influence in the home country (21 percent); Puerto Ricans are the least likely (11 percent).

RESULTS

Demographic and immigration characteristics proved more salient in predicting the likelihood of immigrant participation in U.S. civic and community organizational activities than did the transnational measures. These traditional explanatory variables, however, were joined by one of the transnational measures—participation in home-country organizational activity.

Not surprisingly, more-recent immigrants were somewhat less likely to participate in U.S. political organizations. Respondents with families in the United States (whether all or in part) were more likely to participate. As predicted, respondents reporting having experienced discrimination were somewhat more likely to be organizationally involved (by a factor of two). Somewhat unexpectedly, increasing levels of education had a negative effect on the likelihood of civic involvement. Permanent residents and naturalized citizens were more likely to be civically involved than immigrants without legal status.

One of the measures of transnational engagement also proved to be a significant predictor of U.S. organizational involvement controlling for the more traditional predictors. Respondents who reported membership in organizations focusing on the country of origin were more likely to also be involved in U.S. organizations. This suggests, perhaps not surprisingly, that some immigrants are simply more organizationally engaged. It also may suggest that the distinction that I am making between U.S. organizations and home country-focused organizations is not so rigid.

The factors shaping migrants' long-term intentions about whether to reside in the United States or the country of origins are shaped by a combination of immigration and transnational engagement factors. Demographic characteristics other than, possibly, age had little statistically significant impact on a reported intention to stay in the United States—each additional year of age increased the likelihood of reporting an intention to stay in the United States by about 1 percent in the specification of the model that excluded length of residence in the United States.

In terms of immigration characteristics, more recent immigration diminished the likelihood of reporting an intention to stay in the United States (each additional year reduced this likelihood by 4 percent) and respondents with most of their family in the United States were more likely to report an intention to stay as were permanent residents and naturalized citizens relative to migrants without legal status. Salvadorans were more likely than Mexicans to report an intention to stay (by a factor of more than 1.5). Puerto Ricans and Dominicans were about half as likely as Mexicans to report an intention to stay in the United States. Perceived discrimination had no effect on residential intentions.

The transnational factors had a consistent impact. Respondents who reported engagement in home-country electoral activities were approximately 25 percent less likely than those who did not report an intention to stay in the United States permanently. Involvement in home-country organizational activities was signed negatively but did not achieve statistical significance. Respondents who perceived they had more political influence in the United States were more likely to report an intention to remain in the United States permanently.

Because expectations about long-term residential patterns are so strongly shaped by one factor—year of immigration—I tested a second specification of this model that excluded this variable. The predictive power of the model declined significantly with this exclusion but did not alter the results. The predictive power of location of family increased in significance and magnitude as did the predictive power of where the respondent thought she or he had more influence. Respondents who believed they had more influence in the United States were nearly twice as likely to report an intention to stay in the United States as those who believed they had more influence in the home country.

The findings of the existing scholarship on propensities to naturalize are largely confirmed. Demographic factors dominate the story, particularly in a model that excludes year of immigration. In the specification including year of immigration, years of education has the most explanatory power. My sense is that education both offers substantive skills that are rewarded in the U.S. economy and the bureaucratic coping skills needed to complete the naturalization application process. In this specification, year of immigration also proves significant, with each additional year reducing the likelihood of naturalization by approximately 12 percent. Women were more likely than men to naturalize. Income was positively signed and significant, but had no substantive impact. Family in the United States also proved to be a positive predictor, but of marginal significance.

Only one of the transnational measures proved to be significant: respondents who perceived they have more political influence in the United States were more likely to be naturalized than immigrants who perceived they had

Table 9
Predictors of Respondents' Involvement in U.S. Organizations

Independent variable	Odds ratio	SE
Demographics		
Age	0.998	0.008
Education (grade school or less)		
Some high school	0.873	0.213
HS graduate	0.611**	0.237
Post–high school	0.760	0.254
Household income	1.000***	0.000
Gender (men as control)	1.269	0.164
Immigration characteristics		
Year of immigration	0.965***	0.011
Immigration status (not permanent resident or naturalized citizen)		
Permanent resident	2.001***	0.219
Naturalized citizen	1.553**	0.283
Location of family (most in home country)		
Equally divided	1.486**	0.194
Most in the U.S.	1.838***	0.224
Country of birth (Mexico as control)		
Puerto Rico	1.426	0.310
El Salvador	1.058	0.216
Dominican Republic	0.844	0.250
Experience of discrimination in U.S.	2.016***	0.193
Transnational political engagement		
Home-country electoral behaviors	0.970	0.182
Home-country originally behaviors	1.761***	0.086
Home-country political influence (none)		
Some	0.788	0.289
A great deal	0.613	0.311
Where does respondent have more influence (home country)		
About the same	0.865	0.236
More in the U.S.	0.966	0.227
Constant	69.523***	21.716
Total cases	1,051	
Predicted correctly	77.7%	
R-squared	0.239	

***$p \leq 0.01$, **$p \leq 0.05$; *$p \leq 0.10$.
Source: The TRPI Immigrant Political Participation Survey, 2002.

Table 10
Predictors of Respondents' Prediction of Long-term Residence—Home Country or the United States

Independent variable	Full model		Model excluding year of immigration	
	Odds ratio	SE	Odds ratio	SE
Demographics				
Age	0.992	0.007	1.013**	0.005
Education (grade school or less)				
Some high school	1.215	0.180	1.213	0.170
HS graduate	1.134	0.205	1.061	0.190
Post–high school	1.225	0.213	1.236	0.201
Household income	1.000	0.000	1.000	0.000
Gender (men as control)	1.045	0.138	1.057	0.129
Immigration characteristics				
Year of immigration	0.961***	0.009	Excluded	
Immigration status (not permanent resident or naturalized citizen)				
Permanent resident	1.794***	0.202	1.911	0.189
Naturalized citizen	1.720***	0.248	2.215	0.227
Location of family (most in home country)				
Equally divided	1.110	0.172	1.247	0.158
Most in the U.S.	1.814***	0.188	2.153***	0.173
Country of birth (Mexico as control)				
Puerto Rico	0.455***	0.245	0.509***	0.227
El Salvador	1.493**	0.195	1.365*	0.181
Dominican Republic	0.562***	0.215	0.478**	0.200
Experience of discrimination in U.S.	0.983	0.149	1.025	0.139
Transnational political engagement				
Home-country electoral behaviors	0.739***	0.134	0.780**	0.127
Home-country originally behaviors	0.986	0.060	0.963	0.055
Home-country political influence (none)				
Some	0.857	0.242	0.847	0.228
A great deal	0.753	0.261	0.782	0.245
Where does respondent have more influence (home country)				
About the same	0.880	0.203	0.894	0.189
More in the U.S.	1.763***	0.190	1.892***	0.000
Constant	78.188***	17.188	−1.393***	0.388
Total cases	1,051		1,172	
Predicted correctly	64.2%		63.2%	
R-squared	0.179		0.156	

***$p < 0.01$, **$p < 0.05$; *$p < 0.10$.
Source: The TRPI Immigrant Political Participation Survey, 2002.

Table 11
Predictors of Respondent Naturalization (Among Legal Permanent Residents with Five or More Years of Residence)

	Full model		Model excluding length of residence	
Independent variable	Odds ratio	SE	Odds ratio	SE
Demographics				
Age	1.008	0.011	1.051***	0.008
Education (grade school or less)				
Some high school	1.565**	0.305	1.406	0.273
HS graduate	1.931*	0.349	1.491	0.298
Post–high school	3.827***	0.345	3.048***	0.301
Household income	1.000***	0.000	1.000***	0.000
Gender (men as control)	1.712**	0.224	1.548**	0.197
Immigration characteristics				
Year of immigration	0.879***	0.018	Excluded	
Location of family (most in home country)				
Equally divided	1.494	0.316	2.086***	0.280
Most in the U.S.	1.693*	0.317	3.234***	0.279
Country of birth (Mexico as control)				
El Salvador	1.105	0.289	0.641*	0.251
Dominican Republic	1.219	0.298	0.729	0.256
Experienced discrimination	1.081	0.245	1.152	0.213
Transnational political engagement				
Home-country election behaviors	1.067	0.220	0.989	0.196
Home-country originally behaviors	0.965	0.099	0.770	0.085
Home-country political influence (baseline = none)				
Some	0.887	0.365	0.699	0.332
A great deal	1.261	0.386	0.835	0.349
Where does respondent have more influence (baseline = home country)				
About the same	0.884	0.343	0.948	0.303
More in the U.S.	1.787*	0.304	1.949**	0.266
Constant	252.177***	36.181	−4.505***	0.685
Total cases	546		611	
Predicted correctly	74.0%		72.8%	
R-squared	0.384		0.269	

***p < 0.01, **p < 0.05; *p < 0.10.
Source: The TRPI Immigrant Political Participation Survey, 2002.

more influence in their country of origin. Considering that the behavioral measures of transnational engagement proved significant in the other models, this finding should offer some solace to critics of U.S. naturalization policy. Immigrants who naturalize are distinguished from those who do not based on individual characteristics and their family relationships (as has, arguably, always been the case) rather than because of newly emerging relationships with their countries of origin.

For reasons discussed earlier, I tested a second specification of the model excluding year of immigration. As with the second specification of the residential intentions model, this specification had less overall predictive value. In this model, age attained statistical significance. The highest level of education remains significant, though the magnitude of the impact declines slightly. Location of family members becomes quite significant, with respondents reporting most family members in the United States reporting naturalization more than 3.2 times higher than respondents reporting most family members in the country of origin. In this specification, Salvadoran migrants proved less likely to naturalize than Mexican migrants. As was the case in the first specification, respondents reporting more political influence in the United States were considerably more likely to naturalize than those reporting more in the home country, controlling for the other variables in the model.

CONCLUSIONS

As the post-1965 wave of immigration has begun to mature, the United States is, in many ways, in a new phase of its long immigration history. The current wave of immigration is soon to reach its fortieth birthday. Unlike the post–Civil War immigration wave, the roots of an organized opposition to immigration at current levels—either legal or unauthorized—do not have a foothold in the policymaking process or in mass organizing (Tichenor 2002). So, it is reasonable to assume that immigration will continue at current levels, or increase, for the foreseeable future.

Immigrants today have opportunities to sustain or rebuild an engagement with their sending communities and sending countries in a way that was difficult for most in the past. Transportation and communication networks allow for a sustained transnational engagement for many migrants. The volume of immigration and the networks that facilitate it ensure that many immigrants in the United States live and work around many from the same sending communities. Many continue to have family in these communities. Although a political transnational engagement is the exception rather than the rule among most Latino immigrants, it is important to measure whether this nascent transnationalism is reshaping the process of immigrant civic and political engagement in U.S. politics and society.

Although this question can only be answered rigorously with longitudinal data, the evidence from the TRPI Immigrant Political Participation Survey offers some insights. The expanding opportunities for migrants to be involved in the electoral politics of their sending countries does appear to have an independent effect on their perceptions of long-term connection to the United

States and, in more cases than not, speeds it. Involvement in these activities reduces respondents' evaluations of the likelihood of their staying in the United States permanently. At the same time, this one form of home-country engagement is balanced by perceptions of influence. Migrants who perceive they have equal or more influence in the United States see their futures here unlike those who perceive that their influence is primarily in the sending country. These impacts appear even after controlling for demographic and immigration/settlement related characteristics previously shown to influence questions of attachment.

With one exception, transnational engagement has little impact on U.S. organizational participation. The exception—home-country organizational behavior—quite likely tells a story not of transnationalism, but of political socialization. Individuals who are organizationally active are likely to be active in many arenas. Finally, transnational engagement does shape naturalization propensity, but in a civically encouraging manner. Those who feel the most influence in the United States are the most likely to have naturalized. This indicates that there remains a political dimension to decisions to naturalize. Home-country electoral or organizational involvement are not statistically valid predictors of naturalization, suggesting that Latino immigrants are not using transnational opportunities in ways that some scholars anticipate of a fully realized dual citizenship.

The final lesson of this survey of Latino immigrant transnational attitudes and behaviors is that this new set of resources for immigrant politics must be accounted for as scholars continue to analyze the contemporary process of immigrant incorporation in the United States. The contemporary scholarship analyzes the story of immigrant social and political adaptation as one that occurs primarily in the United States. While transnationalism is the exception in immigrant communities today, and will probably remain so in the future, it nevertheless offers an opportunity (and a new one, for the mass of immigrants) for political socialization and an outlet for individuals' civic energies. As the number of immigrants grows and the concentrations of immigrants from specific parts of the world deepen, it is likely that some will have political experiences shaped by transnational engagements that are distinct from the majority and that these engagements will lead them to different political and civic outcomes. As the data here suggest, that difference can serve as an encouragement to increase connections to the United States and to U.S. civic institutions. It is also possible, however, to envision a scenario where these transnational engagements act as a further barrier to informal and formal connections between immigrants and U.S. politics.

NOTES

I would like to express my appreciation to Ricardo Ramírez, Karthick Ramakrishnan, Taeku Lee, and the participants in the "A Nation of Immigrants: Ethnic Identity and Political Incorporation" conference for comments on an earlier draft of this chapter.

1. I use the terms Latino and Hispanic interchangeably to refer to U.S. residents who trace their origin or ancestry to the Spanish-speaking nations of Latin America. The focus

of this project is Latino immigrants and migrants, so all analysis of Latinos presented here refers to people who were born in one of the four nations included in the TRPI survey described later—Mexico, Puerto Rico, the Dominican Republic, or El Salvador.

2. I would like to express my appreciation to the Tomás Rivera Policy Institute for access to these data. The survey was designed by Louis DeSipio, Rodolfo O. de la Garza, Harry Pachon, and Jongho Lee. A more detailed discussion of the design of the survey and the findings related to the relationships between home-country political activities and U.S. political engagement among Latino immigrants appears in DeSipio et al. 2003 (http://www.trpi.org/PDF/Immigrant_politics.pdf [Accessed June 15, 2004]).

3. These include organizations made up primarily of the U.S.-born—such as the League of United Latin American Citizens (LULAC), the American G.I. Forum, the Young Lords, and the Chicano Movement organizations—as well as immigrant-driven organizations—the Congress of Spanish-Speaking Peoples, the United Farmworkers, and the Cuban American National Foundation.

4. This emerging scholarship of immigrant transnational politics does have some recurring weaknesses, however. First, there is no effort to assess the overall frequency of transnational politics among immigrants. Second, the scholarship of transnational politics often assumes, often uncritically, that such transnational political activity is durable over time and offers immigrants resources they can use to shape not just the politics of their sending communities/countries, but also their communities in the United States. Finally, most analyses focus only on a single sending community or a single country of origin. As a result, it is more difficult to identify general patterns in the exercise or significance of transnational political activity among immigrants.

5. Cuban immigrants were excluded from the survey for two reasons. First, because of Cuba's nondemocratic government, Cubans do not have the same opportunities to participate in Cuban politics that the four nationality groups under study do. Second, the Cuban American-Cuban relationship has been, and continues to be, extensively analyzed (Calvo and Declercq 2000, Croucher 1997, García 1996, Torres 1999, as examples).

6. In a separate analysis, Adrian Pantoja and I have analyzed patterns of transnational engagement among Puerto Rican migrants to see if there is a distinct Puerto Rican pattern of transnational politics driven by the unique relationship of Puerto Rico and the United States (DeSipio and Pantoja 2004).

7. All respondents were at least eighteen years of age and immigrants/migrants from one of the four nations under study. To complete the 1,602 surveys, TRPI completed calls to 10,470 phone numbers. Of these, 4,454 were disconnected, businesses, or had call-screening software in place. Nearly 1,200 potential respondents refused to participate at the point of initial contact. Approximately 2,000 potential respondents were found to be ineligible to participate during the six question screening process (for example, potential respondents who were not of Mexican, Dominican, Salvadoran, or Puerto Rican origin). Initial attempts were made to contact an additional 8,207 phone numbers. These numbers remained available in the sample pool at the end of survey. Contact had not been made for such reasons as reaching an answering machine, the phone not being answered, or reaching a busy signal.

8. As is the case in many surveys, a large share of respondents to the TRPI Immigrant Political Participation Survey fail to provide answers to some specific questions, particularly demographic questions on age and household income (14 percent

and 16 percent, respectively). The final question that resulted in high nonresponse rates was year of initial migration to the United States (13 percent). As will be evident, these nonresponses reduce the overall sample size by as much as one-third. It is reasonable to assume that these nonrespondents are not randomly distributed. Assuming these respondents are similar to those of other surveys, higher-income respondents and older respondents are more likely to be excluded. These respondents are generally more likely to have higher than average levels of civic engagement and naturalization rates. The respondents who did not offer year of initial immigration were more likely than average to report that they were neither permanent residents nor naturalized U.S. citizens. These respondents are generally less likely to have higher than average levels of civic engagement and would be ineligible for naturalization (and excluded from the model).

REFERENCES

Alvarez, Robert R. 1987. "A Profile of the Citizenship Process among Hispanics in the United States." *International Migration Review* 21, no. 2 (Summer): 327–51.

Arellano, Anselmo. 2000. "The People's Movement: Las Gorras Blancas." In *The Contested Homeland: A Chicano History of New Mexico*, edited by Erlinda Gonzalez-Berry and David R. Maciel, 59–82. Albuquerque, NM: University of New Mexico Press.

Barkan, Elliot R., and N. Khokolov. 1980. "Socioeconomic Data as Indices of Naturalization Patterns in the United States: A Theory Revisited." *Ethnicity* 7:159–90.

Bosniak, Linda. 2001. Nationalizing Citizenship." In *Citizenship Today: Global Perspectives and Practices*, edited by T. Alexander Aleinikoff and Douglas Klusmeyer, 237–52. Washington, DC: Carnegie Endowment for International Peace.

Burns, Nancy, Kay Lehman Schlozman, and Sidney Verba. 2001. *The Private Roots of Public Action: Gender, Equality, and Political Participation*. Cambridge, MA: Harvard University Press.

Calvo, Hernando, and Katlijn Declerq. 2000. *The Cuban Exile Movement: Dissidents or Mercenaries?* Hoboken, NJ: Ocean Press.

Croucher, Sheila. 1997. *Imagining Miami: Ethnic Politics in a Postmodern World*. Charlottesville, VA: University Press of Virginia.

de la Garza, Rodolfo O., and Brian Lindsay Lowell, eds. 2002. *Sending Money Home: Hispanic Remittances and Community Development*. Lanham, MD: Rowman and Littlefield.

de la Garza, Rodolfo O., with Fujia Lu. 1999. "Explorations into Latino Voluntarism." In *Nuevos Senderos: Reflections on Hispanics and Philanthropy*, edited by Diana Campoamor, William A. Díaz, and Henry A. J. Ramos, eds., 55–78. Houston, TX: Arte Público Press.

de la Garza, Rodolfo O., and Harry P. Pachon, eds. 2000. *Latinos and U.S. Foreign Policy: Representing the "Homeland?"* Lanham, MD: Rowman and Littlefield.

de la Garza, Rodolfo O., and Jesús Velasco, eds. 1997. *Bridging the Border: Transforming U.S.-Mexico Relations*. Lanham, MD: Rowman and Littlefield.

DeSipio, Louis. 1996a. "After Proposition 187 the Deluge: Reforming Naturalization Administration while Making Good Citizens." *Harvard Journal of Hispanic Policy* 9:7–24.

DeSipio, Louis. 1996b. *Counting on the Latino Vote: Latinos as a New Electorate.* Charlottesville, VA: University Press of Virginia.
DeSipio, Louis. 2002. *Immigrant Organizing, Civic Outcomes: Civic Engagement Political Activity, National Attachment, and Identity in Latino Immigrant Communities.* University of California Irvine, Center for the Study of Democracy. Working Paper 02–08. http://repositories.cdlib.org/csd/02–08. Accessed January 20, 2003.
DeSipio, Louis, and Harry Pachon. 1992. "Making Americans: Administrative Discretion and Americanization." *Chicano-Latino Law Review* 12:52–60.
DeSipio, Louis, and Harry Pachon. 2002. "Are Naturalized Citizens Leading Latinos to Electoral Empowerment? Voting among Naturalized Latinos Registered to Vote in the 2000 Election." Paper prepared for presentation at the Annual Meeting of the American Political Science Association, Boston. http://apsaproceedings.cup.org/Site/papers/032/032004DeSipioLou.pdf. Accessed August 26, 2002.
DeSipio, Louis, with Harry Pachon, Rodolfo O. de la Garza, and Jongho Lee. 2003. *Immigrant Politics at Home and Abroad: How Latino Immigrants Engage the Politics of Their Home Communities and the United States.* Claremont, CA: The Tomás Rivera Policy Institute.
DeSipio, Louis, Harry Pachon, Rosalind Gold, and Arturo Vargas. 1998. *America's Newest Voices: Colombians, Dominicans, Guatemalans, and Salvadorans in the United States Examine Their Public Policy Needs.* Los Angeles and Claremont, CA: NALEO Educational Fund and Tomás Rivera Policy Institute.
DeSipio, Louis, Harry P. Pachon, and W. Andrew Moellmer. 2001. *Reinventing the Naturalization Process at INS: For Better or Worse?* Claremont, CA: The Tomás Rivera Policy Institute.
DeSipio, Louis, and Adrian Pantoja. 2004. "Puerto Rican Exceptionalism? A Comparative Analysis of Puerto Rican, Mexican, Salvadoran, and Dominican Transnational Civic and Political Ties." Paper presented at Latino Politics: The State of the Discipline Conference, Texas A&M University, College Station, April 30–May 1.
Fouron, Georges E., and Nina Glick Schiller. 2001. "The Generation of Identity: Redefining the Second Generation Within a Transnational Social Field." In *Migration, Transnationalization, and Race in a Changing New York,* edited by Héctor R. Cordero-Guzmán, Robert C. Smith, and Ramón Grosfoguel, 58–86. Philadelphia: Temple University Press.
García, John A. 1981. "Political Integration of Mexican Immigrants: Explorations into the Naturalization Process." *International Migration Review* 15, no. 4:608–25.
García, María Cristina. 1996. *Havana USA: Cuban Exiles and Cuban Americans in South Florida, 1959–1994.* Berkeley: University of California Press.
Gavit, John Palmer. 1922. *Americans by Choice.* New York: Harper Brothers.
Glick Schiller, Nina, Linda Basch, and Cristina Blanc-Szanton. 1992. *Toward a Transnational Perspective on Migration: Race, Class, Ethnicity, and Nationalism Reconsidered.* New York: New York Academy of Sciences.
González-Gutiérrez, Carlos. 1999. "Fostering Identities: Mexico's Relations with Its Diaspora." *The Journal of American History* (September): 545–67.
Guarnizo, Luis Eduardo. 1997b. " 'Los Dominicanyorks': The Making of a Binational Society." *Annals of the American Academy of Political and Social Science* 533: 70–86.
Gutiérrez, David G. 1995. *Walls and Mirrors: Mexican Americans, Mexican Immigrants, and the Politics of Ethnicity.* Berkeley: University of California Press.

Huntington, Samuel. 2004a. "The Hispanic Challenge." *Foreign Policy* (March/April): 30–45.

Huntington, Samuel. 2004b. *Who Are We?: The Challenges to America's Identity.* New York: Simon and Schuster.

Jasso, Guillermina, and Mark R. Rosenzweig. 1990. *The New Chosen People: Immigrants in the United States.* New York: Russell Sage Foundation.

Johnson, Hans P., Belinda I. Reyes, Laura Marneesh, and Elisa Barbour. 1999. *Taking the Oath: An Analysis of Naturalization in California and the United States.* San Francisco, CA: Public Policy Institute of California.

Jones-Correa, Michael. 1998. *Between Two Nations: The Political Predicament of Latinos in New York City.* Ithaca, NY: Cornell University Press.

Jones-Correa, Michael. 2001. "Under Two Flags: Dual Nationality in Latin America and Its Consequences for Naturalization in the United States." *International Migration Review* 35, no. 4:997–1029.

Levitt, Peggy. 2001. *The Transnational Villagers.* Berkeley: University of California Press.

Levitt, Peggy, and Mary Waters, eds. 2002. *The Changing Face of Home: The Transnational Lives of the Second Generation.* New York: Russell Sage Publications.

NALEO Educational Fund. 2004. "Four Million Latino Legal Permanent Residents Eligible for U.S. Citizenship as Exorbitant Fee Hike Takes Effect." Press Release, April 30. Los Angeles: NALEO Educational Fund.

Ong, Aihwa. 1999. *Flexible Citizenship: The Cultural Logics of Transnationalism.* Durham, NC: Duke University Press.

Pachon, Harry, and Louis DeSipio. 1994. *New Americans by Choice: Political Perspectives of Latino Immigrants.* Boulder, CO: Westview Press.

Pardo, Mary. 1998. *Mexican American Women Activists: Identity and Resistance in Two Los Angeles Communities.* Philadelphia, PA: Temple University Press.

Portes, Alejandro, and John Curtis. 1987. "Changing Flags: Naturalization and Its Determinants among Mexican Immigrants." *International Migration Review* 21, no. 2:352–71.

Portes, Alejandro, and Rafael Mozo. 1985. "Naturalization, Registration, and Voting Patterns of Cubans and Other Ethnic Minorities: A Preliminary Analysis." In *Proceedings of the First National Conference on Citizenship and the Hispanic Community.* Washington, DC: The NALEO Educational Fund.

Portes, Alejandro, and Alex Stepik. 1993. *City on the Edge: The Transformation of Miami.* Berkeley: University of California Press.

Sánchez Korrol, Virginia E. 1994. *From Colonia to Community: The History of Puerto Ricans in New York City.* Berkeley: University of California Press.

Skocpol, Theda. 2003. *Diminished Democracy: From Membership to Management in American Civic Life.* Norman: University of Oklahoma Press.

Smith, Michael Peter, and Luis Guarnizo, eds. 1998. *Transnationalism from Below.* Somerset, NJ: Transaction Publishers.

Soysal, Yasemin Nuhoglu. 1994. *Limits of Citizenship: Migrants and Postnational Membership in Europe.* Chicago: University of Chicago Press.

Tichenor, Daniel. 2002. *Dividing Lines: The Politics of Immigration Control in America.* Princeton, NJ: Princeton University Press.

Torres, María de los Angeles. 1999. *In the Land of Mirrors: Cuban Exile Politics in the United States.* Ann Arbor: University of Michigan Press.

U.S. Immigration and Naturalization Services. 2003. *2001 Statistical Yearbook of the Immigration and Naturalization Service.* Springfield, VA: National Technical Information Service.

Verba, Sidney, Kay Lehman Schlozman, and Henry E. Brady. 1995. *Voice and Equality: Civic Voluntarism in American Politics.* Cambridge, MA: Harvard University Press.

Yang, Phillip Q. 1994. "Explaining Immigrant Naturalization." *International Migration Review* 28, no. 3:449–477.

THESES ON THE LATINO BLOC:
A CRITICAL PERSPECTIVE

Rosaura Sánchez and Beatrice Pita

Last spring's historic pro-immigrant marches across the United States turned out hundreds of thousands in Los Angeles, Chicago, New York, and Washington, DC, as well as significant numbers in states like Iowa, Georgia, and Tennessee. Most of those marching were Latino. Predictably, reaction has been vocal, and often virulent. Even before the marches, xenophobes like Harvard University professor Samuel Huntington (2004) worried about the rapid growth of the U.S. Latino population, now officially 41 million strong, but in all likelihood closer to 45 million or even 50 million if undocumented workers are counted. Even more alarming to critics is the fact that the Latino population is expected to more than double by the year 2050, when it will reach an estimated 102.6 million (U.S. Bureau of the Census 2004). Although the United States is already a multiracial and multiethnic nation, the implications of this Latinization challenge the imagination. For the first time, minorities will become the majority population.

Especially troubling to Huntington and like-minded critics is what they perceive as Latinos' unwillingness to conform to "America's traditional identity"—in other words, to Anglo-Saxon Protestant culture. A slew of recent publications on Latinos or "Hispanics" describes us as a threat to America's identity, values, and way of life, with most if not all of these critiques arguing as a principal concern that we fail to assimilate into mainstream U.S. culture. But is this demographic change and the cultural ascendancy of the Latino population what really frightens Huntington and others? Or is it rather the specter of a fragmented public—that is, of a lack of unity under the state?

We would argue the latter. Underlying Huntington's fear of the many, of a heterogeneous body politic with a strong Latino component, is a general dread of fragmentation of the state. Given the demographic configuration of the Latino population, now spread throughout the country, this is not fear of separatism, à la Quebec Province, but an anxiety regarding the population's

---

Reprinted with permission of The Regents of the University of California from *Aztlán: A Journal of Chicano Studies* 31, no. 2 (Fall 2006), UCLA Chicano Studies Research Center. Not for further reproduction.

failure to abide the authority of the state. Behind this fear of a failure to consent is the construction of the Latino Bloc as a destabilizing presence. What alarms Huntington and others is not, however, as troubling to some Latinos, who dismiss these fears as groundless. Huntington's essay has compelled Chicano/Latino (Rodríguez 2004) and even Mexican writers (Schwartz 2004; Krauze 2004) to respond defensively, refuting allegations of Latinos as a "fifth column" and stressing that we are, in fact, "assimilating," as previous waves of immigrants have done before us. Huntington and the country as a whole, these Latinos argue, need not fear ethnic/racial fragmentation or separatism, for we are all already on the way to becoming true "Americans," whatever that might mean. Clearly, for these Latino writers, unity under the state is taken as a given; a questioning of national identity is not an issue. Is it, however, as simple as that, or is the issue far more complex?

In any discussion of U.S. Latinas and Latinos (hereafter Latina/os), one of the first issues that arise is whether a population marked by multiple differences should be grouped as one ethnicity or bloc. Is ethnicity itself a significant distinguishing category in today's global society? The irony is that constructing and continually reconstructing this heterogeneous collectivity on the basis of difference implies going not around ethnicity but rather through it (Eagleton 1990, 23). If one hopes eventually to abolish ethnic, racial, and other social markers, one cannot wish them away; one cannot even legislate them away, as the U.S. experience with racism has made clear. Rather, one has to go through these "estranging definitions to emerge somewhere on the other side" (24), where the need for these markers is eliminated. Arguably, then, the very construct of the Latino Bloc needs to be seen as transitional, as inchoative, to be eliminated when it is no longer operative, when it can no longer be used in connection with some type of emancipatory politics, and when it has made way for alliances with other social blocs or forces. For the present, however, it is clear that one is fighting on a terrain always "already mapped out by antagonists" (26), where one is faced with responding to particular, time-specific political and economic relations and categories in order ultimately to move away from broad, unserviceable rubrics like "American."

One of these ready-made categories, mapped out by both the state and the market, subsumes U.S. Latina/os or Hispanics under one label, even though we do not constitute one ethnic group if ethnicity is determined by national origin and/or culture. And yet, as we shall see, there are good reasons—all political in nature—for us to construct ourselves as a nexus, an entity marked not by unity but by difference, by a shared sense of dislocation and oppression. It is an identity born in the context of difference and is itself marked by difference. Present national and international conditions call for the deployment of a Latino Bloc identity, even though it is tentative and will in time melt away. The reasons for constructing the Latina/o population as a bloc are examined in more detail below. The term "bloc," as we argue, is a useful construct that allows us to comment on the diversity and contradictory aspects of this population. It would be foolhardy to claim complete knowledge of a population in flux, but we have a number of critical points to raise in relation to the analytical and political notion of a Latino Bloc. Our strategy here will be to address problematizations through a series of theses or statements that are not meant to be exhaustive but rather to suggest the conditions facing the Latino Bloc. Each thesis will concentrate on at least one site of tension or contradiction within the network of relations. It goes without saying that many of the contradictions that emerge within the social totality are not particular to Latinos and Latinas.

We begin by addressing the notion of the Latino Bloc before moving on to a discussion of particular differences that contribute to the population's diversity. With each thesis we proceed from a generalization to a series of concretizations that seek to be explanatory while also illuminating differences or contradictions. The order of the theses is not meant to be significant, and the underlying premise is of course that all the theses are interrelated and intersect.

THESIS 1

The Terrain for Constructing the Latina/o Population as a Bloc Is from the Outset Mapped out in Negation

A clarification: what we are terming "the Latino Bloc" is not Gramsci's "historical bloc," a term he used to refer not to a bloc of social alliances, as is usually thought, but to the social totality (Boothman 1995, xi). Our use of "bloc" seeks to emphasize the potential for links among various elements of the Latina/o population despite its heterogeneity. The word *bloc* here is more akin to *nexus,* in the sense that it allows for the figuration of a *coyuntura,* a node or juncture of an ensemble of elements. "Bloc," for us, recalls in part Hardt and Negri's definition of multitude in *Empire* (2000) and *Multitude* (2004), although given their rejection of the dominance of class, racial, and ethnic links, their notion of multitude proves inadequate.

The Latino Bloc is, like the multitude, diverse at the level of culture, race, ethnicity, gender, sexual orientation, forms of labor, political views, and class. It arises out of an international experience and is also inherently global in scope as a product of U.S. imperialist policies. Yet it is as much local as global in its migration, residential, and labor patterns. Our concept of the Latino Bloc also borrows from the work of Virno (2004, 76), who opposes "multitude" to "the people," the nation, in effect underscoring the latter's transfer of its rights to the state and its ascribed unity under the state. "Bloc" here is not meant to suggest "the cohesive unity of the people" but, on the contrary, to point to a population alienated to varying degrees from the state. It is this particular difference, in fact, that is at the root of xenophobic and nativist fears about Latina/os in the United States. This negation of "cohesive unity" is, we argue, at the core of the Latino Bloc itself, given its heterogeneity at every level: social, political, and cultural. Paradoxically, it is this heterogeneity that needs to be addressed even as we construct a collectivity-in-difference, a bloc. While recognizing the diverse class composition of the Latino Bloc, we also note in our analysis that social identity as Latina/os is particularly meaningful for those at the lower stratum of the social structure—that is, for working-class Latina/os who face antagonisms grounded in their difference. As will become clear, labor and social relations under capitalism define the Latino Bloc's conditions of existence and negation.

THESIS 2

THE U.S. LATINO BLOC IS A LATE CAPITALIST PHENOMENON, ALTHOUGH ITS EMERGENCE IS LINKED TO U.S. EXPANSIONISM, COLONIZATION, AND IMPERIALISM OF THE NINETEENTH AND TWENTIETH CENTURIES

The immigration of Latina/os and the growth of the Latino Bloc are in large measure results of U.S. imperialist policies and practices that establish enclosures depriving workers of their means of subsistence, historically and currently (Midnight Notes Collective 1992). Since the nineteenth century, capital has sought what Harvey calls "spatio-temporal fixes" (2003, 43)—that is, territorial expansion that brings access to new natural resources, markets, and cheap labor. Such expansion has been achieved through imperialist policies, designed and implemented by the state, that have often implied the relocation of populations en masse. It is useful to recall that the United States's first socio-spatial fix involved the removal of Indians from their lands either through dispossession and relocation to particular areas or through the practice, if not the policy, of extermination. After the acquisition of the Spanish borderlands, from Florida to Louisiana, the United States used a variety of strategies, including inducements to colonization, filibustering, and war, to gain control of Mexican Texas and the Southwest, and subsequently furthered its imperial project by taking it to the Pacific, the Caribbean, and especially Central America. In the process it also gained a significant, albeit disdained, Latina/o population from the former Spanish and Mexican territories.

A majority of U.S. Latina/os are of Mexican extraction. But the growth in numbers of other Latina/o groups owes much to twentieth-century U.S. interventions in the Caribbean and Central America, as well as to the mid-to-late-century military hostility to liberal or left-leaning governments, from Guatemala in the 1950s to Chile in the 1970s. Likewise, U.S.-backed military coups and reigns of terror in Argentina, Uruguay, and Chile have led to the emigration of thousands of Latin Americans to the United States, other parts of Latin America, and Europe. More recently, neoliberal policies throughout Latin America, enforced through trade agreements and conditions on loans from the international financial institutions, have increased unemployment and imposed austerity measures that have spurred millions to emigrate in search of jobs and subsistence. As a secondary consequence, this has enabled the United States to continually replenish its internal labor reserve through successive waves of Latin American immigration.

THESIS 3

THE LATINO BLOC IS A HETEROGENEOUS, TRANSNATIONAL, TRANSCULTURAL, MULTIRACIAL, AND MULTILINGUAL POPULATION

"Latino" cannot operate as a simple ethnic designation because we cannot claim one national origin. Our origin is multinational and multiracial. Our Latina/o identity is trans-American, linked to the continent of the Americas and more specifically to Latin America. In this sense we are a transcontinental and transnational population, deeply divided by class, national origin, race, language, residence, and political orientation. Issues of gender and sexual orientation further divide us. We are not a nation but a conglomeration, a social construction, what Hall might call "a politically and culturally constructed" grouping that is continually reconfiguring itself (1996, 443). We are a composite, made up of multiple positionings—that is, of concrete social locations—and assuming multiple ideological perspectives and identities. We are U.S. citizens and noncitizens, documented and undocumented. The diversity of the Latino Bloc will only increase during the coming decades as even more Latin American immigrants come to the United States in response to the labor shortage brought on by retirement of the baby boomers.

The ethnic and racial diversity of the Latino Bloc is a crucial difference that further underscores the need for the notion of "bloc." If ethnicity generally designates a national origin, as in the case of Irish Americans, then the Latina/o multitude includes some twenty-one ethnicities: not only the nineteen Latin American republics and the colony of Puerto Rico but also people of peninsular Spanish origin in the United States. The state, for its own purposes, constructs these various ethnicities under one rubric, as Latinos or Hispanics (the latter term being preferred by the U.S. Census Bureau, the press, and marketing experts). This constitutes the population as a macro-ethnicity in relation to geographic and linguistic origin, much as Asian Americans or African Americans are constructed by continental origin, whether those origins go back 500 years or five years. The Census Bureau recognizes the heterogeneous mix of ethnicities when it breaks down the Latino population for comparative statistics into five groups: Mexican, Puerto Rican, Cuban, Central/South American, and Other Spanish.

Racially, the Latino Bloc is unique in that it includes Latin American immigrants who are indigenous, white, black, mestizo, mulatto, Asian, and Middle Eastern. The Census Bureau, recognizing that a number of Latina/os are black, has rather clumsily formulated several new categories including "Non-Hispanic Blacks" and "Non-Hispanic Whites." Today, however, the "white" designation, so important to Californios who sought the right to vote as white citizens in the nineteenth century and to mid-twentieth-century Latina/o activists who questioned the designation of "Mexican" as a race, is likewise being rejected by many Latina/os who, for valid cultural and political reasons, prefer ethnic or culturally based designations.

Our preference for designating the population as the Latino Bloc and continuing to use the Latino/Latina labels requires turning to the term "Latino" itself. Of course the term is closely linked historically to a geographic area,

Latin America, and to the Latin origin of Spanish and other Romance languages. This geographic area has historically been known by various designations: Spanish America, Hispanoamérica, Indo-América, América Latina, Latinoamérica. It was in the nineteenth century, when Napoleon III began seeking to counter Anglo-America's imperialist designs on the whole of the continent, that French-influenced intellectuals in Latin America, concerned with the danger of conquest by the Anglo *coloso del norte* and wishing to be linked to what was deemed a superior and more kindred French culture, began using the term "América Latina" in opposition to "América Anglo-sajona."

Today, "Latina/o" is likewise used in negation, to distinguish what is not Anglo; more recently it has also been used to signal that one is black but not African American. Nevertheless, "Latino" is never equivalent to "Latin American," as the former designation is a U.S. phenomenon. The term "Latina/o" is thus geographically, culturally, and linguistically situated, and, for that reason, fraught with issues of misrepresentation. As a socio-spatial-political identity, "Latino," like "Hispanic," continues the erasure of indigenous peoples of the Americas. This is nothing new. The term "Latin America" itself reconfigures and disidentifies the pre-Columbian populations that are still very much a part of the continent and whose indigenous cultures and languages have survived widespread mestizaje and even genocide. The term also elides from the equation descendants of African slaves and other people of African, Middle, Eastern, and Asian descent in Latin America. The diversity of the Latino Bloc in the United States is closely linked to the diversity of Latin America but, unfortunately also recapitulates racist practices in Latin America.

Given the heterogeneous composition of the Latino Bloc, there is as yet no amalgamating identity, nor, often, even a willingness to be seen as one group. In its changing taxonomies, the state, too, has used a variety of terms to classify Latina/os as a separate entity. For example, fifty years ago government agencies employed terms like "Spanish speaking" or "Spanish surname." However, not all Latina/os speak Spanish: some are English-monolingual, while others speak indigenous languages or Portuguese rather than Spanish. The use of the Spanish surname as an indicator is even less accurate, as Asian and European immigration to Latin America, the retention of indigenous names, and intermarriage have all produced many non-Spanish surnames. U.S. Latina/os themselves have throughout the years used a variety of general terms, including designations like "Latin American," "Spanish American," "Spanish," "Hispanic," and "Hispano." The Census Bureau's preferred term, as well as that of advertising and the media, is "Hispanic," and while some Latina/os approve of this designation, others have a visceral negative reaction to the label, particularly in the Southwest.

Many Latina/os prefer to be identified by national origin, as hyphenated Americans. Some people of Mexican origin, the largest group within the census category of Hispanics, prefer "Latino," "Chicano," or "raza," the latter two being self-assigned and politically charged identities in use since the 1960s. With the growth of the Mexican-origin population the term "la raza" has become increasingly widespread, and it may extend even further as this population moves beyond the U.S. Southwest. Are we suggesting that "bloc" is akin to "raza" in its current U.S. sense? No, the term "raza" is both racially and culturally rooted, but it excludes those Latina/os not falling into the perceived category. Is an Ecuadorian of Korean origin or a Lebanese from Colombia or an Armenian from Venezuela or a Jew from Argentina to be considered "raza"? For some of us, she is, but not for others. The unwieldiness of the "raza" label suggests the need for a more inclusive designation, like that of "Latino Bloc."

Why then seek an umbrella identification if we are divided by so many differences? The rationale is fundamentally political. We need an identification that will interpellate us to participate in collective action, like the recent nationwide pro-immigrant marches; in this regard strict national-origin identity could prove to be divisive and counterproductive. In some areas of the United States where diverse Latina/o populations are in close contact with each other, there is greater acceptance of the term "Latino." In that case, why include "bloc"? The term "Latino," unfortunately, also suggests a cohesive group. Since this is decidedly not the case, there is need for a classifier that points to a nexus of diverse groups, such as "bloc."

Most important, such an identity would be of our own making. Historically, we have been identified by others, often in exclusionary if not derogatory terms. We have been subjected to racial profiling by the police, by the Immigration and Naturalization Service (*la migra*), and by white supremacists. We are often criminalized and viewed wholesale as illegal immigrants, as foreign to the body of the nation. Perhaps it is time to assume a self-designation, a strategic essentialism, as it were, for overtly political and social reasons. Perhaps it is time to constitute our own political identity, fully aware that we are a multitude, differentiated by national origin, race, place of residence, generation, class, and political orientation, and deeply divided with respect to fundamental issues such as immigration policy, social and economic domestic policies, and U.S. foreign policy. The underlying and troubling challenge facing us is undoubtedly whether we are capable of uniting in broad and sustained strategic alliances.

THESIS 4

The Latino Bloc Is Marked by Cultural Exchange and Adaptation

In the growing Latina/o population, there is no concrete cultural particularity to which we can point. A variety of Latina/o cultures coexist within the United States, distinguished not only by divergent national origins but also by urban/rural, regional, and state residence (Tejano culture, for example, is different from Nuevo Mexicano culture). Is culture really the issue? As Eagleton reminds us, to the colonizer the culture of the colonized or oppressed is never the issue; in fact it is rather unimportant (1990, 29). What about assimilation? Much is made of cultural assimilation, but that issue is ultimately not what troubles nativists like Huntington. Nevertheless, because culture and cultural difference are elements that can be strategically deployed in the building of a

Latino Bloc, they warrant discussion, especially in relation to the questionable paradigm of assimilation versus failure to assimilate.

Since immigration to the United States has been a constant from the beginning of the nation-state, scholars have often measured the impact of cultural contact in terms of language acquisition or loss, national and ethnic identification, and cultural values. Often in these studies class-related changes are conflated with acculturation, with some degree of social mobility and acquisition of so-called middle-class values taken as evidence of acculturation and wrongfully termed "Americanization"—as if there were ever just one culture in the United States.

History teaches us that whenever there is sustained contact between different populations, sociocultural exchange takes place, even between enslavers and the enslaved. While language and culture are not synonymous, the impact of cultural contact on language can serve as a useful example. All languages reveal in their borrowings contact with other populations, be it through invasion, conquest, commerce, relocation, or co-habitation on the same island or continent. Just as there are no "pure" languages in the world, there can be no "pure" cultures. Linguistic borrowing always involves adaptation or translation. Cultural adaptations likewise involve new constructions, like the creation of fictive traditions that in time are taken to be historically grounded. Borrowing within cultural interaction is equally complicated. Often the process involves translation, as occurred during the Spanish colonization of the Americas. For example, native cultural practices or rites were often "translated" by missionaries to hasten conversion to Christianity, as when they constructed an indigenous-looking Virgen de Guadalupe (Gibson 1964). The opposite can also be the case: dominated or enslaved people can engage in translation for purposes of maintaining a culture, as in the renaming of the African *orishas* with Catholic saints' names, a practice still alive today in Santería. Clearly, in cases where a language or culture is imposed by force, strategic translation may lead to the adoption of elements of the master's culture in an attempt to resist it. Historically, particular cultural practices have been viewed as suspect and dangerous, as in the case of the Native American Ghost Dances of the late nineteenth century. In these instances, culture becomes a site of resistance (Bonfil 1987, 109), a space for maintaining diversity and difference, and often also a rationale for persecution. But even then the process of exchange continues.

New cultural contacts continue in today's so-called era of globalization through mass population flows, forced or voluntary. Millions, the subaltern of the world, must migrate to stave off starvation, to seek employment and social mobility, to escape from war, turmoil, and particular political regimes, and to flee natural disasters. In all of these cases, groups coming into contact are never on an equal footing. In fact, contact between different populations in the United States has rarely if ever been peaceful and harmonious; on the contrary, it has been marked by strife and violence. Contact with whites, for example, has been deadly for Native Americans. Blacks endure continuing racism, highlighted most recently when the Katrina hurricane devastation in New Orleans made the connection between race/class and governmental indifference only too clear. A painful narrative at best, the U.S. history of interracial, intercultural, and international contact continues to be written in equally violent ways, at home and also abroad, as is clear from present-day U.S. military engagements throughout the world.

U.S. society has always been marked by diversity and stratification. In this context, assumptions about what constitutes "American" culture have been skewed in one direction by politically and economically dominant groups. Through control of education, the media, and political institutions, they have tried to impose one language, English, and the idea of one culture on the rest of the population, fomenting in the process the myth of American culture as one distinct culture. But this dominant construct of an "imagined community" (Anderson 1987) has not erased the regional, racial, ethnic, or social/cultural differences that are most evident in segregation practices. The U.S. mainstream still seems unable to come to grips with this continuing cultural diversity. For that reason, the myth of a "traditional" U.S. culture and an "essential" U.S. identity has been served up to every entering first-grader in U.S. public schools and promoted in both commercial and state advertising, despite recent nods to multiculturalism.

Closer scrutiny of the term "assimilation" itself would reveal the fallacies inherent in this notion, but for purposes of brevity it might be best to simply suggest that there are different types of assimilation. In the case of Latina/os there is no doubt that we have been absorbed as a labor force since the nineteenth century, but to what degree have we been included culturally and socially? The interactional playing field has never been even, given that the particular give-and-take or negotiation is always conditioned by stratified social relations and ideological vectors. Yet the Latino Bloc has responded with vigor, borrowing, adapting, and translating, while still maintaining a series of cultural differences that have enabled it to survive in a terrain marked by labor inclusion and social exclusion.

Let us take a concrete example that turns out to be quite telling. The arrival of U.S. settlers in Texas and the Southwest made wheat more easily accessible in that region and in the northern part of Mexico. As a result, the corn tortilla was exchanged for a "flour tortilla" in these areas. This transfer of resources—the adoption of wheat flour—did not lead to a predominantly bread-consuming population among people of Mexican origin, as would have been the case if Anglo cultural practices had simply been appropriated. Rather, the new resource, wheat, was adapted and incorporated within an existing cultural grammar that called for use of the tortilla, not only for tacos but also as an implement for eating. The tortilla of Mexican *norteños* and Chicanos is not an Anglo phenomenon—it is not a pancake, crêpe, or blintz—nor is it exactly like the corn tortilla of central and southern Mexico. The ingredients and the process for making it are different. The flour tortilla is a displaced, transformed corn tortilla, if you will.

Change inevitably occurs within both dominant and minority cultures. The effort to maintain things a certain way, to achieve homeostasis, is bound to fail because no culture that is alive has remained the same permanently. U.S. Anglo hegemony too will see its end, undoubtedly, but what will replace it?

The past no doubt has something to teach us in this regard. Arrighi and Silver (1999), examining the similarities and differences in the transitions from Dutch to British hegemony in the eighteenth century and from British to U.S. hegemony in the early twentieth century, suggest that the U.S. era has already seen its apogee. Will the new hegemony be an Asian one? Will it lead to the fragmentation of the western part of the United States? Quite possibly. We have no crystal ball to consult, only history. Like Benjamin's "angel of history" (1968, 257), we are condemned to look back at the pile of ruins before us, the residue produced by the U.S. era of empire, even while being propelled into an uncertain future.

That said, should we then dismiss notions of cultural interaction as irrelevant? Perhaps by the year 3000 that will be the case, and identities as "Anglos" or "Latinos" will be superfluous and nonfunctional. At this historical juncture, however, we simply cannot afford to do so, given social conditions and xenophobic practices persisting in this country. We are compelled to work our way through them. As long as social stratification continues to be constructed on the basis of race, ethnicity, language, native or immigrant status, and class, there will be a need to mobilize in terms of particular identities. Perhaps in the future, geography or political orientation, DNA markers, or, more likely, social location will be the key critical factors to consider, and we can dispense with ethnic/racial markers. But until then, ethnic, racial, and cultural identifications will be important organizing and survival strategies in any political context.

THESIS 5

THE LATINO BLOC IS HIGHLY DIVIDED BY ISSUES OF HOMELAND AND NATIONAL ORIGIN

A 2004 student rally in downtown San Diego to protest the raising of college and university tuition brought out youth wearing t-shirts that proclaimed: "Latino, No. Chicano, Sí." Students wanted to make a statement about their identity as Chicanos—that is, as persons of Mexican origin. Specific national-origin identification is undoubtedly important and ultimately defining for many Latina/os, especially for first-generation Chicana/os. A border city, San Diego has a large number of first-generation Mexican residents who have immigrated to the United States and continue to maintain close ties with the "homeland." First-generation Latina/os often have family members still in the country of origin, and many travel as often as possible to and from these Latin American regions. They are often hesitant to take up an identity other than that of national origin. However, this is less true of their offspring. Second- or third-generation Chicana/os do not see Mexico as their homeland; in fact, the myth of the "homeland" no longer holds for those born in this country. Clearly, over time and after several generations, origin itself can be a fuzzy indicator.

"National-origin" identity and adhesion to a foreign state are two different matters. Marchers who waved the banner of another country in last spring's demonstrations, a gesture often misunderstood, were making a statement more of ethnic pride than of allegiance to another nation-state. National-origin identification can, however, prove highly contentious. Native-born Chicana/os, for example, sometimes find themselves in antagonistic relations with first-generation students of Mexican origin in high school. These divisions within the Latino Bloc are at root class-based divisions, although they masquerade as national-origin and generational issues. On the other hand, crisis situations make our commonalities clear and can bring out Latina/os as a collectivity, as occurred in the Chicano Moratorium against the Vietnam War in 1970, in the march against Proposition 187 in Los Angeles in 1994, and in the recent mass marches that highlighted the working-class character of immigrants (evident in the slogan "Somos trabajadores, no criminals"). While national origin has been foregrounded, other core issues are obviously in play in these cases and beg closer analysis. Class, in fact, is the node or linchpin upon which hinge all the other factors that make up one's identity as Latino or Latina—national origin being just one among them.

Political identity based on national origin or race is undoubtedly a strategy for organizing, but this approach thus far has not effected significant structural changes or transformed our social location within the system. Nevertheless, one has to recognize that this identity, once constructed, has served various purposes, as is evident in the reforms gained by the civil rights movement. Today, it would seem, politicians on the right see racial or ethnic identity as running counter to their interests and would like to see it disappear. In California the year 2002 brought failed attempts to limit the state's ability to collect information about an individual's race or ethnicity through Proposition 54 (the Racial Privacy Initiative). Why, at this historical juncture, is this information perceived to be threatening? The reasons are self-evident. Statistics based on identity are the basis for challenges to the state regarding issues of access and distribution: for example, denial of political representation, exclusion or low representation of particular groups in institutions of higher learning, denial of voting rights, and so forth. Clearly, those advocating "merit" as the only criterion for access and arguing that we live in a color-blind society would prefer that we not have official evidence that contests that assertion.

The U.S. Armed Forces, on the other hand, see an advantage to retaining these categories and are, ironically, using them to attract "volunteers" from ethnic communities (as when an army recruiter in San Diego decorates his truck with a bumper sticker saying "The Army of Juan"). Business interests have also found the simulacrum of "Hispanic" identity to be a useful marketing tool, especially in the creation of market niches to attract customers to food or entertainment products. The appropriation of difference at all levels by the market has a not-to-be-overlooked consequence: the flattening of identity to the point of meaninglessness. Ethnic identity, manipulable like any discourse, flexible enough to be used against us or in our favor, is yet a tool that we cannot at this point give up as a political strategy. Perhaps when over 50 percent of the population in this country is Latina/o—and that day is fast approaching—the term will become truly insignificant, and other considerations, such as social class location, will be foregrounded as key elements of identity. Until then, it is important that identification as part of the Latino Bloc be an instrument that we implement for redress and progressive social transformation.

THESIS 6

THE LATINO BLOC, SHAPED BY REPEATED MIGRATORY WAVES, FACES RECURRENT XENOPHOBIA

The category of national origin is intimately tied to the issue of immigration. As previously mentioned, it is the continuing influx of immigrants from Mexico and Latin America that Huntington and others find especially troubling (Huntington 2004, 32). Of course the Latino Bloc does not consist entirely of immigrants and their descendants: some Latina/os are the descendants of Tejanos or New Mexican Hispanos or Californios who were here before the U.S. invasion and appropriation of the Southwest, even before the United States was formally constituted. Others descend from early Native American populations that resided in the Southwest and mixed with the incoming Spanish/Mexican settlers; these Latina/os can trace their origins in the Southwest back to the pre-Columbian era. For this reason, as Huntington warily notes, Latin American immigrants, especially those of Mexican origin, proffer irrefutable ancestral claims and do not see their geographic shift to U.S. territory as unprecedented. Nevertheless, in view of the significant number of foreign-born within the Latina/o population (some 40 percent), geographical mobility, relocation, and location mark the Latino Bloc decisively.

One could argue facetiously that all the people of the United States at some point are the product of mass migrations and contact between different groups that go back several centuries, if not millennia. Huntington (33) himself recognizes that the rate of nineteenth-century immigration to the United States, especially from Ireland and Germany, was greater than the rate of Latina/o immigration in the late twentieth century. Most of these nineteenth-century immigrants were of European extraction, but they were poor, unemployed men and women, which made their "whiteness" questionable. They too faced xenophobic reactions, especially the Irish and the Chinese. The "whitening" of these immigrant populations since then (even of the "model minority," the Chinese) has served to blur that past.

Today, however, the specter of a perceived nonwhite immigrant majority, whether documented or undocumented, is again setting off alarms and leading to cries of "invasion" by ideologues. These neoconservatives are right about one thing: given our numbers and fertility, the Latino Bloc will undoubtedly change the face of this nation, both literally and figuratively. A broader perspective is called for, however. As of 2006, there are more than 42 million Latina/os in the United States, but this population is still smaller than the combined population of German (58 million), Irish (39 million), English (33 million), and Italian (15 million) descent in this country. The statistical difference is enormous, but ideologues like Huntington do not fear the present; it is the future that concerns them, in view of the continued influx and the increase through reproduction. The more salient question is whether the new Latina/o look, this "colorizing," will be politically and economically meaningful or merely cosmetic.

U.S. Census Bureau statistics (2003) indicate that over half of the estimated 15 million Latina/o immigrants currently in the United States entered this country after 1990. This rapid increase in immigration in the last decades of the twentieth century, as previously mentioned, is linked to specific economic, political, and social factors. While some immigrants are professionals or artists seeking career advancement, business people with cross-border interests, or political exiles, the majority of the arrivals are "economic immigrants" coming to the United States for wage labor. Among them are the many undocumented workers who face the perils of crossing the Arizona desert, the barbed-wire fence, the Rio Grande River, and the Southwest freeways inside car trunks, trailers, converted gas tanks, door panels, dashboards, and airliner wheel wells, day after day, year after year. They may stay in the Southwest or go to other states where they are not welcome but their labor is. Attempts by undocumented immigrants to cross the increasingly militarized U.S. border are made every day more difficult by the low-intensity warfare that they face and, more recently, by emboldened anti-immigrant vigilante groups.

And yet, despite the continued harassment, hostility, and low-wage exploitation they encounter, these immigrants still fulfill their purpose in going north: they contribute to the sustenance of the families left at home. Remittances by Mexican emigrants worldwide now exceed $20 billion a year and are second only to petroleum as Mexico's largest source of foreign exchange (Dickerson 2004). This immigration must be viewed in the context of the unemployment rate in Mexico, so high that 1.3 million more Mexicans are without jobs each year. This situation is not, of course, particular to Mexico or Latin America, but is a worldwide phenomenon with millions of Africans, Asians, and Eastern Europeans also migrating globally for employment and sending remittances home. More important, these immigrants contribute significantly to the U.S. gross national product and, as emphatically noted in the 2006 marches, pay taxes.

The post-1990 immigration influx to the United States has triggered a wide spectrum of xenophobic reactions among certain segments. It has spurred the passage of anti-immigrant legislation such as California's Proposition 187, intended to deny health and educational services to undocumented individuals. Congressional attempts to deny citizenship to children born to undocumented immigrants in the United States, although unconstitutional, likewise resurface every few years, as do proposals for criminalizing undocumented status, for repatriation, and for extending the border wall. Today, virulent anti-immigrant movements and armed vigilante groups like the Minutemen, the Border Patrol Auxiliary, the Friends of the Border Patrol, and the Save Our State group are multiplying across the country. This practice of xenophobic scapegoating has ample precedent in U.S. history and has been especially strident in periods of economic crisis (Rosales 1996, 85). Since the 1980s, when economic restructuring led to the closure of many U.S. plants, which were subsequently "outsourced" to Mexico, other parts of Latin America, or Asia, thousands of immigrants have been rounded up and repatriated as well (Hondagneu-Sotelo 1994, xv). Latina/os, both citizens and immigrants, have long suffered racial profiling, racism, segregation, and discrimination at the level of residence, education, employment, and language use. Today, like other minorities, they suffer from heightened police brutality as well.

Xenophobic reactions, of course, are not deployed with surgical precision and often do not distinguish between documented and undocumented immigrants, nor between foreign-born Latina/os and those born here. The entire Latino Bloc is seen as foreign, and in the process it is criminalized, much as happened in the past with Asians and as is still happening today with people of Middle Eastern descent. In this post-9/11 period, fear of penetration of the U.S. homeland and the ostensible security vulnerability at the southern border figure prominently on TV news programs and radio talk shows. Worrisome too is the xenophobic logic at work in the pernicious conflation of foreigner/ Latino/terrorist/gangbanger. Racist stereotyping of Latina/os, as if all were potential terrorists, might unintentionally serve to build greater group solidarity and identification as Latina/os. But it has also served to divide the Latino Bloc further, as some nativist Latina/os join vigilante movements against immigrants. What is crucial, however, is that all Latina/os, whether documented or undocumented, foreign-born residents or native-born citizens, are subject to subordination, discrimination, and harassment. Ultimately, the status and the rights of each one are linked to the status and rights of all (Gutiérrez 1995, 174). In developing contestatory political strategies to counter racism, discrimination, and exploitation, it might prove useful to consider border crossing as a human rights issue and even as a radical act of civil disobedience.

Today, as in the past, immigrants to the United States face varying degrees of hostility and rejection on arrival. The reception is clearly better if one is European or Canadian. But even among immigrants from Latin America, there are marked distinctions that further divide us. Puerto Ricans, titularly U.S. citizens, are "free" to move between the island and the U.S. mainland, often in a continuous migratory cycle; when settling on the mainland they join a community of close to 4 million Boricuas in the United States. Then there are Cuban immigrants, who are considered "refugees" because of Washington's anti-Castro policies and are granted asylum once they reach U.S. shores. On the other hand, Salvadorans and Guatemalans who left their birth countries for political and economic reasons had to survive here as undocumented immigrants for up to two decades, until 1999, when they were allowed to petition for permanent residency as political refugees.

Issues of migration, place of origin, and residential status (first-generation, second-generation, third-generation, etc.) have always been important and, as noted earlier, have served not only as divisive wedges within the Latino Bloc but also as key concerns for a population subject to harassment and discrimination by mainstream society. For this reason, an awareness of the history of immigration has been a necessary first step in raising our consciousness of being part of a transnational Latina/o community in the United States.

THESIS 7

The Latino Bloc Is Primarily an Urban Population

Latina/os now reside in every state of the union, although they are still heavily concentrated in particular cities, states, and regions. The largest group, the Mexican-origin population, has a long history in the Southwest and is still concentrated there, but people of Mexican descent are now found all over the country, including in the Northeast, where they live alongside Puerto Ricans, Dominicans, Central Americans, South Americans, and Cubans. The prominent position now accorded to the Virgen de Guadalupe in Saint Patrick's Cathedral in New York City attests to the growing numbers of Latina/os, especially *mexicanos/as*, in the area.

In a shift from past patterns, Latina/os are now primarily an urban population, with nine out of ten living in metropolitan areas (U.S. Bureau of the Census 2003). The numbers are striking in some cities, like San Antonio, Texas, where Latina/os already represent a majority population. Within these metropolitan areas, however, the neighborhoods where Latina/os tend to reside are highly contained, ethnically and racially. Thus, whether residing in the inner city or outside the urban core, Latina/os tend to live in segregated neighborhoods, in enclaves that are often distinguished by the geographic origin of their inhabitants—a particular nation, a state or province within that nation, or even a specific city, town, or village. Place of origin is thus a critical aspect of identity for first-generation Latina/os, as residing in place-linked enclaves allows for cultural familiarity.

Residential segregation is not only racially or ethnically marked, but also class-determined. If urban residence often means living in run-down, overcrowded homes in areas marked by poverty and violence, it also affords access to low-income housing and low-wage work opportunities. These jobs, once mainly in manufacturing, especially in garment factories, are increasingly found in the service sector, where Latina/os work as hotel staff, janitors, domestics, gardeners, and restaurant workers, often the only jobs open to them. In the past, Latina/os, like African Americans, were unable to rent or buy property in particular neighborhoods, as much for racist as for economic reasons. Many of these inner-city areas have since become predominantly low-income and Latina/o, whites having exited to less diverse and more affluent suburbs. Opposing forces can also be at play, however, when low-income inner-city areas become gentrified and trendy. As real estate prices rise, Latina/os are pushed to the margins, outside the central city and out of long-established Latina/o communities, as has happened in the Mission district in San Francisco, Echo Park in Los Angeles, and Spanish Harlem in Manhattan. Ethnic enclaves also suffer fragmentation when city planners zone these areas for the construction of freeways, waste dumps, junkyards, factories, and other industrial and commercial establishments. Concentration of the Latino Bloc in these metropolitan areas undoubtedly foments resentment and hopelessness, but, ironically, it also generates survival skills and a broader sense of the complexity of the world.

Spatial fragmentation is further compounded by territoriality. Urban gangs, through which youth seek identity in a hostile environment, carve out their own "turf" in urban areas. The existence of gangs, while symptomatic of a need for urban youth to belong, is also, unfortunately, closely linked to intragroup and intergroup violence. Youth and location also link up in other problematic ways, because poverty and unemployment inevitably facilitate access to the informal economy and alternative moneymaking opportunities, such as theft and drug dealing, that pay much more than minimum wage. These practices land our youth in the prison system, where racism, gang affiliation, and the drug trade exacerbate tensions and polarize inmates. The gang factor is often sensationalized and used to justify racial profiling, police harassment of youth, and the all-too-frequent cases of police shootings in our barrios and ghettos. Gang affiliation is increasingly being used as well to target undocumented youth, both Mexican and Salvadoran, who are then repatriated back to their countries of origin; the urgency of these deportations is torqued up with claims of a potential for "terrorism." Deportation or prison is the only option open to many immigrant youth, both men and women, but native-born Latinos (and increasingly Latinas) do not fare much better; they, like African Americans, are more likely than whites to end up in prison for similar crimes (Davis 1997, 267). Little progress has been made in creating new options for the young. Nor has the justice system become any more just, as it is still more likely that a court will find a person of color guilty than a white person, and the sentencing practices of the courts are likewise skewed by the melanin factor.

THESIS 8

THE FACTOR THAT MOST DIVIDES THE LATINO BLOC IS SOCIAL LOCATION—THAT IS, CLASS

As suggested earlier, social position or class, more than race or national origin, cuts across and divides the Latino Bloc in crucial ways. In the United States, class is generally both an economic and a political category, and class issues are often skirted in favor of a focus on race or ethnicity. In a multiethnic society with a dominant white population, the slippage from class to race is easy to understand; after all, the two are intimately interconnected. Class, in fact, is viewed more often than not through the lens of race or ethnicity. But within the multiracial, multiethnic Latino Bloc, class differences serve both to fragment us and at the same time to unite us across ethnicity (that is, national origin) and race. It is thus a strategic category that we can use to maneuver politically, especially now that the myth of a classless U.S. society is being called into question even by the mainstream press (Kinsley 2005; Wessel 2005).

While some theorists might view class as an outmoded category, there is an increasing, even mainstream, recognition that class hierarchies and divisions characterize the U.S. social fabric. For the most part, class is defined in terms of income, or degree of access to goods and services. Varying notions of "poverty" are more likely to be studied than class inequality. While these economic indicators do provide a sense of social location, it is the increasingly transnational capitalist relations of production that are crucial and that allow us to see the Latino Bloc as a primarily working-class population. After all, it is the labor capacity of Latina/os, along with their potential for consumption, that concerns capitalists, for despite mechanization, informational technologies, and finance capital investments, capital "must still depend on workers to make a profit" (Midnight Notes Collective 1992, xiv). Latina/o workers have undoubtedly felt the impact of deindustrialization, unemployment, de-unionization, and subemployment, like other U.S. workers. It is this crucial positioning as labor that places Latina/os in a particular relation to capital.

The distorting effect of media-constructed images notwithstanding, class location serves to organize the experiences and practices of everyday life. For that reason the class location of Latina/os says a good deal about our level and quality of education, our place of residence, our access to opportunities and to consumer goods and services, our access to health care, and our cultural capital. Analysis of social issues strictly on the basis of race, ethnicity, culture, or language often leads to limited, band-aid solutions. Even affirmative action struggles were a limited effort, and our trust in state measures to at least partially ameliorate glaring disparities proved misplaced. Poor educational attainment in the context of racism and segregation led in the past to our focus on the desegregation of schools. "Integration programs" in many cases involved the bussing of students and led to a renewed segregation through the integration solely of minority students. Critics have since recognized the need to rethink both causative factors and solutions for low educational performance. As critical race theorists like Bell have noted, in the past we expected too much from school integration, as if such measures alone would ensure racial equality and opportunity (1995, 305). The problem, then as now, is that we need schools with excellent teachers, conscious of the language and social needs of our communities, and solid programs to prepare our children for success, not to ensure their educational failure. Neither desegregation nor resegregation, unfortunately, provided a remedy. Quality schools are likely to remain out of our reach because of our social location, the lack of political clout that comes with our particular social standing, and, more broadly, the ongoing neoconservative trend against public spending on educational programs.

Even the social ills that we suffer are not evenly distributed, for class status determines who gets the proverbial short end of the stick. Consider, for example, the racism suffered by blacks or Latina/os of different classes. The racism that an African American professional might be subject to has little in common with that endured by Rodney King as he was beaten by the Los Angeles police in 1991 or by James Byrd, dragged by a pickup driven by members of the Aryan Brotherhood through the streets of Jasper, Texas, in 1998. Even within our own communities, we are not all equal and class can be more significant than race or ethnicity. A wealthy Latina/o or Mexican often has no problem oppressing or exploiting a working-class Latina/o or Mexican. In fact, national origin or race tends to become increasingly irrelevant for capitalists, managers, and higher-income individuals, unless these traits can be manipulated opportunistically. And yet the fact that one cannot axiomatically find refuge or empathy within one's own racial or ethnic community can also lead to a sense of resentment and awareness, and as such can signal a step in the development of a broader, more critical class perspective.

Social location or class is obviously intrinsically tied to all the previously mentioned theses regarding the Latino Bloc. It is intimately linked to emigration, immigration, residence, education, employment, unemployment, language choice, and everything else, including racial/ethnic identity. Our class contradictions divide us as Latina/os, inasmuch as the Latino Bloc is socially heterogeneous and includes more than working-class Latina/os. But class location can also serve to unite us across race and ethnicity with other working-class collectivities. It is this transracial, transethnic perspective that is called for to find viable solutions to our social problems.

THESIS 9

Like Other Racial Minorities, the Latino Bloc Is Subject to "Not Feeling at Home" within the United States

Across time, immigrants have come to the United States with hopes of having more options and making better lives for themselves and their offspring. The children and grandchildren of these immigrants, however, do not necessarily share these expectations to the same degree as first-generation immigrants. Second- and third-generation Latina/os are in fact less likely than their grandparents to see the United States as an unrestricted "land of opportunity." Like U.S. blacks, by the second generation young Latina/os no longer harbor illusions about the United States being a color-blind society, and they see notions of equal and unrestricted access for all as myths. Critical race theorists, among others, note that the dominant society and the state proffer notions of meritocracy, pretending that racial remedies of the civil rights era have worked, but those of us who are Latina/os, African Americans, and Asian Americans are painfully aware that racism is constitutive of this society and is not a thing of the past (Bell 1995, 306). Increasingly, as well, U.S. Latina/os, like other minorities, are beginning to see the close relationship between policies and practices at home and policies and practices abroad. Identifying as part of the Latino Bloc may make a broader transborder/international awareness possible.

Racism and class stratification contribute to disidentification and a sense of feeling like "a foreigner in one's native land," as Tejano Seguín noted in 1858 (1973, 177). This sense of rootlessness, of not feeling at home, is not a nineteenth-century phenomenon but an ongoing reality (Mosely 2005; Moraga 2002, 44). It is in part linked to the particular social and economic conditions encountered within this economy. Global capitalism makes fearful strangers of us all, as noted by Virno (2004, 34). It is the very experience of not feeling at home and the absence of a viable sense of a national community that make us seek protection "among our own," especially when our very citizenship is placed in question if we happen to be the children of undocumented workers. When Huntington criticizes Latina/os for forming enclaves, he loses sight of the fact that within an alienating society there is a demonstrable need for an alternative space, a refuge, that will enable individuals to protect their cultural practices and traditions, a place where they might feel more at home. In these communities Latina/os create social spaces where they are able to retrieve practices rooted in their past or produce new cultural practices in response to emerging contexts. These spheres are political as well as cultural sites and are potentially spaces of resistance, for in these local communities unity and identity can be redefined, if not outside the state, then parallel to it.

For most U.S.-born Latina/os, "not feeling at home" seldom triggers a desire to migrate to the homeland of parents or grandparents. Often the parents' homeland is foreign to them. For some Chicano cultural nationalists of the 1960s and 1970s, the sought-after refuge was the mythic homeland, Aztlán. It was a "homeland" within the U.S. nation-state and was meant to legitimize one's roots in the region of one's residence—that is, the U.S. Southwest. In fact, the Chicano movement of the 1970s was primarily linked to struggles for entitlements under the state and did not advocate secession or a return to Mexico.

Disidentification with the state and society at large undoubtedly leads to a search for alternative forms of identification, as for example in gang affiliation and loyalty. There are also other types of alternative identifications that are generated by participation in social movements that go beyond the local. It is perhaps through transnational, transracial, and transethnic political struggles that members of the U.S. Latino Bloc can address and counter the feeling of not being at home in the United States and begin to feel at home in the world.

THESIS 10

The Latino Bloc Is Divided by Issues of Gender, Sexism, and Sexuality, and by Patriarchal Structures

One of the key internal differences dividing the Latina/o multitude is gender, which cuts across all other differences of national origin, race, and class. Internationally, the last few decades have seen a growth in the number of women migrating, in contrast to the pattern of previous decades, when immigrants were more likely to be male. In a period of flexible accumulation (Harvey 1992, 147), labor-intensive low-wage industries in the United States employ large numbers of women, particularly Latina and Asian women. It is thus no surprise that women, especially from Mexico and Central America, are migrating in larger numbers to fill these jobs. In fact, official estimates of recent undocumented immigration from Latin America indicate that these immigrants have been disproportionately female (Sampaio 2002, 53). The influx of women has clearly increased the number of Latinas in the United States, whether immigrant or native-born. Because not all employment is officially reported, especially among domestic workers, the actual numbers are undoubtedly higher than the official estimates.

Global capital is, in fact, what draws these women to the border and beyond. Women provide the bulk of the labor in the maquila industries along the U.S.-Mexico border. Once there, and facing cyclical layoffs at these plants, more and more of these women make their way to the United States to work as domestics, janitors, seamstresses, and nannies. Many are housekeepers or live-in maids, often earning less than the minimum wage. Hondagneu-Sotelo notes that over 68 percent of the estimated 100,000 domestic workers in Los Angeles are Latinas, a situation mirrored in other metropolitan areas of the country (2001, 17). Often working "off the books" because of their immigration status, these domestics earn poverty wages and are subject to abuse and discrimination.

The need to send remittances home is primarily what drives these women north, despite the risks. In light of the growth in remittances from immigrants to their families, clearly labor exportation—increasingly gendered—has served as a sort of "spatial fix" for Latin American economies burdened by high rates of unemployment and debt. Nonetheless, the outflow of women from Latin American communities has negative consequences as well. Recent reports indicate that more and more women coming to the United States from Central America and Mexico are leaving their own children behind with relatives and neighbors, often for extended periods of time (Nazario 2002). Once the mothers are able to obtain legal residence, they often take steps to have their children join them in the United States.

In some cases, as noted by Nazario, domestic violence at home, compounded by economic factors, leads women to migrate. This, ironically, subjects them to further abuse and violence on the dangerous road north, and once they reach the United States, they often find the same patterns reproduced. Well into the twenty-first century, patriarchal structures continue to dominate our homes, and Latina women continue to be subject to both physical and psychological abuse, not only at home but also on the street and in the workplace. Among Latina/os, incidents in which rejected lovers or husbands kill their women and children are all too numerous, although admittedly violence against women is not Latino-specific. Women's work outside the home, however, has made many less willing to endure machista practices and more aware of marginalization and abuse.

While Latinas' experiences are multiple, diverse, and complex, it is important to develop a critical awareness of the dilemmas faced by Latinas and women in general in both the domestic and labor spheres. In part because of transformations in their social location and in family relations, Latinas are increasingly unwilling to put up with sexism, domestic violence, and subjugation. Growing awareness of domestic violence as a crime is leading Latina women to speak out against the rape and abuse not only of women but also of young children, violence often perpetrated by family members, friends, or clergy. They are also more apt to unite with other women, working-class or otherwise, gay or straight, both locally and internationally, across racial, ethnic, and national lines, to fight oppression of any type. Class, however, like race and ethnicity, continues to divide women, and Latinas are not exempt from participating in the exploitation and oppression of other women, whether Latinas or not.

THESIS 11

The Latino Bloc Is Marked by Internal Political and Social Contradictions

As the U.S. Latina/o population grows, it also becomes more diverse politically, with political differences frequently tied to differences in social positioning or class status. Upwardly mobile Latina/os are often more apt to accept neoconservative policies advocating retrenchment and increased repression at home, along with higher military spending and intervention in defense of the interests of oil corporations and military contractors. That these policies should bring destruction to hundreds of thousands and lead to the recruitment of Latina/o youth to die on the front lines seems of little interest to those whose middle-class children are unlikely to "volunteer" for military service.

Along with the general U.S. population, the entire Latino Bloc is, of course, subject to government and corporate-sponsored disinformation. The warping effect of the dominant ideological mindset becomes evident when Chicana/os cheer the nomination of Alberto Gonzales, a legitimizer of torture, for U.S. attorney general simply on the grounds that he is a Texas Latino. There is still a strong if misguided belief that a Latina/o in higher office is there to serve "the people" and therefore is good for Latina/o interests. Those who believe this will no doubt ultimately be disabused of this notion. If ethnicity blinds us to the point that we cannot distinguish between those who serve the interests of ethnic minority communities and those who do not, then clearly our ethnic identity is being used against us. Increasingly we see how easily black, brown, and Asian individuals who advocate hegemonic policies (the Ward Connerlys, Clarence Thomases, and Alberto Gonzaleses) make their way into the higher echelons of power. A real danger lies in thinking that matters will be different once the Latino Bloc constitutes a majority. It would behoove us to remember what material conditions were like for blacks in apartheid South Africa, where they were in the majority.

If the wide spectrum of ideological positionalities within the Latino Bloc appears to negate any notion of political unity, the social location of the majority of Latina/os does perhaps provide for and map out a different story. It is this multitude's labor and its productive and reproductive power that will allow it to transcend its political and social contradictions.

CONCLUSION: MULTIPLE INTERNAL CONTRADICTIONS AND THE UTILITY OF BUILDING BLOCS

For some, the specter of a Latino Bloc is haunting the United States. Yet at this historical juncture, it is an entity that cannot be legislated, exorcised, or wished away. We are here to stay, as are all U.S. minority and majority populations. The numbers, cultures, views, tastes, and languages of the Latino Bloc will undoubtedly profoundly affect the United States, just as in another era the Arab presence in the Spanish peninsula had a lasting impact. Our numbers suggest that we will eventually tilt the scales in the direction of a Latina/o ascendancy, but not completely. This will never be a homogeneous land; it never has been and it never will be. Heterogeneity (cultural, racial, ethnic, linguistic) will continue to define it.

But cultural diversification in and of itself is nothing to cheer about if social stratification and racism persist; if the state wields power in ways that pit one sector against another as we struggle to survive in the same violent economic/geographic spaces; if some of us are oppressed or oppress others, are exploited or exploit others. Even acceptance of cultural diversification within the United States is meaningless if it comes at the cost of exploitation and military intervention abroad. Our problems are at bottom not cultural; they are social, economic, and political, and however much we might think that culture is constitutive of the world around us, it is time to see that culture is not genetic or inherent but is shaped by our daily reality. Unemployment, lack of health care for all, violence in our schools and streets, domestic violence in our homes, hawkish politicians in power, war mongering, racial profiling and police brutality, exploitation of cheap labor here and around the world, homophobia, prostitution of children, and the rapid destruction of the environment and thus our planet—all of these and more are problems that we need to address collectively. We must not allow these issues to be facilely reduced, as they historically have been, to "cultural differences," or taken as a "clash of civilizations."

The future of the Latino Bloc is open, but, we would argue, its construction and utility are likely to be closely tied to the productive and reproductive power of its members. Given their history and racial/ethnic heterogeneity and the critical role of the labor they provide, we would like to envision these Latina/os as agents of resistance—that is, following Linebaugh and Rediker (2000), as the "motley crew" of history that challenges the colossus of capital and, in the process, the current configuration of the state. To this end, building blocs will be crucial.

WORKS CITED

Anderson, Benedict. 1987. *Imagined Communities: Reflections on the Origin and Spread of Nationalism.* London: Verso.

Arrighi, Giovanni, and Beverly J. Silver. 1999. *Chaos and Governance in the Modern World System.* Minneapolis: University of Minnesota Press.

Bell, Derrick. 1995. "Racial Realism." In *Critical Race Theory: The Key Writings That Formed the Movement,* ed. Kimberlé Crenshaw, Neil T. Gotanda, Gary Peller, and Kendall Thomas, 302–12. New York: New Press.

Benjamin, Walter. 1968. "Theses on the Philosophy of History." In *Illuminations,* 253–64. New York: Schocken Books.

Bonfil, Guillermo. 1987. "Los pueblos indios, sus culturas y las políticas culturales." In *Políticas culturales en América Latina,* ed. Néstor García Canclini, 89–125. Mexico City: Grijalba.

Boothman, Derek. 1995. "A Note on the Translation." In *Further Selections from the Prison Notebooks,* by Antonio Gramsci, xi–xx. Minneapolis: University of Minnesota Press.

Davis, Angela Y. 1997. "Race and Criminalization." In *The House That Race Built: Black Americans, U.S. Terrain,* ed. Wahneema Lubiano, 264–79. New York: Pantheon Books.

Dickerson, Marla. 2004. "Funds Sent to Mexico Hit Record." *Los Angeles Times,* July 30, C1.

Eagleton, Terry. 1990. "Nationalism: Irony and Commitment." In *Nationalism, Colonialism and Literature,* ed. Terry Eagleton, Fredric Jameson, and Edward Said, 23–39. Minneapolis: University of Minnesota Press.

Gibson, Charles. 1964. *The Aztecs under Spanish Rule.* Stanford, CA: Stanford University Press.

Gutiérrez, David. 1995. *Walls and Mirrors: Mexican Americans, Mexican Immigrants, and the Politics of Ethnicity.* Berkeley: University of California Press.

Hall, Stuart. 1996. "New Ethnicities." In *Stuart Hall: Critical Dialogues in Cultural Studies,* ed. David Morley and Kuan-Hsing Chen, 441–49. London: Routledge.

Hardt, Michael, and Antonio Negri. 2000. *Empire.* Cambridge, MA: Harvard University Press.

———. 2004. *Multitude: War and Democracy in the Age of Empire.* New York: Penguin.

Harvey, David. 1992. *The Condition of Postmodernity: An Enquiry into the Origins of Cultural Change.* Cambridge, MA: Basil Blackwell.

———. 2003. *The New Imperialism.* New York: Oxford University Press.

Hondagneu-Sotelo, Pierrette. 1994. *Gendered Transitions: Mexican Experiences of Immigration.* Berkeley: University of California Press.

———. 2001. *Doméstica: Immigrant Workers Cleaning and Caring in the Shadows of Affluence.* Berkeley: University of California Press.

Huntington, Samuel P. 2004. "The Hispanic Challenge." *Foreign Policy,* March/April, 30–45.

Kinsley, Michael. 2005. "The Upward Mobility Myth." *Los Angeles Times,* June 5, M5.

Krauze, Enrique. 2004. "Huntington: El falso profeta." *Letras Libres,* April, 24–26.

Linebaugh, Peter, and Marcus Rediker. 2000. *The Many-Headed Hydra: Sailors, Slaves, Commoners, and the Hidden History of the Revolutionary Atlantic.* Boston: Beacon.

Midnight Notes Collective. 1992. "The New Enclosures." In *Midnight Oil: Work, Energy, War, 1973–1992.* Brooklyn: Automedia.

Moraga, Cherríe. 2002. *Watsonville.* Albuquerque: West End Press.

Moseley, Walter. 2005. "What We Forget about Watts." *Los Angeles Times,* August 9, B13.

Nazario, Sonia. 2002. "Sharing a Fear: Will Their Children Forget Them?" *Los Angeles Times,* October 6, A7.

Rodríguez, Gregory. 2004. "Mexican Americans Are Building No Walls." *Los Angeles Times,* February 29, M1.

Rosales, F. Arturo. 1996. *Chicano! The History of the Mexican American Civil Rights Movement.* Houston: Arte Público.

Sampaio, Anna. 2002. "Transforming Chicana/o and Latina/o Politics: Globalization and the Formation of Transnational Resistance in the United States and Chiapas." In *Transnational Latino Communities: Politics, Processes, and Cultures,* ed. Carlos G. Vélez-Ibáñez and Anna Sampaio, 47–72. Lanham, MD: Rowman and Littlefield.

Schwartz, Stephen. 2004. "Ser hispanófilo." *Letras Libres,* April, 28–29.

Seguín, Juan Nepomuceno. 1973. "A Foreigner in My Native Land." In *Foreigners in Their Native Land: Historical Roots of the Mexican Americans,* ed. David J. Weber, 177–82. Albuquerque: University of New Mexico Press.

U.S. Bureau of the Census. 2003–2004. *Current Population Reports: Hispanic Population.* Washington, DC: U.S. Bureau of the Census.

Virno, Paolo. 2004. *A Grammar of the Multitude: For an Analysis of Contemporary Forms of Life.* Trans. Isabella Bertoletti, James Cascaito, and Andrea Casson. New York: Semiotexte.

Wessel, David. 2005. "As Rich-Poor Gap Widens in U.S., Class Mobility Stalls." *Wall Street Journal,* May 13, A1.

PART II
VOICES

The Coyote and the Chicken

Luis Alberto Urrea

There are things, unlikely as it seems, that unite the Mexican consular corps and the Border Patrol. In consulates, names of certain Border Patrol officers are spoken with respect, even affection—Ryan Scudder of Tucson is called a gentleman; Mike McGlasson of Yuma is looked on with respect; Ken Smith, at Wellton, is mentioned as a kind of patriarch of the wasteland. The Wellton boys like the Calexico consul and the Yuma consul, and they have a pretty good feeling about the Mexican Beta Group cops, who are the elite agents investigating narco and Coyote crimes on the Mexican side. Aside from that, they seem to see lots of the other Mexicans as communists and thieves.

But the two things that most unify the two sides are each one's deep distrust of its own government, and each side's simmering hatred for the human smugglers, the gangsters who call themselves Coyotes.

The sign is printed in black and blue and red on a white banner.
It faces south.
They have spent good money on it.

For the Coyotes Your Needs
Are Only A Business And
They Don't Care About Your Safety
Or the Safety of Your Family.
Don't Pay Them Off With Your Lives!!!

The sign has been posted by the Mexican government at Sasabe, Sonora. It is as absurd a placard as might have been posted by the U.S. government. Policy wonks in Washington, D.C., are as ineffectual as policy wonks in México, D.F.

There is no real border here, just a tattered barbed wire fence, a dusty plain, and some rattling bushes. Walkers face the Brawley Wash and the Sierrita Mountains coming up from Mexico.

From *The Devil's Highway* by Lius Urrea. Copyright © 2004 by Luis Urrea. By permission of Little, Brown and Company. All rights reserved.

Don Moi never bothered with Sasabe. He wasn't a walker. For Don Moi, the conspiracy was a thing of buses: the Tres Estrellas and Transportes Norte del Pacífico bus lines. Then a quick night tossing and turning in a Sonoita or San Luis or Douglas motel. A wad of colorful Mexican pesos and a nice lunch, and back home on the bus. It was all *Playboys* and American cigarettes, a tequila and maybe some girls. And so long, boys! I'm going home!

The border was the problem of others.

The Sasabe sign, which many of the walkers can't read, is the only thing Mexico is doing to try to stop them from crossing. The Mexican army patrols the borderlands, sort of, though nobody can find them, probably because the Coyotes pay the soldiers off. Coyote gangs have more money than the Mexico City sign painters. What do Mexican soldiers care if *alambristas* (wire-crossers) walk into Arizona? Any one of the soldiers might very well head north himself at some point.

For a while, the Mexican government offered the walkers survival kits with water and snacks, but the uproar from the United States put a stop to that. Americans saw these attempts at lifesaving as a combination invitation to invade and complimentary picnic basket. They were further astonished to learn that Mexico City officials put condoms into the boxes. Of course, Mexico City claimed this was a gesture of deep consideration for the health of all involved. Gringos were deeply alarmed that the illegals were not just coming over to work, but to get laid. They're coming for our daughters! They're coming to make welfare babies! They're coming to party, party, party!

Fifteen hundred walkers a day depart from under the Sasabe sign. The writer Charles Bowden, on a visit to Sasabe in 2003, counted five thousand walkers in one afternoon.

Although our Wellton 26 did not cross at the sign, their trail leads to the region surrounding it. The Lukeville/Organ Pipe border was too busy for them, so they scooted off to the side and tried to backtrack to the Lukeville paths once they were in the United States.

No matter where they entered, they had only to step over a drooping bit of wire fence, or across an invisible line in the dust. Near the legendary crossing at El Saguaro, there is often no fence at all. Along the Devil's Highway near Tinajas Altas, there is nothing but a dry creek bed and a small sign telling walkers: *Y'all better stay out or else we'll be, like, really really bummed!*

Tucson's newspapers described their entry as having been "somewhere between Yuma and Nogales." This is a safe bet—a cursory glance at a map will reveal that most of the state lies between Yuma and Nogales. Several accounts say they crossed at a tiny burg called Los Vidrios, not to be confused with the Vidrios Drag.

A woman named Ofelia, or Orelia (depends on who you ask), Alvarado, runs a small truck stop at Los Vidrios. Many walkers stop at her store before they cross over. Near Mrs. Alvarado's store are signs that warn walkers "USA Prohibido!" Walkers see them, scratch their heads, and continue. At best, the signs imply, in bad Spanish:

TO USE IS PROHIBITED!

To use what? The trail? The sign? The desert? Spanish? Nobody, it seems, told the Yanquis who put the signs up that in Mexico, "USA" is spelled "EEUU."

Mrs. Alvarado never saw the Wellton 26. She told reporters that a young man had gone a few days before they did, and he'd returned, burned black and vomiting blood, after they'd left. He told her God was coming to get him.

So Los Vidrios, as generally reported, was not their crossing point.

Most of the survivors say they crossed at El Papalote. That would be a tiny scatter of wrecks and huts whose name translates as "the kite." The trail probably led them into the Quitobaquito Hills. These confusions and guesses should suggest why it's so difficult to enforce immigration law on the border. Of the men confirmed to have survived from the group, none can agree on where, exactly, they entered the United States. Perhaps only one person knew where they were trying to go once they were here, and that was their Coyote.

From El Papalote, it seems like the myth of the big bad border is just a fairy tale. One step, and presto! You're in the EEUU. Los Estados Unidos. The Yunaites Estaites. There's nothing there. No helicopters, no trucks, no soldiers. There's a tarantula, a creosote bush, a couple of beat saguaros dying of dry rot, some scattered bits of trash, old human and coyote turds in the bushes now mummified into little coal nuggets. Nothing.

The smugglers tell the walkers it's just a day's walk to their pickup point. If they are crossing into Organ Pipe Cactus National Monument, it's literally a walk in the park. A couple of hours, heading north for Ajo, Arizona. Cold soda pop and a ride to work.

How bad can it be? A day of thirst, some physical struggle—they've lived like that all their lives. The place may be alien to them, but the situation feels like home. After all, they tell themselves, America's a country with a state called Nuevo México. Other states are called Red, Snowy, Mountain, and Flowery; several of them were going to Flowery, and some of the others were going to Northern Caroline to see about making cigarettes. The state of Nuevo México even has a capital city called Holy Faith: Catholicism, New Mexico.

And then there's the hilarious Chi-Cago. ("Piss." And, "I Shit.") It's funny until they feel the cold of winter.

Illegal entry is the sole reason for Sasabe's or El Papalote's or Vidrios's existence. The vans lined up under the spindly cottonwoods have driven from Altar, Sonora, full of walkers. Don Moi was quite familiar with Altar. The bus stopped there, and he often hit the cell phone to check with his bosses: should the walkers hop off in Altar and grab a guide for the Sasabe line, or should they go on to Sonoita, to take part in a more complex conspiracy? Several of our Wellton 26 stopped over in Altar, and it was the merest whim of the head Coyote that put the Yuma 14/Wellton 26 on the bus to Sonoita instead of in a wasted Ford van heading for Organ Pipe. Maybe the Big Man was watching MTV; maybe he was heading for the toilet, or looking for a smoke. He had his phone in one hand, he spoke one word, and on they went to their ordeal.

By the time they were finally rescued, they could have been in Miami.

The ne'er-do-well fence jumpers that galloped into El Paso and San Diego on a quest for chocolate shakes and Michael Jackson cassettes are no more.

The New-Jack Coyote is largely the inadvertent product of the Border Patrol's extremely effective interdiction and prevention policies. Good old Operation Gatekeeper is the mother of invention. San Diego's Border Patrol beefed up the border fence, then placed massive floodlights along it, illuminating the no-man's land between the United States and Mexico. Then, in a burst of creative thinking, it ceased the endless patrolling of the hills and river valleys of the region. Instead, the Border Patrol parked trucks at half-mile checkpoints all along the fence. Each agent is in sight of the next, and all of them are in constant contact as they observe the line. Helicopters still hover, and their versions of the Oscar sensors blip, and night-vision electric eyes scan. The fence in the west extends into the ocean. In the east, it terminates in the wasteland of deserts and mountains.

Unimaginable developments followed. In the region of San Ysidro, the last small town before you get to the Mexican border, at the last U.S. exit off I-5, a big sparkling suburb has sprung up. In this area formerly notorious as a human hunting ground, a dangerous waste of crime and panic, junkies and gunfights, there are now soccer fields and two-story houses that look like they could be in a subdivision of Denver. At the end of all the cul-de-sacs in the development, there is a high wall, and football-stadium floodlights pointing south. Some of the new Latino middle class once crossed that very land in a mad scuttle; now, teens in the neighborhood climb up on their backyard sheds to watch the action in the Tijuana River floodplain.

The hundreds of walkers who once ran this gauntlet are now forced to move east. They rarely try to swim around the western barrier, and if they do, they land in a state park where "fishermen" casting into the surf are often armed feds. The only way to go is out there, back of beyond, away from civilization. And if you go far enough, the fence devolves into a two-foot-high road barrier you can step over. Farther still, and you're in territory much like Sasabe. There are approximately two thousand miles of this kind of terrain to enter.

This new paradigm—walkers crossing Desolation in place of jumping urban fences—has made Altar the largest center of illegal immigration on the entire border. The central park plaza in town is full of Coyotes and walkers. A five-minute visit to the park will garner several offers to cross. Coyotes hawk destinations like crack dealers in the Bronx sell drugs: voices murmur options from a memorized menu, "Los Angeles, Chicago, Florida."

The backs of the Altar vans have plastic milk jugs of water for sale. On the front of each van is a sign made of masking tape, and it says "Sasabe," or "Frontera."

"Carolina Norte. Carolina Sur. Nueva York."

The main grocery store in Sasabe, hardly a supermarket, is winkingly called "Super El Coyote."

The Mexican government's border sign near Sasabe doesn't actually say "Coyotes." It uses the hipper slang of the border. It says, "Los Polleros."

A *pollero* would be a chicken-wrangler. The level of esteem the smugglers hold for their charges is stated plainly. They're simply chickens.

Of course, if you know Spanish, you know that the word for "chicken" is *gallina*. *"Pollo"* is usually reserved for something else. A *pollo*, as in *arroz con pollo*, has been cooked.

Now, more than ever, walkers need a Coyote.

In the new organized crime hierarchies of human smuggling, the actual Coyotes are middle-management thugs. The old Coyote, the scruffy punk leading a ragtag group of Guatemalans into San Diego via the bogs and industrial parks of Chula Vista, is rapidly becoming extinct. You will still encounter a dope fiend who will walk you into the infrared night-vision RoboCop scrub for fifty bucks, or the homeboy in the Impala who blusters you through the line by being a "Chicano" heading home to the barrio after "hitting the bars," but he's being replaced by the new breed. And woe to that crackhead if the Young Turks get hold of him. He'll be found with his hands tied behind his back and a .9 mm slug in his brainpan.

Even asking questions about these criminals is considered dangerous. Queries into the Coyote operation behind the Yuma 14 catastrophe, for example, elicit three different warnings about being "shot in the head." One gets the feeling that the entire world of Coyotes is waiting, waiting to merge with the *narcotraficante* underworld immortalized by Norteño music and movies such as *Traffic*, waiting to hook more deeply into the white slavery and sex slavery and child-labor rings of the world, waiting for a human-smuggling visionary to unify them.

Gangs are so in control now that walkers who want to go alone, without a pollero to guide them, must pay a fee just to enter the desert.

Criminals are at the gate of Disneyland: they're scalping tickets, and they're scalping each other.

The criminal operation that lured the Yuma 14 and their companions into the desert and abandoned them was not the biggest, by far. But it was well established, and it operated out of Phoenix, Arizona, and the Mexican state of Hidalgo. It was a family operation. The main man, the Tony Soprano figure, lived in the United States. Or maybe he lived in Hidalgo. He liked to wear cowboy boots, and he kept his figure slim. Or he was never seen by the troops. A voice on the phone.

In Phoenix, it was Luis Cercas.

Luis Cercas, at the time of the Yuma 14 deaths, had contacts in Florida, Illinois, and California. He had a Florida associate, Don Francisco Vásquez, and another roving associate was placed in Mexico. He was the brother of Luis, Daniel Cercas, and he lived in Hidalgo.

Like all of the smugglers, Daniel had an alias, "El Chespiro," derived in part from "Chespirito," the cloying little red cricket of Mexican kids' TV. (Chespiro! Did some of the walkers think Don Moi was in touch with the television star? Did some of them secretly believe that Chespirito, the red cricket, was a massively powerful gangster? It made a kind of sense to the Mexican mind. Stranger things had happened.) This Chespiro never met the bottom-feeders of the gang face-to-face; he kept in contact via cell phone. All payments went to Chespiro, and all payouts allegedly came from Chespiro.

Chespiro sent people to Sonoita from all over Mexico. A sister-in-law worked in Phoenix, running the administration of the corporation. She organized pickups and human deposits in the double-wides and barrio apartment safe houses. One of these drop-offs is known to have been on Peoria Street in Phoenix.

A step beneath Luis and Chespiro Cercas and their sister-in-law were the soldiers and drivers and guides.

In the Yuma 14 case, the Coyote was a shadowy and notorious figure known as El Negro (with the wonderful Mexican bandido name of Evodio Manilla). He had the universal black mustache. He was short and thin, with an "aquiline" nose and a haircut that in reports sounds like it was a mullet. He wore gold chains around his neck, and he had a curious head-bobbing walk. He had three vehicles, and all of them might have been white. El Negro was also alleged to be the brother-in-law of Luis. *Bada Bing!* It's a family thing.

El Negro apparently worked his way up from an early life as a guide. It was said he never crossed into the United States for any reason once he achieved middle-management status. At the time, he was about twenty-eight.

El Negro, dreaded enforcer and manipulator of Sonoita, Sonora, had a driver known as El Moreno. The Black Man and the Dark Man. Scary. El Moreno affected the black border mustache like his boss, and his round face had a scar slanting down the left side. The combination of the scar and the 'stache made him a really convincing bandido. El Moreno was described as "robust" in the investigation documents.

In Sonoita, El Negro and El Moreno lived together in criminal bliss in a house described as being "around the corner" from an evangelical temple on the west side of town. Local directions are simple: go to the road to San Luis Río Colorado; El Negro's house is there, between the *templo* and a disco called Angelo. Jesus Christ on one side, and party hardy on the other. El Negro sometimes danced at Angelo with his girlfriend, Lorena. Lorena seems to be one of the only people in Sonora not involved with the smuggling gang.

Immune to prosecution, Chespiro oversaw El Negro and El Moreno via long-distance cell phone, and they in turn commanded a small army of soldiers. These were secondary drivers, guards, enforcers, and *guias* ("GEE-yahs"), or guides. Today, these guides are what we used to think of as Coyotes.

They actually cut sign, make trails, and lead the walkers into the desert. Young men, mostly, who are as disposable as the pollos. They can die as easily as the walkers, and the organization will not be hurt. There are always more fools willing.

Smugglers pay locals, like drug lords in the inner city pay off shorties and grandmothers, to cover their operations. Runners. Lookouts. Imagine living in a burning cement brick oven in Sells, Arizona; a guy comes along and offers you two hundred dollars to let him park his van behind your house for two days. Maybe he offers you five hundred dollars to go sleep at your mom's trailer while he waits. You'd be crazy not to take it.

The Cercas crew had a favorite illegal entrant pickup spot in the United States: mile marker 27, on Highway 86, on the O'Odham reservation. Or mile marker 27, or 21, on Highway 85. No one can agree. The Devil's Highway forecasts are always for sun, heat, and impenetrable fog.

But wherever the pickup spot was, when a load of walkers was due, a woman named Teresa would drive up and down the road after dark. Thin, with long black hair, she is our Mata Hari. Teresa must have been bold—even cops don't like to be out there in the dark. The guía would gather his chickens at the mile marker post, and Teresa would then spot them on the drive-by. She'd speed-dial a transport on her cell phone, and one or two vans would depart from their prearranged parking spots.

The walkers, squeezed out of the urban corridors, are relying more and more on the reservation. They cost the Indians millions of dollars a year in cleanup, rescue, enforcement, and land restoration. Hundreds of pounds of garbage accrue yearly: bottles, pants, tampons, paper, toilet paper. Corpses. And the Migra barrels through in their trucks.

This may help to explain some of the frayed relationships between the Border Patrol and the O'Odham people on the rez.

The Cercas gang's western operation centered on Yuma and Wellton, their central operation delivered walkers to the Mohawk rest area on I-8, and the eastern operation—which ultimately killed the Yuma 14—targeted Ajo.

Ajo (Garlic) is a small mining town not far from Why. (Locals quip: "Why not!" And: "Good question!") It's near the reservation. And it's a straight shot to Gila Bend in one direction, and Tucson in another.

The Cercas drivers got Teresa's call and sped onto 86, mindful of Border Patrol vehicles or the unlikely sheriff's cruisers. Cut north on 85, pull up at marker 27, throw open the doors, and hustle 'em in, slam the doors, and be gone. If you were slow or ill, and you missed the van, there you were, waiting for whatever fate would find you.

Recently, a young woman was found dead beside I-8. Someone had dragged her out of the desert and left her like a bag of litter on the shoulder. It is entirely possible that she simply couldn't manage the fast upload into the van and was left to stare at the stars as they drove away. One can imagine the tiresome complications of dealing with a dead or dying woman in Phoenix. The Coyotes are stone-cold pragmatists. Perhaps somebody kicked her out of the van. It was a big freeway—she still had a shot. By desert standards, it was a tender act.

The Cercas's vans would hustle onto I-10 and deliver their loads to Phoenix, where the illegals would squat in safe houses guarded by gang-bangers until they could be shuffled off into wider America. Their United States travel was arranged by big brother Luis, King of the Freeway. All it took was a van, a truck, a car with a big back seat or a roomy trunk. A rear seat on a Trailways bus.

Luis, Daniel, El Negro, and El Moreno plied their trade in the vast reaches of the Cabeza Prieta wilderness. El Negro, El Moreno, and the Dark-Head Desert. It sounds like a Mexican translation of an H. P. Lovecraft story.

It will shock no one to learn that Don Moi was said to be yet another relative of the prolific Cercas family.

So this was their system:

The Cercas familia controlled the operation from Phoenix; fixers in other states procured jobs for a fee; Daniel recruited the polleros and the guias for transport of walkers to these jobs, and he oversaw the tides of money, and he made the complex arrangements for housing and transport; Don Moi recruited the walkers—his title was *enganchador,* or the hooker; El Negro enforced and organized the shady doings in Sonora; El Moreno supervised the transport to the launching pad, where the walkers stepped off on a forsaken piece of desert on the brink of El Camino del Diablo, and he sometimes drove.

At the bottom, there was the guía.

A Soccer Season in Southwest Kansas

Sam Quinones

Because Garden City High School had trouble finding white students who could kick the ball, Juan Torres was the field-goal kicker for the school's football team for one sweet year and knew the rarified world of privilege and glory that comes with playing America's sport in western Kansas.

In the year 2001, Juan Torres and Miguel Benítez, both sophomores, had the strongest legs on the school's soccer team. So they were made the kickers for the football team, as well. Miguel had the stronger leg and was used for kickoffs. Juan was reserved for field goals. Even so, the coach showed little confidence in Juan's leg. Toward the end of one game, down by two points, the team was close enough for a field goal but the coach opted to try for a touchdown. The attempt failed, and Garden City lost. "We could have won that game if they'd put me in," Juan said.

Despite their essential roles, Juan and Miguel were strangers on the team. No one called either of them anything but Kicker. This was how Garden City had evolved since the beef plants had brought Mexican and Salvadoran immigrants to town. Native Garden City—which is to say, the city's white and assimilated Mexican-American residents—depended economically on the immigrants and were mostly polite. But neither group knew much about the other with whom it had come to share streets, schools, and, occasionally, neighborhoods. An awkward coexistence was expressed in a million little ways, and one of these was the way the football players grew to call each of their two young kickers simply, Kicker.

But when Rockhurst High School came to town, Juan Torres earned a place in history. Rockhurst is a Jesuit school in Kansas City, a school reputed to recruit its players as early as middle school, put them on weight plans, and field kids of enormous size every year. By the time Rockhurst came to Garden City that season, no one had scored against them. There was no question who would win the game. But as no one had scored against Rockhurst so far,

---

Published in *Antonio's Gun and Delfino's Dream: True Tales of Mexican Migration*, by Sam Quinones (Albuquerque, New Mexico: University of New Mexico Press, 2007). © 2007 by Sam Quinones. Courtesy of University of New Mexico Press.

Garden City's coaches decided they would try a field goal if the team got close enough. Sure enough, in the first quarter, the team found itself at Rockhurst's twenty-yard line. They called on their sixteen-year-old Kicker.

"I was so nervous," said Juan. "I actually thought I was going to get hit by one of those kids. They snapped the ball, and I just ran up there and closed my eyes and kicked it and hoped it went in. I didn't even see it go in. I just heard the crowd cheering."

Garden City lost the game 40–3.

A tall fellow with confidence beyond his years, Juan Torres possesses the handsome jock cache that, as a senior two years after his field-goal glory, made him a presence on campus in a way that some of the smaller, thinner Mexican kids were not. Still, he spoke of his year on the football team the way a kid remembers a favorite summer vacation. On the road, you ate your fill at restaurants, and sometimes you even went to steakhouses. The school held pep rallies for you. The cheerleaders and the trainer were always at your games. Everyone on campus wanted to know you. It was intoxicating. Most of the Mexican population in town slaughtered cattle for a living and spent mostly unnoticed lives, unless they committed a crime, which was then duly reported in the *Garden City Telegram*. By joining the football team, it was as if Juan had been allowed into a special club, the benefits of which he'd been only partially aware of until then.

Most of all, he remembered wistfully, "it was great to play on Friday night, under the lights, and have your name announced over the speakers."

Two years later, in 2003, in the sky over western Kansas one afternoon in September, the sun had beaten away any errant wisp of cloud and was now beginning its decline in the west. Had a breeze not trickled in from somewhere, the soccer field might have been deadeningly hot, as September afternoons often are on the High Plains of Kansas.

Coach Joaquín Padilla shielded his eyes, looked into the sun, and yelled at his players to send the ball forward. On the field before him ran the Buffaloes, the varsity soccer team for Garden City High School, in white uniforms with black numbers. A slower opponent was outhustling his boys. Padilla groaned, turned away, and stomped the grass, as his players gave up on another loose ball.

Joaquín Padilla is a short, affable man now in his fifties, with gray hair and a mustache. Twenty years ago, as Mexican immigrants were arriving to Garden City, he'd come to town, hired as a high-school guidance counselor. Over the years, he had pestered the administrators and school board for an activity in which the immigrant students would want to participate. The school created a soccer team in 1996.

Soccer at Garden City High had gone largely unnoticed since then, however. Padilla's players insisted some students on campus didn't even know the school had a soccer team. In Wichita, Kansas City, and Topeka, soccer was a middle-class, white sport. But out here on the High Plains it was as foreign to the native white residents as the immigrants who played it. Southwest Kansas was farming and cattle country, which made it football country. Soccer was the sport Mexicans brought with them, and Mexicans went out for it. A few white school administrators attended soccer games, but players suspected they did so out of obligation.

As the 2003 season got under way, the team suffered the kind of indignity soccer players at Garden City High School were used to by now. A girl from the school's yearbook staff showed up at practice with a digital camera she didn't know how to use. She told the players that everyone on the staff who knew how to operate the camera wanted to take pictures of the football team, so they'd sent her to shoot the soccer team. She asked if any of them knew how to work the camera.

The varsity team she would photograph was made up of eleven children of Mexican immigrants, five of Salvadoran immigrants, one Vietnamese, and an Anglo. Padilla hoped this team would be different. Every year, he usually lost eight or nine players, who'd be academically ineligible or whose families would leave for work in other states. Each fall Padilla would start anew, patching together a team from whoever was left and whoever had moved into the area over the summer. But this year he'd lost only three guys, and eight of his returning players were seniors.

Juan Torres had dropped football to concentrate on soccer and had been the team's leading scorer the previous year. Rey Ramírez was a quick forward and played a lot of midfield as well. Hugo Blanco was small but fast. Armando González and Elbin Palencia alternated at the other forward spot. Luis Posada was a midfielder whose speed allowed him to cover enormous territory. Carlos Reyes, a thick, tough junior, and Pablo López, a thin sophomore, were at midfield. Defense was a solid wall made up of Rudy Hernández, Hernán Macías, and Servando Hernández. Backing them all up was Miguel Benítez, the goalie, who had remained as the football team's now all-purpose kicker.

These kids, or their parents, had come from different parts of Mexico and El Salvador. They were out on the desolate High Plains prairie of Kansas for one reason: IBP, the world's largest beef slaughtering plant. It was a few miles out of town and employed some four thousand people, virtually all of them Latino immigrants.

Seniors Tri Dang and Chuck Dodge were the team's only non-Latinos. Tri came to Garden City when he was nine. His father was a former officer in the South Vietnamese Army who had spent years in a communist reeducation camp after the war and who also worked at IBP. Chuck was born and raised in Garden City, and, alone on this team, his family had never worked in the beef plant.

Years before, when they were ten and eleven years old, seven of Padilla's players had played on a team that traveled around southwest Kansas playing other youth squads. That had been the start of organized youth soccer in Garden City. So by now, they knew each other's game. They were talented and fast. For all these reasons, Padilla allowed himself to hope. None of his teams had ever won even a first-round playoff game, but Padilla thought this team could advance beyond regional playoffs. He wanted the school to notice the team and by extension the Latino student body. This would only happen if the team did well.

Yet early in the season he watched as his boys played timidly. They showed up out of shape for practice in August. On this sunny September afternoon, they wilted when opponents pushed them out of plays. When his team won anyway, 1–0, on superior skill not effort, and the sun went down and his players walked off the field, Joaquín Padilla was not pleased.

His mood did not improve two nights later, when Garden City played Great Bend, another High-Plains town. Padilla's guys seemed to collapse when they couldn't score easily and discovered instead that Great Bend battled them all game long and won 3–0.

By the end of the first week of the 2003 season, the Buffaloes were 2–1. But Padilla believed they could easily have been 1–2. It was not the way he liked to start a season, and this year especially.

What bothered Padilla most was that there seemed to be a lot of Mexico in the way his kids had played soccer up to now. As the season progressed, this became one of his favorite subjects, and he would go on eloquently about it for quite a while.

Padilla had grown up in the town of Pátzcuaro, in Michoacán, several hours west of Mexico City. Pátzcuaro is the center of a region where people make handcrafts—guitars, furniture, and copperware. As a boy, Padilla learned to guide tourists around the area. As the artisans would pay him 20 percent of whatever they sold to his tourists, it was a lucrative business.

One day, he met a busload of tourists from Kansas. Among them was Henry Watkins, a railroad foreman, rancher, and state legislator. Watkins took a liking to this boy and asked Padilla if he'd like to come back to Kansas to live and go to school.

Padilla talked it over with his parents. Learning English would make him a better tour guide. So in 1962, at fourteen, alone and speaking no English, little Joaquín Padilla moved to the town of Erie, in eastern Kansas. Every morning he'd milk cows on the Watkins farm, then hop a bus for school. He sat in the back of his classroom, lost and bewildered, the only Mexican in the school. But he was a plucky kid. He memorized words and what they meant. He could understand the math and science. He would read to his English teacher during lunch break, and she would listen and correct him. Within six months, Padilla was pulling Cs. At year's end he was speaking English.

That summer Padilla returned to Pátzcuaro. He now knew enough English to be a great tour guide. But Kansas had changed him. "I went back to the same house, and I didn't find myself," he said. "The lake was there, the mountains were there, the trees were there, the house was there. Everything was the same, but I was not. When August came, I said, 'I can't stay here.'"

He returned to Kansas, leaving his family, who remain in Pátzcuaro to this day. Over the next seven years, he lived with two other families. The father of one of these families was the high-school basketball coach. So Padilla played on the basketball team and ran track at his high school.

Upon graduating, he received a track scholarship at Pittsburg State University in eastern Kansas, where he studied psychology. That led to a master's degree, and when he'd finished that, the school had an opening teaching Introduction to Psychology. At twenty-four, ten years after coming to the United

States speaking no English, Joaquín Padilla stood before a college class of a hundred Kansas freshmen and taught them the basic concepts of psychology.

Padilla therefore had distinct ideas about what was possible in life. The cardinal sin, he felt, was to let life happen to you. That was how it was in Mexico.

"Mexicans are taught to be submissive. In Mexico, we're taught not to compete," he said. "A lot of those ideas come over here with families."

Mexican immigrants showed remarkable daring in coming to the United States. But once here, Padilla believed, many immigrants settled too easily into the enormous and oft-replenished Mexican enclave. The enclave helped immigrants find work and housing, then insulated them and did not force them to change.

As bilingual guidance counselor, Padilla would watch as, paralyzed, his students stared at the list of elective classes from which they had to choose three per semester. They'd ask Padilla what he recommended. He would tell them the choice was theirs.

"But the classes are all in English. There's a lot of Americans in there," they'd say.

"Of course," Padilla would answer. "If we were in Japan, there'd be a lot of Japanese."

He noted ruefully how they dropped the classes when they got difficult.

His players would buy their shoes through Padilla because he had a coach's discount through a catalogue. This was also often a tortured, drawn-out process, as some of his players anguished over what shoes to buy. On the field, too, his players seemed afraid to assert themselves—particularly when the other team was tall and white. They gave up on loose balls and took an elbow in the chest without giving one back.

Padilla felt this was part of a fear of standing out that was widespread among Latino students at Garden City High School. It was why the school, with a thousand Latino students amounting to a huge vein of soccer potential, had only about thirty boys go out for the varsity and junior varsity soccer teams each year. No Latina had ever gone out for the cheerleading or dance squad. The school newspaper, which published an article a week in Spanish, had no immigrant kids on its staff. The school formed special activities to get Latino students to participate; Latin Lingo began as a dance squad for Latinas.

Some students' poor English held them back; others were academically ineligible. Just as often, though, Latino students suffered from feelings of inferiority. "You know in Mexico how most people look down on poor people," said Artemio Rodríguez, a junior, whose parents came from Jalisco. "They think it's that way here, that white people look down on them. I think it's self-imposed. They always stay to themselves."

On campus, being Mexican had come to mean showing less interest in school and participating less. A Latino student who got good grades or did after-school activities was a "coconut": brown on the outside, white on the inside. Many soccer players, therefore, preferred the more comfortable Sunday adult leagues in town, playing against other immigrants—though competition was uneven, injuries were common, and college coaches never scouted these leagues.

With few boys to choose from, Padilla felt he couldn't ask of his players what a football coach would have demanded. His players whined about running sprints. Padilla would relent. Players were late or sometimes didn't show up at all. Football players would have been cut for any of these infractions, but Padilla said little.

"If we ran them hard... we wouldn't have a kid out here," he said, one day watching an unfocused practice. "It's a fear of excelling, of achieving."

Like any coach, Padilla compared his sport to life. Neither soccer nor life was determined by "Lo que Dios diga—Whatever God wishes." "It's you who makes things happen or not happen," he said. "This is hard for them to buy into."

Still, Padilla had faith in soccer in the United States. Until they joined the team, certain of his players had never showered in a locker room, competed face-to-face with white people, or stayed in a motel far from family. In the United States, soccer fulfilled the mission of student athletics in a way that football and basketball often didn't anymore. Those sports, in fact, tended to teach Old World lessons: that your behavior has fewer consequences if you belong to a privileged elite. In the United States, soccer was assiduously ignored and was therefore more egalitarian. Soccer players didn't often get the breaks on grades afforded a star running back, but that was a good thing. They had to work hard for recognition. Because of this, Padilla felt, soccer scholarships could offer real educations and open more important doors in life. But, again, the team needed to do well for the scholarships to come.

It was for all these reasons that his team's hesitant play distressed him in the first weeks of the 2003 season. This year was the culmination of a lot that Joaquín Padilla had been waiting for since he started the soccer program.

"This is the year," he said. "This is it."

This would indeed be a different kind of year for soccer in Garden City, Kansas. A high-school soccer season in the High Plains heartland where football was king would afford glimpses of America, of the Mexico within it, and of what had become of the country's melting pot.

Somewhere west of Wichita, the eastern United States ends and the West begins. Rolling hills bow to semiarid, flat land; the tall grass of eastern Kansas becomes short and scruffy out in the western part of the state. These are the High Plains. They stretch out before the Rocky Mountains from South Dakota down to Texas. At their center is western Kansas.

On the prairie, the trees that grow are thin and weather-nagged and mean nothing to the wind. A fall wind can rally across the plains and blow unobstructed for hundreds of miles. As remarkable as the flatness of western Kansas is its weather. It changes insanely. This part of Kansas has seen rain, snow, and hard sunshine, all in the same day.

Two hundred miles west of Wichita—equidistant from San Francisco, California, and Norfolk, Virginia—in the very middle of what Americans consider their heartland, lies the town of Garden City, Kansas.

The town, twenty-nine thousand people, is flat, too. Surrounding it are the cattle feed yards and the farms and the natural gas wells that make up the region's three principal industries. The largest edifices in Garden City are the water towers—each broadcasting the town's name across the prairie— and the white grain storage elevator. Only two-lane state routes bisect Garden City; no interstate comes anywhere near the town. Garden City's restaurants are mostly of the Burger King, Subway, and Lonestar Steakhouse chain variety that have crept across the country, homogenizing city and small town alike.

Garden City has always been a regional shopping center and is today the home to the only Target and Home Depot stores for 180 miles. Downtown Garden City is usually empty, and people are rarely seen out walking. Nor is there much to do at night, which people say is one reason the region has among Kansas's highest teen pregnancy rates. Seven miles away is the town of Holcomb, famous as the setting of *In Cold Blood,* Truman Capote's chronicle of the murder of a farm family.

This part of Kansas has always scared people away. The 2000 census showed that the state had 2.68 million people. Of these, only about 350,000 souls were brave enough to live west of Wichita.

The first European to see the region was a Spanish explorer named Francisco Vásquez de Coronado, in 1541. An Indian guide told Coronado that he would discover an Indian land of unimaginable wealth, of fish the size of horses and rivers six miles wide. Instead he found a few hundred Indians in huts and oceans of buffalo. Coronado recognized that the land had rich black soil that could, with effort, be farmed and where trade routes could be developed. But the Spaniards wanted gold and weren't inclined to settle for less. Coronado and his crew strangled the guide who'd led them there, turned around, and went home.

Three centuries later, in the late 1800s, the pioneers in western Kansas would understand how Coronado felt. Promoters of the region had to invent ploys and get-rich-quick schemes to attract settlers, because people tended not to stay, and without people the region had no future. Those who responded to these come-ons hoped for a place to escape limitations, to reinvent themselves. They were black "Exo-dusters" leaving the collapse of Reconstruction in the South; Mennonites from Austria escaping persecution; Czech, German, and Bohemian peasants; city folk from the east looking for fresh air to breathe.

Out on the plains, their lives became an epic grapple with nature. Blizzards froze them and their livestock. Their crops withered under hailstorms in July, then droughts. Con men fleeced the settlers. Rattlesnakes dropped from the roofs of their sod houses onto their dinner tables. Children died from the flu, from pneumonia, and scarlet fever. Walls of prairie fire could race across the flatlands, swallowing pioneer homes. As the pioneers slept, centipedes entered their ears, and fleas nipped their legs. Poor farming techniques withered the land, and by the 1930s terrifying dust storms moved across the High Plains, turning day to night and filling homes with silt. Only the most willful people, or those with no choice, stayed and survived.

One of the best tellers of their stories is a man named Craig Miner. Miner is a tall, thin historian with wispy white hair who teaches at Wichita State

University. His great-grandfather, William Miner, came from Connecticut in the mid-1880s, looking to be a land speculator. He invested in extending street rail lines between the towns of Ness City and Sidney, a scheme that failed when Sidney blew away in a tornado. He founded the town of Harold, which disappeared when a railroad planned for the area failed to materialize. Two generations later, Miner's father was a lawyer and moved the family to Wichita.

Miner's father would take him to the family farm in Ness City. Miner remembers the lights of the harvesters at night crawling like huge insects across the fields. The farmers he met were leathery men conversant in the exotic themes of truck engines and bull castration.

"I was a city kid. I had that imagery about western Kansas—which may be partly a myth and maybe always was—as where double-distilled U.S. of A. is," Miner said. "Of course, I didn't have to live there, which everyone was always reminding me."

Studying history, his romantic notions of western Kansas faded as he discovered stories of immigrants' spirits crushed by land fraud and mean weather. Through Miner's books pass marauding Indians gang-raping pioneer women, towns that choke to death on the dust of failed crops, and locusts—which one year formed a cloud 250 miles wide and 20 miles deep, devouring even children's clothes, and driving people insane.

Yet much of what Americans think of themselves and the origins of their country is bound up in the land Miner described. The hard land promoted the values of self-reliance, directness, frugality, and calloused hands. It sculpted a classless society where weather and economics humbled all, regardless of station. Thus, no region outside New England contributed more of this country's historical icons: pioneers, sod houses, family farms, fields of corn and wheat, small towns and Main Street, Sioux and Cheyenne Indians, buffaloes, Dodge City, cattle drives, cowboys, the Santa Fe Trail—all of it the subject of ballads, novels, and a hundred western movies.

Southwest Kansas was America in another way, too. No one who stayed here remained the same. As recently as the 1950s, a woman suffering through a drought could be found in Miner's book, *West of Wichita,* writing: "Those who can stand it [here] have had to learn that man does not modify this country; it transforms him, deeply."

In 2003, tourism to Kansas was rising. A principal reason for this, state officials discovered from tourist surveys, was that Americans longed for something rooted and authentic to nourish their lives amid soulless chain stores, nonstop shopping, and twenty-four hour news cycles. Naturally, they looked for it in Kansas.

"People have that yearning for that Grant Woods sort of family—homesteader, pioneer stock that's independent and honest and sort of free of all this load of junk," said Miner one October day, sitting in his university office. "We imagine (these families) are not on the Internet getting spam. They're out there on their tractor, close to nature, close to God and heaven and livestock. We think about them earning their own way, independent of the taxpayer. We'd all like that to be true."

But western Kansas had been changing in ways relevant to this story for at least fifty years.

In the 1950s, the invention of the turbine water pump allowed them finally to suck water from the massive Oglalla Acquifer, a sea of underground freshwater that stretches under the High Plains from South Dakota to Texas and New Mexico. New irrigation systems let them spread that water across wide swaths of land and decreased the threat of drought. Farmers could grow huge amounts of grain—corn, milo, and alfalfa—which could be fed to cattle. With that came the cattle feed yard.

In 1951, a Garden City farmer named Earl Brookover built the first cattle feed yard in Kansas, with large pens in which cattle ate locally grown grain from a trough. Cattle fattened faster and more efficiently—on high-protein milo, corn, and alfalfa—than when they grazed aimlessly on the range. Dozens of ranchers opened feedlots across the High Plains. The Irsik family, another feedlot operator near Garden City, built the first processor that turned corn into cattle feed. Today, there is feed yard space for a million head of cattle within a sixty-mile radius of Garden City.

Poets would find potent symbols of America's vanished frontier in these yards, with their acres of penned and tagged cattle that once roamed the range. The cowboy was now as penned in as the cattle. He rode from yard to yard, culling the sick head.

Still, the feed yard changed the American diet. The price of beef dropped. On rangeland, cattle exercised as they grazed, making their meat lean and tough, so not much of the animal was usable for anything other than hamburger or pot roasts. America's hamburger tradition was due to the fact much of the range-fed cattle was appetizing only when it was ground up with some of the animal's fat. But in feed yards, cattle didn't move much, so their meat was fattier and thus more tender and better tasting. Demand for beef rose. This added protein to the U.S. diet. Cattle producers could now harvest more profitable specialty cuts—brisket, chuck, inside skirt, flatiron, and flank steaks—from all over the animal.

Brookover's idea was to keep in Kansas what was raised in Kansas. Up to that point, Kansas and a lot of rural America resembled the Third World: its commodities—cattle and corn, in this case—were shipped away to be transformed into more profitable products elsewhere. The feed yard transformed Kansas corn into a more profitable product—cattle. Thus a bit more of the wealth that these rural communities produced remained in the area.

By the 1970s, southwest Kansas was a cattle center unlike anything early settlers could have dreamed. Yet it was only a hint of what was coming.

The man who completed the transformation of southwest Kansas—and changed America in the process—was a tall, jowly fellow with a slow Iowa drawl named Andy Anderson.

Anderson cofounded a company known as Iowa Beef Packers—later IBP. Anderson had intense energy and creativity where building things was concerned. He'd been a butcher, then a meat wholesaler in Los Angeles. Anderson had no schooling in engineering but would become an expert, and endless tinkerer, in the science of meat-packing and refrigeration. He built the meat-packing plant of the future.

Meat-packing began in the big cities, near large populations of workers, many of whom were Eastern European immigrants. Legions of well-paid union butchers in Chicago, Omaha, and Kansas City slaughtered the cattle that came in on trains from the High Plains. Anderson and IBP moved the meat industry to the small town in the American heartland where the cattle were raised. Anderson retired from IBP in 1970 and died in 1990 at the age of seventy-one. But by then, he and IBP had reinvented the way meat was slaughtered and sold. They'd also ended butcher unions and brought millions of Mexican immigrants to the heartland.

In 1960, Anderson and his partner, Currier Holman, used a U.S. Small Business Administration loan to form IBP in the town of Denison, Iowa. Anderson applied assembly-line principles to the disassembly of cattle. In this factory, the jobs of slaughtering, cutting, vacuum wrapping, and boxing the meat for shipping were mechanized and consolidated under one roof. His factories broke down these tasks until anyone could do them. A production line would send a cow carcass on a hook through the plant. A worker would make one cut, then the carcass moved to the next worker, who made another cut, and so on, until the skeleton remained. The cuts were then sealed in plastic and boxed for shipment.

Boxed beef was easier and more sanitary to ship than the swinging carcasses that were touched by dozens of hands before they were eaten. Packaged in plastic, the meat kept fresh, and it didn't lose weight, as happened when carcasses were handled excessively. Also, only the edible parts of the animal were shipped to market. In the old days, retail butchers might throw away the small quantities of unsalable fat and bones that came with the large slabs of beef. An IBP factory could accumulate great quantities of this detritus and sell it in bulk for use in other products. More than forty products—from perfume to shoes—are today made from one cow.

After Brookover's success, feed yards spread across the High Plains. They supplied the huge numbers of cattle Anderson's factories required to run efficiently. IBP built or acquired boxed-beef factories in small towns in Nebraska, Iowa, Kansas, and Minnesota. In 1980, the company built the ultimate expression of Anderson's innovations: the plant near Garden City, which can slaughter eight cattle a minute.

To IBP, rural towns had an advantage in addition to their oceans of livestock: they had a nonunion culture and were mostly in states that had outlawed the union shop. Unions correctly viewed IBP's plants as a threat to the skilled tradesmen they represented. The two sides waged fierce, occasionally bloody battles for two decades.

The tale of IBP's rise to dominance in the meat industry is too long to fully recount here. It is studded with antitrust investigations, lawsuits alleging price fixing, armies of injured workers, and fines from the Occupational Health and Safety Administration. In 1974, company cofounder Currier Holman was convicted of conspiring with a Mafioso to bribe the company's way into the New York meat market. Consumer groups decried IBP's cozy relationship with federal regulators, whom they said watered down investigations of the company's pricing and labor tactics. Meanwhile, IBP's competitors needed similar plants, and their battles with meat unions further wracked the industry.

By the end of the 1980s, IBP and Anderson's boxed-beef factories had closed urban meat-packing plants and busted the unions. The skilled union butcher in the city was replaced with a low-skilled assembly-line worker earning less than a third of the wages in the heartland.

IBP applied its model to pork as well. Tyson, the chicken titan, was mechanizing poultry slaughtering and locating chicken plants in small, nonunion towns in Tennessee, Arkansas, and North Carolina. Meat plants would come to Joslin, Illinois; to Lexington, Nebraska, and Jamestown, Tennessee; to Storm Lake, Iowa, Guymon, Oklahoma, and Fort Morgan, Colorado.

Mechanized meat plants allowed rural America to retain even more of the wealth from the product it generated. But slaughtering cattle at a ferocious pace without union protection made meat-packing the most dangerous job in America. Workers were prone to repetitive-motion injuries, knife cuts, and stress. They came home with their hands frozen in a grip. Turnover was high.

While these towns had the poultry and livestock the factories needed, they lacked people willing to do hard, fast, nonunion work. The only people who would work these jobs in the required numbers—the people the heartland needed to extract the wealth from what it produced—were from Mexico and Central America. It again attracted immigrants—this time not from villages in Czechoslovakia or Austria, but from Mexico, El Salvador, and Guatemala.

Once in the heartland, many of these immigrants later moved on to its cities, forming the core of the working class in Denver, Nashville, Memphis, Des Moines, Wichita, Oklahoma City, and Kansas City. By the beginning of the twenty-first century, the mass movement of Latino immigrants to the heartland, which the meat plants had ignited, was one of the country's most important demographic trends. The Midwest hadn't seen this kind of influx of foreign-born workers in a century. The South hadn't seen it since slavery.

"It was the IBP revolution," said Don Stull, professor of anthropology at the University of Kansas, who studied meat-packing and the effect of immigration on Garden City. "You could credit or blame IBP—depending on your point of view—with bringing immigrants to these areas. They certainly were the industry leader with all these innovations that lowered wages, busted unions, and sent packing plants out to the country. We have IBP to thank for the modern beef-packing industry."

Perhaps the first rural town in the American heartland that Mexicans sought out in large numbers was Garden City, Kansas. IBP's plant opened with twenty-three hundred jobs, and that number soon jumped to above three thousand jobs. Garden City's population almost doubled. A town that in 1980 was 82 percent white was by the year 2000 almost half Hispanic. New languages befuddled schoolteachers. Hundreds of workers slept in their cars at first. Then trailer parks were built.

Garden City, and the towns of Dodge City and Liberal, formed meat-packing's golden triangle, with five plants in all, employing twelve thousand people and slaughtering about five million head of cattle a year. The companies were desperate for workers; one company briefly advertised in the Garden City High School newspaper. They first recruited workers from Texas and New Mexico. They arranged for newly arrived Vietnamese refugees to settle nearby, giving jobs to anyone. In time, though, many of the Vietnamese took their savings and left southwest Kansas.

By the late 1990s, workers in these plants were mostly from Mexico and Central America. Kansas ranchers and farmers of bygone eras had relied on their own labor to extract wealth from the region. That was now Latino immigrants' job, which was an alarming development for a state that had prided itself on its classless society.

But a lot of what Americans imagined as quintessentially American about the heartland had, in western Kansas at least, been fading for some time.

Two-thirds of Kansas farms were on the government dole. Farmers in Finney County, where Garden City was the county seat, received $151 million in government subsidies between 1995 and 2003—more than any county in the state. Most Main Streets were empty, thumped by farm crises and then finally sucked out of western Kansas towns and regurgitated onto the floors of numerous Wal-Marts. The local bar and grill had bowed to Applebee's, the faux hometown diner with fifteen hundred branches nationwide and plans for a thousand more. Boot Hill in Dodge City and the Dalton gang's hideout a few miles away in Meade—symbols of the untamed American spirit—had been made into fun parks for tourists.

Much of what these prairie towns had been was now found only in their historical museums. These museums were always worth a visit, as much for the conversation with the old ladies who ran them as for the wondrous displays of church organs, tractors, Victrolas, and old stoves. Museums reminded visitors of how small-scale and locally owned America had been. The photographs in these museums were especially telling. They were reminders that a generation ago the people here had been as thin as rails.

By 2003, an obesity epidemic was in full bloom across southwest Kansas, as it was across the country. Doctors in the area reported hundreds of patients who were seventy-five to one hundred pounds overweight. Women five feet nine weighing 250 pounds were almost common. Garden City High School served pizza, French fries, and Pepsi and called it lunch. Unpleasant parallels could be drawn between the feed yards where thousands of cattle fattened at the trough all day and the "All-You-Can-Eat" buffet at the Golden Corral restaurant in Garden City.

Obesity was especially unsettling to see in western Kansas, which had been so associated with wizened pioneers and gratification postponed. Viewed from western Kansas, it did not seem coincidental that Mexicans came to the heartland just as Americans were attaining unprecedented sizes. It wasn't that the immigrants weren't fat—many of them were. It was that, in the words of one doctor, "physical activity is left to the immigrants, for the most part."

As the twenty-first century began, the sparse prairie of southwest Kansas again offered a clear view of an America under construction. It was different from that which earlier pioneers had created. Its values included not gratification postponed, but excess consumption; not self-reliance, but dependence on others' labor; a class, not classless, society.

What seemed closest to the American spirit that southwest Kansas had forged was the attitude of the Latino immigrants who'd come to work as hard as it took to get ahead. Even behind the great symbols of authentic Americana, there was often a Mexican doing the heavy lifting and ensuring that Kansas looked as the country expected.

Pheasant hunting, for example, was a time-honored western Kansas tradition. With wild pheasants long dead, however, pheasant farms had popped up—worked by Mexican immigrants. These farms raised pheasants but sold fantasy. Farmers bought the birds, then rented their land to groups of lawyers and businessmen from Chicago, Denver, and Kansas City. These lawyers and businessmen came to southwest Kansas with shotguns they didn't always know how to use, looking for pheasants and the illusion that they were roughing it on the High Plains. Meanwhile, the immigrant workers said nothing to upset the effect the lawyers sought.

Perhaps the best example of this dependence, however, was in the town of Liberal.

Liberal is the hometown of Dorothy in *The Wizard of Oz*. The book's author, L. Frank Baum, never lived in Kansas, but he set his story there to emphasize his heroine's innocence. During the 1980s' farm crisis, Liberal was persuaded to build a Land of Oz to draw tourists. The town stages its OzFest there in October.

OzFest 2003 featured Robert Baum, great-grandson of L. Frank Baum, and five tiny actors, now in their 80s, who had played Munchkins in the film. Organizers held look-alike contests for kids dressed as Dorothy, the Cowardly Lion, and the Tin Man.

Moving invisibly through the crowd was the handyman at the Land of Oz, a man named Eduardo Barrios. Barrios grew up in the state of Durango, in northwest Mexico. A taciturn fellow of fifty-four, Barrios lived and worked for many years in Southern California. In 1999, he came to Liberal, where two sisters live. He found work at the National Beef plant, but then cut his hand. The company patched him up, gave him some money, and sent him on his way. The Land of Oz hired him.

Today not much happens at the Land of Oz without him. Barrios paints the Yellow Brick Road yellow and the Emerald City green. He mows the lawns, cleans the bathrooms, and replaces the toilet paper. Were it not for Barrios changing the light bulbs on one display, a vision of Glinda the Good Witch would never appear. And if you look behind the curtain at the Land of Oz in Liberal, Kansas, you will find not a frumpy white professor, but Eduardo Barrios, a Mexican immigrant, tending the dials on the tape deck that pipes in the Wizard's booming voice, creating the icon Americans most associate with what is theirs.

On a sunny, breezy afternoon in October, the calls of soccer players echoed like wind chimes on a field near the western Kansas town of Great Bend.

The Garden City High School soccer team was again playing the team that a month before had made them look weak. This time, though, Garden City seemed to have found itself. There was a new urgency to the way they played. It was startling to see Rey Ramírez and Rudy Hernández push opponents out of the way, to watch Luis Posada buzz back and forth, covering the entire field in seconds.

The intervening month had been a good one, the kind that Joaquín Padilla had expected of his squad as the season started. Since that early loss to Great Bend, the team had won all its games. Now at midseason, its record stood at 8–1.

Winning, it seemed, had jolted them awake and helped them shed the losing attitude. The hesitancy of a month before was gone. They confidently elbowed opponents or streaked together down the field with the ball, like a pack of gazelles in perfect choreography, then turned together to backpedal.

Most players would say the tougher attitude emerged during two close wins a month apart in which the team had ample opportunity to give up but did not.

The first was a home game against Dodge High School. Trailing Dodge 2–1 with six minutes to go, Juan Torres tied the game with a magnificent bicycle kick—flipping in the air with his back to the goal and kicking the ball in for a score. Hugo Blanco scored with two minutes left to win it. The team went on to win its next five games.

Then, in early October, Garden went south to play Liberal High School. The team took an early 2–0 lead. Liberal surged back to lead 3–2. With three minutes to go, Juan beat defenders to a loose ball in front of the Liberal goal and scored, tying the game. In overtime, Servando Hernández rocketed a penalty kick from thirty-five yards out that the Liberal goalie couldn't corral. The ball caromed off the goalie, and Juan was there to kick it in for the 4–3 win.

"The attitude began to grow that we can beat anybody," Padilla said. Luis Posada believed the team was no longer intimidated by higher expectations. "People expect us to win, and we expect to win," he said.

This was new for Garden City High School soccer. Since the team's inception, soccer had long been a metaphor for Mexican immigrants' standing in town. The team's annual mediocre showings were due, as Padilla said, to losing a lot of players each year. But also, on campus, soccer was considered low class. No one at school cared much about the team. Few Latino students, nor even many players' parents, attended the home games. So as each season went on, players would grow demoralized, stop caring, and lose. All this would, in turn, support the idea that soccer was as unworthy of attention as the immigrant population in town.

Even the team's one decent year—in 2000, when it went 12–4—wasn't much recognized. Attendance didn't rise; few people came to the team's one playoff game, which it lost. Soccer, after all, wasn't football, and it was simply too soon after the school's football team had won it all.

The story of Garden City High School's rise to football greatness was well known to all the soccer players. Most of them were not so young as to have missed the football team's one truly great year in 1999. Four years later, the soccer team felt it still competed with the wistful memories of that championship year that the town fervently clung to. When it came to football's glory days, Garden City was like a jilted lover who refused other suitors hoping the one great romance would return.

Garden City had spent the 1970s and 1980s developing a losing tradition in football that seemed unshakable. As the 1990s approached, administrators vowed to change that. They hired a coach named Dave Meadows from a winning high school in Oklahoma. Meadows's job, he was told, was to win, period. Wanting to retain nothing from Garden City's losing years, Meadows brought his entire coaching staff with him from Oklahoma. Meadows was made the school's athletic director. He was an old-style southern football coach and had a dictatorial way about him. This miffed a lot of folks, but they stifled their criticism as the new coach crafted the school into a statewide football force.

Under Dave Meadows, Garden City's team made the state playoffs eight of the next ten years. It played for the state championship in 1998, losing to Olathe North, from Wichita. The next year Garden City won it all, beating Olathe South High School 14–7. The team's trophy stands next to Sodbuster—the stuffed, full-size buffalo that is the school mascot—that is enclosed in glass in the school's main hallway.

High school football never reached the level of religion in Garden City. After all, as one parent said, "this isn't Oklahoma." Still, the great 1990s enshrined the football team as the town's central social preoccupation and unequaled source of civic pride. There was resistance to starting a soccer program for fear that it might detract from the football team. At public events, mayors mentioned the football team's record and its Friday night opponent. Hundreds of parents joined the booster club each year. They would travel the many hours it took to go to games in Wichita, Manhattan, and Salina.

At school, football players formed a privileged caste. They were expected to remain silent on the bus to away games, concentrating on the task ahead. But they were winked at when they did poorly in class, and they roamed the halls during class uninterrogated. The booster club ponied up money for them to eat at steakhouses while on the road. Football players got the pep rallies. Cheerleaders pined to date the star players. Students ached to say hello to them in the halls; teachers clapped them on the backs.

As much as anything, the sign of the football team's status was that it played at the school's stadium, under the lights, with bleachers and a scoreboard. Soccer, meanwhile, played on a nondescript field attached to Kenneth Henderson Middle School a mile away. The field had no scoreboard, no snack bar, no dressing rooms. Nor did it have lights. Games, therefore, had to begin at 3:30 PM. The field had only one bleacher, though this had been more than ample seating for the dismal attendance at soccer games.

To the town's credit, winning football games at any cost did not interest Garden City. In 1999, the very year the team won the state championship, Dave Meadows was pressured to resign. Meadows was feared, but not loved. When he was found to have supplied two players with a salve usually applied to injured horses—an ointment known as DMSO—outraged parents and teachers mobilized and forced him out.

But the school's football team had never been better than mediocre since then. Meadows's successor had been fired after only two losing seasons. By

2003, the school's football dominance was a memory. What hadn't changed, however, were the traditional privileges that the 1990s had conferred on the football team. Both the local and student newspapers, for example, spent far more prominent space on the football team than on soccer, though in 2003 the soccer team was having a stellar season.

This unequal treatment of football and soccer is true of most U.S. high schools. Football is more popular, has a longer tradition, and is a bigger money earner. Thus, it gets more attention and larger budgets. At many schools, the inequality stops there. Most high school soccer teams are made up of middle- or upper-class white kids, who feel socially equal to their football peers. But at Garden City, the inequality in the two sports simply magnified the town's class and racial differences. The recognition of football reflected the class of the kids who played it. Likewise, when soccer went begging, it seemed to emphasize to the players their status on campus. Just as meat-plant workers never made the papers, no student at Garden City High School had ever been recognized or popular because he played soccer.

It was easy for Padilla's players to dwell on this inequality. As Rey Ramírez put it, "Their parents own farms and cattle feed yards. Our parents work for their parents."

But as the fall of 2003 progressed, a few things began to happen in Garden City. First, the football team once again began to lose. At homecoming, the team's record was 1–4. Attendance dwindled. Who wanted to watch a losing team? Students now came late to the games and left once they had an answer to the evening's central question: where are the parties?

Observant folks discerned that the town's demographics meant football's glory days probably would not return. The city was growing, but the Anglo population was declining. Replacing them were families from Mexico and Central America. By 2003, their children made up more than half the two-thousand-student body at Garden City High School. Immigrant kids quietly acquiesced before school traditions, of which the football team was the most important, but the sport they prized was not football, but *fútbol*.

"When the school was defending state champion, there were easily seventy kids—sophomores, juniors, and seniors—who went out for the football team," said Brad Hallier, the high-school sports reporter for the *Garden City Telegram*. "Now you're looking at forty or fifty kids. Liberal, same thing, and they're a football town, too. Maybe five families move out, and ten Hispanic families move in. How many of them have played football in their lives? Pretty much all they know is soccer."

It was in 2003, as Garden City football declined, that soccer ascended. The early loss to Great Bend jolted players awake. They stopped focusing on what they weren't getting and began to ask more of themselves. By the second Great Bend game, players were charging for loose balls. In fearless and elegant slides, they would launch themselves feet first at the ball, stealing it while leaving opponents sprawled on the ground. That October afternoon, they easily beat Great Bend, and their record stood at 9–1.

Now, for the first time, the soccer team became the talk of Garden City High School. Suddenly people noticed the sport, and thus the immigrant kids who played it. Soccer players were startled when teachers stopped them in the hall to ask how they'd done the day before. They could hear other kids talk about the team in the halls. Students put up posters with newspaper articles and photos of players in action, urging the team on.

As excitement built around the team, the city commission took up an issue related to soccer. The commission decided to name the soccer field at Kenneth Henderson Middle School for a member of the community. Several Latinos were mentioned as possible candidates, including a former street-department worker and a radio DJ. Hearing of this, the family of Martín Esquivel thought the field ought to be named for him.

Esquivel was born in Somberete, Zacatecas, and grew up in Ciudad Juárez. In 1976, at the age of nineteen, he came to Garden City and found work in a small meat plant. Later, he helped build the IBP plant and was hired at the plant when it opened.

In 1977, Esquivel organized the town's first soccer team, made up of Mexican immigrants. The team traveled to play in Texas and elsewhere in Kansas. It was a rag-tag crew. Still, soccer in Garden City began with that team Martín Esquivel founded. Ten years later, Esquivel was shot and killed by a young man he confronted who had been bothering his sister, Manuela.

In the fall of 2003, his sister, Manuela Esquivel, drew up a petition asking the city to name the field for her brother. Taking the petition to IBP, McDonald's, the local schools, and the Sunday adult soccer leagues, the Esquivel family came up with fifteen hundred signatures and presented it to the city. As the Buffaloes' season went on, in the background was the debate over how to name the field where the team played.

Meanwhile, the team won game after game. Attendance climbed beyond the demoralizing fifteen or twenty spectators. The school moved bleachers from the football stadium to the soccer field to handle the overflow. Toward the end of the season, even the cheerleaders, white and Asian girls, started coming to the home games, urging the Buffaloes to "F-I-R-E, Fire Up!" After each win, the students in the crowd, now numbering in the dozens, lined the field, and the players ran by high-fiving them all. This became a tradition, and the line of students grew longer with each win.

All this had an almost physical effect on the players. They walked taller on campus. "Around here it's always been football, football, football," said Rey Ramírez, midway through the season. "But the other day, the athletic director asked me how we'd done the night before, and I said we'd won and he said, 'All right! High five!' It caught me off guard. I've never seen anybody show excitement for soccer other than us."

The team was something for immigrant kids to be proud of, and some of its glory reflected on them. "It seems like it shouldn't matter, but it did," said one student. ESL students met the team at their bus before it headed to an away game. Kids who'd never attended soccer games before began showing up at home games. After a while there were enough spectators that for the first time cheers were chanted in unison, in Spanish. One frigid afternoon in late September, dozens of students huddled together wrapped in blankets to watch an entire home game despite a lacerating wind and temperatures in the 30s.

By midseason, the school newspaper, *The Sugar Beet,* for the first time wrote long stories about the team and ran them with photographs. The posters in the school hallways got bigger with each victory.

One result of that was some Latino students gradually began to lose their fear of participating. One of these was a girl named Vanessa Ramírez. Vanessa, pretty and bright, was a lively sophomore. Her mother was eight-months pregnant with her when she swam across the Rio Grande to enter the United States. Her parents came to Garden City and found work at the IBP plant. On Valentine's Day of 1988, Vanessa was born.

By the early 1990s, the Mexican community in Garden City had grown so large that Vanessa didn't learn English until the third grade. This enclave had been most of what she'd known up to then. But her bubbly personality allowed her to move beyond the limitations of the Mexican enclave at school. In eighth grade, she had tried out for choir—the first Mexican-immigrant student to do so.

In ninth grade, her grades fell, and Vanessa lost some of her ambition and spirit. Much of this had to do with her parents, who saw no future for her in school and told her so. "I'm not smart," she said. "I get told that every day at home: 'You're dumb.' They call me *burra, pendeja* (dope, idiot). 'Why are you in school? Just drop out and get a job.' My dad just told me yesterday, he said, 'Soon you'll be sixteen, and you can drop out.'"

But as the soccer team's season electrified the Latino students at Garden City High School, one of those it transformed was Vanessa Ramírez, now a sophomore. By midseason, she was the team's most faithful fan. She began to regain some of that fearlessness that her parents' low expectations had discouraged. She never missed a soccer game. She painted her face in school colors and made T-shirts supporting the team. She carried a large school flag to home games and ran up and down the sidelines with it when the team scored.

Vanessa recognized this as radically new behavior for the child of Mexican immigrants at Garden City High School, but she didn't care. "Hispanic students isolate themselves," she said one afternoon at a home game late in the season. "They say, 'I'm going to look stupid if I participate.' They feel like they don't want to be involved in school. They just want to be involved in their own little world. They're scared."

As the team kept winning, more immigrant students began to consider after-school activities. More boys spoke of trying out for soccer the following year. Several Latinas were actually planning on going out for the girls' soccer team in the spring. Five girls promised to become the first children of Mexican immigrants to try out for the school's cheerleading squad next fall. Whether they'd make it was an open question. The parents of Asian and white girls had money to send them to cheerleading camps that most Mexican girls' parents couldn't afford. Still, the chutzpah it took to even plan on it was impressive. It was as if a Mexican boy were talking about trying out for quarterback.

The ringleader in this was Vanessa Ramírez. Inspired by the team, Vanessa vowed to play soccer in the spring and try out for cheerleader next fall.

Though her grades were sagging, she showed no signs of listening to her parents' opinion of her scholastic abilities, but instead met with a University of Kansas counselor and now spoke of attending college to study nursing.

"I know we can do something for this school," she said. "It's not only them (the white students) at this school. It's us, too. We're part of it. It's just that we feel neglected. We feel they don't pay attention to us. Whatever we do isn't going to count. That's why we never try for anything. We're just as capable of doing something as they are, we just haven't realized it."

Through that fall, the Garden City Buffaloes won game after game. The school took notice. So did the *Garden City Telegram*. The paper's reporter, Brad Hallier, understood the sport and explained the fine points to the school's other coaches, who were caught up in the excitement. Finally, more or less all of Garden City—immigrants and whites—awoke to what was happening. The Spanish-language radio stations mentioned their success. The mayor stopped asking about the football team and now inquired how the soccer team had done each week.

Among the townspeople, though, one white couple needed no prodding to follow this team. They were Andy and Sidni Musick, and they watched the team's success that fall with a mixture of bitterness and satisfaction.

Sidni Musick has a grandmotherly look about her, with long gray hair often kept in a bun or ponytail. She teaches English as a Second Language (ESL) at Garden City High School. All her students are immigrants, and in 2003 these even included one or two of Padilla's players. She is also the advisor to the school's Asian Club. Andy Musick is bald, with a mustache and goatee, and works as a church musician and substitute teacher.

The Musicks are among the few white people in Garden City who live in an entirely Mexican neighborhood. There are people in town who would describe the Musicks' attitudes on politics and society, including the issue of immigration from Mexico, as "bleeding-heart liberal."

The Musicks had been a driving force behind the youth soccer team in 1996 that included many of the players who were now on the high-school team. That youth team marked the first time in Garden City that immigrants and the native white population—children and parents—were thrown together socially, outside a school or workplace. Then, abruptly, the team dissolved when Latino families took their children to form another team. The white kids dropped soccer for other sports.

The experience had challenged some of the Musicks' ideas regarding Mexicans and the American melting pot. Now, seven years later, watching the 2003 Garden City High School soccer team made up of kids from that team, the couple still wanted answers for the break-up of the experiment into which they'd put so much work.

The Musicks' involvement with soccer began when their son, Theo, was six and playing in a parks-and-recreation league. Andy Musick had never played soccer, but he learned to coach it. Eventually he became a certified soccer referee. The rec league was informal, and the teams rarely practiced. So as Theo grew, Andy Musick looked about for more competitive soccer for his son.

The way Andy Musick tells it, when he'd referee rec-league games, one of the coaches, Juan Rucker, was particularly critical of his calls. Rucker is a Mexican immigrant, a proud, intelligent man who had played high-level amateur soccer in Mexico. He had no children in the soccer leagues but volunteered to coach a team anyway.

One day after a game, Musick said he approached Rucker and proposed they work with, instead of against, one another. Rucker agreed. They set about forming a team of the more talented kids in the rec league. Their idea was to practice regularly and travel to play better teams far from Garden City. They chose the best players for the team.

What they formed was meant to be a traveling soccer team, not a social experiment, but it became both. About half the players chosen were white, the other half were Mexican and Salvadoran. On the team was the nucleus of players that would make up the 2003 team for Garden City High School: Juan Torres, Rey Ramírez, Carlos Reyes, Miguel Benítez, Hernán Macías, Rudy Hernández, and Chuck Dodge.

Those involved in the team remember it, by and large, as a pleasant and beneficial experience. The team practiced twice a week and played teams in Lawrence, Emporia, Dodge City, and Liberal. Once, though, at a tournament in Topeka, the players, tiny nine- and ten-year-olds, were greeted with calls of "beaners" and "taco vendors" from white parents. The Dodge City coach was equally nasty. At the Dodge City game, the opposing team's parents' insults got so vicious that a referee finally ordered them off the field.

The Musicks said they dove into the team's organizational details. They arranged lodging for the boys on their trips. They recruited parents to drive the team to games. They helped put together fund-raisers. During the summer of 1996, the couple was busy arranging nonprofit status for the team.

That summer, Andy Musick invited a soccer coach from Wichita to hold a three-day camp for the kids. Rucker had been away for several weeks. Musick arranged the camp, then called Rucker to tell him that the camp was scheduled. Rucker showed up, but left without saying a word. The Musicks never heard from him again.

Suddenly, the Latino players stopped coming to practice. Just like that, the biracial traveling soccer team ended. The immigrant parents took their kids and formed a team with Rucker—a team that itself fell apart a short while later.

The Musicks never understood what happened. They ran into a wall of what in Mexico is called *hermetismo*—which translates into a social silence, an unwillingness to give direct explanations, combined with a desire to avoid confrontation. Immigrant parents looked away when they saw the Musicks in stores or at school.

"Even when we had their kids' personal items, like socks or something, we called them, and parents never returned our phone calls," said Sidni Musick.

Sidni Musick says she heard later through her students' grapevine that parents were telling their relatives not to let their children take her ESL class because she was prejudiced. Meanwhile, the immigrant players stopped saying hello to Theo Musick at school.

Rucker said he broke with Andy Musick over the soccer camp because money the kids had raised for uniforms was used to pay for it. "We'd done three car washes for uniforms, and I didn't think that money should be used for the summer camp," Rucker said.

If true, the Musicks say no one told them. Andy Musick's family had been migrant farm workers in Oklahoma. He remembered his folks as direct and straightforward. "I thought Mexicans would be the same as my family," he said. But years later, Andy Musick still had no explanation for the split, except for from one boy, who'd told Theo Musick that they were going to form a team just for Mexicans. When Theo reminded the boy that he was not Mexican, but Salvadoran, the boy replied, "Well, we Hispanics got to stick together."

Undeterred, Andy Musick continued to referee adult-league games on Sunday. Then players began calling him racist for the calls he made against them—though all the players in the games he refereed were Latino. After a while, the league stopped calling him to referee.

To the Musicks, wrapped up in the episode were Mexicans' complicated feelings toward America and toward white people whom they perceived as wealthy by definition. Perhaps, too, there were attitudes, accepted implicitly from years of PRI government education, that gringos will always want to usurp what's Mexican. Also part of the mix may have been Mexican envidia— or envy, usually involving someone feeling that he doesn't get enough credit or attention, or that someone else gets too much. "Maybe this is why IBP has been so successful in keeping unions away," said Sidni Musick.

Americans talk often about racial diversity, but it isn't an idea that seems to appeal to many Mexican immigrants. On occasion during the 2003 season, when Tri Dang dribbled the ball downfield, some of the Mexican fathers of his own teammates made fun of him by babbling in imitation Chinese.

"I think there was prejudice against us because we were white," said Sidni Musick, talking about the team seven years after its demise. "Prejudice because they perceived the fact that we had more money, when in reality we probably didn't. There was a perception that we thought we were better than they were. I think they thought they were inferior. When I see people kind of duck and turn away now when I come by, I can see that they're embarrassed."

Sidni Musick also thought the experience a result of Mexican immigrants' unwillingness to let go of Mexico and be absorbed into America. She saw this in the vehemence with which her ESL students—with better futures and better educations in Kansas than ever possible in Mexico—spoke of the United States taking Mexican territory 160 years earlier.

"The people who are treated the worst [by Mexico] are the ones who turn around and are the most loyal to Mexico," she said. "It's an interesting human puzzle."

One mother remembered the traveling team well. Sylvia Trevino is Juan Torres's aunt. She is a frank, strong woman. Both Juan and her youngest son, Sergio, played on the traveling team. She often sold candy and made enchiladas to raise money for the team. Race was part of what split the traveling team, Sylvia said. The bitter welcome the Mexican kids received in places like Topeka and Dodge City hardened these views.

"I think that's what made it so racial among the kids. They grew up with it," she said. "They want something that they don't have to share with anybody. 'This is just for us.' The white kids truly knew they weren't wanted. It kept going into the high school. I listen to the guys talk. They see it as a Hispanic game, a Hispanic sport—'We're the best and nobody can do what we can do.'"

Youth sports often get tangled up in the egos of parents who covet athletic success for their children. Andy Musick may well have wanted more success and playing time for Theo, who played goalie, than the Latino parents thought right. He may have considered himself a coach of the team, while Rucker may have believed his experience meant that he alone was the coach. Some of the Latino parents may have felt the white kids were not as skilled as their children.

All of which is to say that there are probably many reasons why the town's first biracial soccer team dissolved. Yet the result was undeniable: it chased a generation of white kids out of soccer in Garden City. Left without a team, they went on to other sports, and from that moment, soccer in Garden City has been an almost exclusively Latino sport. The city recreation department still holds weekly games at which every child in town is welcome, but these games aren't competitive, and children don't develop many skills. There are more competitive leagues for older kids, but no one who plays in them is white. Thus the high-school team will also likely be uniracial for years in a way that would be unacceptable for any other team sport.

Also watching the Garden City High School team's season unfold was Adam Hunter, who was beginning his third year as soccer coach at Dodge City Community College, seventy miles away.

Hunter was twenty-eight, an outgoing fellow with a gruff baritone, and short-cropped reddish-blond hair. He was from a small town near Wichita, and he'd gone to college on a soccer scholarship. Upon graduation, he found a job coaching the boys' and girls' soccer teams at Dodge City High School. In 2001, the community college hired him to start a soccer program, wanting to attract Latino immigrant kids and generate some scholarships for them at four-year colleges.

Hunter's job was to recruit kids from the meat-packing towns of Dodge City, Liberal, and Garden City. He didn't speak Spanish. Nor had he much contact with Mexican kids besides the few with whom he'd played. But he didn't figure his new job would be too complicated.

"Go pick the players you want and coach them," he told himself.

That proved to be only half the job. The other half, Hunter came to find out, was administering pep talks and seat-of-the-pants psychology to Latino players from meat-packing towns to get them to accept the scholarships that four-year colleges were begging them to take. So far, these talks had failed, and Hunter was at his wits' end.

"There's definitely a pattern developing," he said one October morning in his office at the school's physical education department.

He had coached three great players in his first two years. Plaques honoring them were affixed to a wall of his office.

"All three of these plaques are for Garden City guys," he said. "All three are our only All-Conference players to ever play here. All three had, or could have had, scholarships to a four-year college. But all three aren't playing anywhere now. All three live with their moms. In fact, every single Garden City kid who's come here to play is back with his mom."

One of these plaques belonged to Guillermo Tamayo, a good-hearted fellow, tall and thin, from La Piedad, Michoacán, with whom Hunter was particularly close. Guillermo's parents had brought him to the United States when he was sixteen. He had been a kicker for the Garden City High School football team in 1999, the year it won state. He was also a tenacious, driven soccer player.

When high school ended, Guillermo figured he'd follow his parents into the meat plants. They wanted him to work there. Hunter, though, had seen him play, offered him a scholarship, and urged him to come to Dodge City Community College. So Guillermo went, without giving much thought to what he was going to study.

Junior college transformed Guillermo. It removed him from the immigrant enclave and his home. Selecting auto technology as his major, he found the classes and the auto lab intimidating at first. But in time, his confidence grew. After two years, he virtually managed the school's auto lab that he'd once been terrified to enter. He had never thought of going beyond high school, yet here he was doing well in college. For the first time, he had to cook for himself, wash his clothes, and pay bills. At first, he went home every weekend, but as he grew accustomed to school, his visits home became monthly.

Guillermo figured his schooling would end after two years at Dodge and he'd go to work in the meat plants. "But when Hunter heard of us stopping school and going to work, he didn't really like that," Guillermo remembered one day, as he sat in a Denny's in Wichita. "He told us that we'd be doing a job because we had to, not because we enjoyed it. He was saying, 'Get an education, and you do the things you like to do.'

"My parents were saying, 'Quit school and start working.' That was their attitude. They had bills to pay. They think that even if you don't have education, as long as you work, you can go through life."

Being away from his family had given Guillermo other ideas. Several schools offered him soccer scholarships. Pittsburg State University, in southeast Kansas, had a top automotive engineering program, which interested Guillermo, but the school had no soccer team. With prodding from Padilla and Hunter, Guillermo tried out for the university's football team as a field-goal kicker. The school's coach liked his kicking, but Pittsburg State didn't give scholarships to junior transfers. The coach told Guillermo he could only fund his senior year. Guillermo decided to attend the school anyway.

He worked that summer in a meat plant in Dodge City and lived with Hunter to save money. The coach persuaded him to take out the first bank account anyone in Guillermo's family had ever had.

That summer, though, Guillermo didn't save as much as he hoped. As fall approached, he had second thoughts about college. Hunter urged him to take out a student loan. Guillermo was terrified of debt—even at the lowest interest rates. His parents moved to Hot Springs, Arkansas, and were telling him to come down and find a job. Two weeks before the 2003 term started, Guillermo pulled out of Pittsburg State and moved to Hot Springs. He told himself he'd attend the school in the winter.

But by midfall, Guillermo pushed off his entry date a whole year. He was battling mightily to decide what to do. Hunter would give him more pep talks over the phone, urging him to leave his parents and go to school. Meanwhile, Guillermo was working at McDonald's.

It drove Hunter crazy. Hunter had begged, cajoled, and browbeaten many of these players to get them to go on to a four-year school. By now, he was getting very practiced at this, though no more successful for the trying.

It wasn't just the star players from Garden City like Guillermo whom he had trouble persuading to stay in school. In his office, Hunter had a roster from his first two years. He ticked off the names of Mexican-immigrant kids from Dodge and Liberal, as well. Every one who finished the two years of college, and several who didn't, had turned right around and gone back home. Just three weeks before, Hunter's star player in the 2003 season, a premed student from Liberal, had left the team to go home and work in a meat plant. Kids who were passing calculus and engineering classes would suddenly leave school and go home. Most of them returned to work in the beef plants in Dodge, Liberal, or Garden City. At twenty or twenty-one, they had wives, children, or both. Their futures were becoming as narrow and hardened as the chutes down which the cattle went to slaughter in the meat plants.

At first, this so confounded Hunter that he was on the phone constantly with Joaquín Padilla, out in Garden City. But Padilla had had no better luck with his kids. In six years, only one of his Latino players had gone on to a four-year college. Several of his players were at the plants. It drove Padilla crazy to see this, too, but leaving the enclave and making the jump into the unknown of a four-year college, competing with white people, was too much for a lot of these kids. Padilla commiserated with Hunter but couldn't help much.

"There's a leap that they have to take themselves, but a lot of them don't," Padilla said.

Still, Hunter kept on. The four-year colleges had offered to his players only partial scholarships, and each kid would have had to put up money, sometimes many thousands of dollars. That's what student loans are for, Hunter told his players. But like Guillermo, a lot of them brought from Mexico a terror of debt that years in the United States had not diminished. On top of that, many of these kids feared leaving family. At home, their mothers and sisters cooked and cleaned for them and did their laundry. In Mexico, this syndrome—the way mothers spoil their sons—was called *mamitis*. Several of his kids were afraid to cut that cord and go far away to a school where few people spoke Spanish and they'd have to compete scholastically with white people. So they returned to mom and to the packing plant. This gave them what they wanted now, regardless of what it sacrificed over the long term.

"What I try to explain to them," Hunter said, "is this: your parents came here so you wouldn't have to do what you're trying to do right now. Your parents didn't move up here so that you can go to work in the packing plant, too."

Even there, Hunter found he was only half-right. Certainly, many parents didn't want their kids in the plants, and many wanted their kids to get an education. But a lot of parents, he discovered, also didn't want their children far from home. Southwest Kansas has no four-year colleges, so these parents' attitude sentenced a lot of kids to a junior-college education, at most. Hunter rarely got a chance to convince the parents otherwise. In Mexico, poor, uneducated parents felt intimidated around schools and rarely participated in school activities. This attitude survived in the Mexican enclave in the United States. Few parents of Hunter's players attended their games.

So while soccer in the United States opened a door to a better future, Hunter's Latino players couldn't bring themselves to leave the comfort of the Mexican enclave to walk through it. Three years after starting a soccer team to get Mexican-immigrant kids into college, Dodge City Community College was instead turning out second-generation meat-plant workers, some with AA degrees.

One of these, it turned out, was Padilla's assistant coach for the 2003 season, a young man named Anselmo Enríquez. Anselmo had been the best soccer player ever at Dodge City Community College and the best to come out of southwest Kansas. He is a high-cheekboned, handsome fellow, with a powerful left leg and delicate touch with the ball that, though he was never the fastest guy on the field, allowed him nevertheless to dribble through slaloms of defenders. The second of those plaques on Hunter's wall was his.

As a freshman in 1996, Anselmo had been a member of Garden City High School's first official soccer team. That team was made up mostly of Mexicans, many of whom were timid and tiny kids. They spoke little English and were thoroughly cowed by their taller, older white opponents. Over the next three years, though, they improved and began beating some of the white schools that once had crushed them. His senior year, Anselmo was second in the state in scoring with twenty-three goals.

"Sometimes you feel like you're less when you come to the United States," he said one afternoon, watching the Garden City team practice. "But once you win, you begin to inflate with pride. You feel you can play on the same level. You feel that you've got two legs, just like them."

After high school, Anselmo took a scholarship at Cloud County Community College, four hours north of Garden City. For the first time, he was away from Mexicans and among middle-class white kids. Anselmo's mother had cut beef at a meat plant; his white teammates' parents were doctors and lawyers who drove BMWs. What struck Anselmo was that these kids who had everything only wanted to drink. Every night, it seemed, they were out getting drunk. The next morning, after wind sprints, they'd be bent over throwing up. Anselmo never threw up after wind sprints. He tried to get along with his teammates, but he didn't have money for endless parties. He didn't drink, smoke, or use drugs. He took soccer seriously.

Moreover, Anselmo had come to Garden City from the state of Durango, where his father had been a state-police officer. One day, when Anselmo was about eleven, his father and an uncle went to town to buy fertilizer. They were stopped by a group of men claiming to be state-police officers as well. They arrested Anselmo's father and drove off with him. The next day he was found shot to death, presumably on the orders of a local drug smuggler. With that memory in tow, Anselmo, his brothers and mother moved to Garden City, where relatives lived.

Anselmo's background distanced him ever further from his privileged Cloud County teammates. Their behavior seemed to him frivolous and wasteful. What Anselmo also noted was how his teammates couldn't wait to leave home for college, in part so they could drink and carouse away from their parents. "Mexicans, we're very close as a family. White people, you leave home, and you don't care," he said. "There in Cloud County, I don't even think the white guys remembered their parents. When they had free time, they wouldn't even go visit their parents. They'd just drink. Me, as soon as I had a chance, I'd come visit my mom in Garden City, then go back to school."

That semester, his mother lost a job and was on unemployment. Anselmo didn't feel right in Cloud County. So after the season, he dropped out and went home. He took a job in the IBP meat plant. The next year he accepted a scholarship at Hunter's soccer program at Dodge City Community College.

That year, Anselmo again displayed his left leg and his spectacular dribbling. He led the team in scoring. Four-year colleges from South Dakota, Oklahoma, and several in Kansas rushed to offer him scholarships. But, again, none offered a full scholarship. Student loans were out, as Anselmo, too, feared debt. That closed a lot of options. He didn't want to again be far from his family. He got his girlfriend pregnant, and their daughter was born. His mother still needed money. So, in the end, Anselmo Enríquez did not accept a scholarship to a four-year school. He went home to his mother's house and the graveyard shift at IBP.

What Anselmo wanted most was to coach high-school soccer and maybe succeed Padilla someday. Padilla encouraged this, but told him he needed a four-year degree. As the 2003 season began, Anselmo was getting older and had a daughter. The graveyard shift at the meat plant in Garden City became Anselmo's path of least resistance. Thus, the best soccer player southwest Kansas ever produced could be found at IBP, shipping boxes of beef until seven in the morning.

As Adam Hunter kept recruiting Latino players from the beef towns, he watched his best former players, whose All-Conference plaques adorned his wall, drop by the wayside. True, their lives weren't done yet, but things didn't look good. He had been unprepared for this part of coaching soccer in the new American heartland.

"Guillermo's down in Hot Springs, when he could be in college right now, in a dorm somewhere, possibly on a football team, or certainly somewhere playing for a school's soccer team, being their leading scorer," Hunter said. "Anselmo was All-Region, our leading scorer. He had chances to get out of here and go to school. He decided to go back to Garden and work in the plant. He knows soccer. He wants to coach. He doesn't want to be doing what he's doing, but he's doing it anyway, and I don't know why."

Alba Torres, however, had seen this so often that she was not surprised. She was Juan Torres's mother. For many years now, her life's project had been protecting Juan, her only child, from a similar fate.

Alba is a short, light-skinned woman with, where her son is concerned, a monumental capacity for work and sacrifice. Education was the point of being in America, Alba believed. She was one of eleven children growing up in a village in Chihuahua where her father had been the postman. Alba had left school as a child, but as an older girl went back to finish elementary school. She had even swallowed her pride at age nineteen and attended a junior high school for three years—with students six and seven years younger.

She divorced Juan's father when Juan was just an infant and raised her son alone. She often worked two jobs, leaving Juan with his aunts and uncles. Juan was born in Dodge City, but Alba had taken him back to her hometown in Chihuahua after her divorce. Eight years later, they visited her brother in Kansas. She saw Juan could get better schooling in the United States, so they stayed.

Over the years, Juan grew into a skilled soccer player. He was graduating after the 2003 fall semester, and Adam Hunter was offering him a soccer scholarship at Dodge City Community College. So for Alba, the decisions he'd make over the next few months were what she'd been working toward all her life.

"I don't want him to just do two years at a community college," she said. "I want him to get a four-year degree. I've always told him, 'I can't give you what you want, but you'll have it once you have an education.'"

The choices young Mexican men around her were making scared Alba. Mexican immigrants now made up almost half the population of Garden City. This, and the proximity to Mexico, kept the families around her emotionally in Mexico, she felt. They lived in the American heartland as Mexicans, returned home often, and therefore certain attitudes they brought with them didn't change.

Among the most harmful of these, Alba believed, was to minimize the importance of higher education. The way Alba saw it, the problem was that college required young people to be poor for a few years as they went to school. This was unthinkable to many immigrant kids. In Mexico, the United States was where people with no education were supposed to get rich. Millions of uneducated immigrants had been proving this for decades by returning to Mexico at Christmas laden with new clothes, cars, tennis shoes, stereos. The stories they told of the United States made more kids in these villages want to go north to test their mettle. These stories didn't often include the indignities immigrants endured as dishwashers, drywall hangers, and factory workers at the bottom of the U.S. economy. It didn't matter. They were living proof of the lesson Mexico had imparted to its poor for at least two generations: menial work in the United States was worth more than a profession at home.

The strange thing was how these attitudes were impervious to the American crucible of western Kansas. It was as if something had broken down. This region that had changed people so fundamentally for more than a century now had ceased to do so.

On one hand, these immigrant kids consumed what the United States was selling; they avidly ate at McDonald's and bought Ford Explorers when they got older. On the other, the Mexican enclave that formed in Garden City quarantined them from America's most liberating ideas. Immigrant families, Alba saw, clung to Mexican ways of thinking regarding issues as mundane as debt and banking and as transcendent as education, work, civic involvement, and what they dared hope for the future. Alba felt it ironic that these attitudes had been part of what had kept Mexico poor, which is what immigrants had left Mexico to escape.

Out on the High Plains of southwest Kansas, these enduring Mexican attitudes combined with the beef plants to create a mixture as hazardous as heroin. In beef plants, a young man without much schooling could earn up to thirteen dollars an hour. Turnover at the plants was high, so these jobs were easy to get. It was quick money and far more than he could make in Mexico. In southwest Kansas, these wages were enough for that young man to make car or house payments.

Once he had a car or house payment, though, that same young man couldn't stop working. For the beef plants were also the *only* place around where someone without much schooling could earn thirteen dollars an hour. The result was disturbing: some Mexican families had two generations working in the plants.

This was unheard of among Vietnamese meat-plant workers. Like Mexican immigrants, the Vietnamese who came to Garden City were poor. They had been peasant farmers with little education and came speaking no English. Yet second-generation Vietnamese were moving into higher rungs of the U.S. economy much faster than Mexicans.

The Vietnamese enclave was never as large, nor as continually replenished, as the Mexican. But Vietnamese immigrants had another distinct advantage over Mexicans, tough as it was: they came from farther away. They had to cut ties to Vietnam and move into America. Vietnamese parents used the meat plants to save money to leave meat-packing and start businesses in Houston or Atlanta, or buy fishing boats on the Gulf Coast. Meanwhile, they emphasized education. Almost all the Vietnamese children in Garden City went to college. They took student loans and combined them with family savings and scholarships to attend public universities far from family, sometimes in other states. This they did routinely. One thing they never did was join their parents at the beef plants.

At least Tri Dang had never seen this happen.

"I think it's just different expectations," he said, sitting one afternoon at a McDonald's. "My dad would slap me if I said I wanted to go into IBP."

Tri had come to the states with his family when he was nine. Tri's father had been an officer in the South Vietnamese Army. The Vietnamese government began expelling those who had worked or fought with the South Vietnamese government. The Dangs were allowed to leave in 1995. They flew from Vietnam to New York, and from there to Garden City, where IBP had a job for his father.

Now a senior, Tri had the best grades on the soccer team, was the shortest player—standing "five feet three on a good day"—and possessed an endearing and self-deprecating sense of humor.

"I'm not a Tri," he told Padilla once, "I'm a bush."

In Garden City, the Dangs found housing in a trailer park. Their neighbors were mostly Mexican immigrants who also worked at the meat plants.

"Walking home they'd make fun of you," Tri said. "There were a lot of fights. They'd say 'Chino, chino, japonés' (Chinaman, Chinaman, Japanese)."

In time, though, Tri learned a little English. The kids from the trailer park were in his ESL class. Pretty soon, he and the Mexican kids bonded in their status as immigrants. By his senior year, the number of Vietnamese students at school had dwindled to fifty or so. Tri's friends were mostly Mexicans. The taunting turned into good-natured ribbing, and the racial jokes were made now in fun.

At eighteen, Tri listened to rap music and spoke a hip-hop English with an accent, as did his Mexican friends. But their paths in life were diverging. This was not something that came up when they joked around.

Tri was taking calculus and writing classes at the local community college to prepare for college. He planned to move to Columbia, Tennessee, where his sister now lived, and study at Middle Tennessee State University. He could help his sister with the beauty salon she owned. His sister, his father, scholarships, and loans would pay for Tri's schooling at Central Tennessee.

Tri had always had an A average. School wasn't that hard, even when he didn't speak much English, and, anyway, his parents accepted nothing less. But Tri doubted any of his Mexican friends planned to attend college.

"The way they think, if you can't get an education and go higher, there's always IBP. They always got IBP to back them up," he said. "Some of the guys go to Dodge City Community College on soccer scholarships, but finally they end up at IBP or Wal-Mart."

Alba Torres saw that her nephews and other young Mexican men thought this way. So as Juan grew up, she went to great lengths to push him toward college. In the ninth grade, Juan saw friends dropping out of school to work and begin buying things. He wanted to do the same. Alba said no. Terrified that he would leave school, she enrolled in a class to study for her GED high-school equivalency exam—to show him that it could be done. For two hours a day she took GED classes, and at the end of a year, she earned her diploma. Juan stayed in school.

She wouldn't let him work part-time until his senior year. Alba knew mothers who couldn't wait for their sons to leave school so they could contribute to the family income. They criticized her for not letting her son work. But Alba had seen young men grow hooked on the short-term cash, buy cars, go into debt, marry, have children. In the end, their commitments kept them from returning to school.

One of these was her nephew, Álvaro Torres. Álvaro was the third great Garden City player Adam Hunter had coached; the third plaque on Hunter's wall was his. Álvaro was a handsome, intelligent young man. After high school, he accepted a scholarship at Dodge City Community College and was one of the team's stars. Then he hurt his knee before his second season. He dropped out of school and went to work at IBP. Eventually his knee recovered, and he could play. But by then Álvaro had three children with three different women and had to pay child support.

He found an easy job in the shipping department at IBP, where a cousin was manager. As Álvaro moved into the plant, it began to take up most of his time. IBP managers often asked workers to come in early and stay late. A worker couldn't plan much of a life beyond the plant. By 2003, school and soccer seemed distant memories to Álvaro, who saw his future increasingly bound up in his meat-plant job.

This drove his mother, Sylvia Trevino, nuts. Sylvia had grown up in Garden City and was raised by her grandparents, who were from Mexico. In eleventh grade, Sylvia had dropped out of high school to support her grandparents, as they were getting old. Her working life began. She did many jobs, and then in 1982, she entered the Monfort meat plant. She hurt her back lifting boxes on the second day. A couple years later, cutting brisket with a dull knife, she hurt her hand. Neither pain disappeared through a decade of working at the plant.

Sylvia married Alba's brother, Álvaro Torres Sr., whom she'd met through friends. He also found work at Monfort, working on the killing floor and developing over the years a variety of hand pains. As the years went by, they had three children.

"I've always wanted to go to school," Sylvia said, sitting in a recliner at the house she and her family share with Alva and Juan. "But you can't work at (a meat plant) and go to school. You can only do one."

Then one day she couldn't take it anymore. She entered a cosmetology program at Garden City Community College. Finishing that, she took the first job she could find, while saving money to open a beauty salon. This happened to be at the Head Start program for infants and toddlers.

Head Start proved to be Sylvia's calling. She was bilingual, and this made her invaluable to the agency. Sylvia never did develop much of a hair-cutting business. She threw herself into her new job, visiting immigrant families with toddlers, taking them to doctors when the kids were sick, urging the parents to educate themselves about health care.

When the Monfort plant burned down in 2000, Álvaro Torres Sr. got the push he needed. His hands now in constant pain, he left meat-packing and found work with the Garden City Street Department.

With great effort, two of the Torres-Trevino family had left the meat plants. Yet they watched in horror as their sons moved to the plants in their place. Álvaro was already at IBP. Their youngest son, Sergio, a high-school senior, wanted to work at IBP when he graduated in the spring.

This was a different Kansas these immigrant kids were growing up in. The America on display on the High Plains heartland of Kansas was no longer rail-thin; the Protestant work ethic of postponed gratification no longer seemed quite so powerful. Kids in the Mexican-immigrant enclave were often urged to take the quick money—the thirteen dollars an hour—and sacrifice the future for the present. Meanwhile, all around them was an America that seemed to be saying that that was the right thing to do.

How much money one's parents had was a central concern among kids at Garden City High School. The wealthy kids were white, and they were the ones who received endless recognition, often for football. These kids had fancy new cars. White kids in class talked often of spending hundreds of dollars of their parents' money on clothes at The Buckles—Garden City's only young-people's upscale shopping option. Sylvia's son, Sergio, came home one day and told his mother of a girl who had blown the clutch in her car. The repair job cost three thousand dollars. She had the car fixed and at school the next day.

"The only thing they can see is the dollar signs," said Sylvia, of her sons and their friends. "They don't want to wait for the long term. They want fast money. They want something that's going to put nice clothes on their back, get them nice cars. As parents, we give them everything they need, but we can't give them the life-styles of the rich and famous. But when they get out of school, they want that right away.

"[Plus] they don't think they can do certain things. I think it's a fear of moving on, a fear of failure. Guillermo Tamayo's a prime example. It's fear that kept him where he's at. My son [Álvaro] is at IBP because they feel it's a necessity. But if him and his wife worked and found jobs somewhere else where they could both go to school, they could do it. Álvaro could work anywhere else. He's real good at computers, but [IBP] is where he wants to go because he wants the fast buck.... Once you get into the meat-packing plant, nothing matters as much as money: 'If I want something, I just buy it.' Leaving that is really hard."

As if in reaction to this, Sylvia had returned to school. Now forty, she was getting an AA degree in early-childhood development at Garden City Community College. As Sylvia struggled with homework each night, her children asked her why she worked so hard at it. She planned to get her bachelor's degree at Fort Hays State College in the same major. It might take five years to complete, but she didn't mind.

Alba, meanwhile, had been preparing herself to accept that one day her son would leave home for college. She began this conditioning in 2000. That year Juan received an invitation to play for a national soccer team of fourteen-year-olds and travel to Australia. With teenage melodrama, Juan let his mother know the trip was his life's dream. The thought would have tested any Mexican mother: to watch her son leave home alone to fly on an airplane halfway around the world; plus the trip cost four thousand dollars. Finally, though, Alba realized that her son might return with bigger ideas of life's possibilities.

To raise money, Alba sold enchiladas, tamales, and cakes to friends. The *Garden City Telegram* ran a story about Juan's Australian quest. Teachers and parents found clients for Alba's enchiladas. In the end, selling enchiladas wasn't enough, and her brother borrowed the rest of the money she needed from a bank.

The trip was a disaster. The coach who chaperoned the team turned out to be only twenty-one and liked to drink. Alba worried incessantly. Juan lost his luggage, and she had to send more money. The telephone charges—since he was calling home twice a day—amounted to a thousand dollars. In all, Alba laid out eight thousand dollars for Juan's trip to Australia; it took her two years to pay off the bank loan. Yet Alba got used to the idea that he would leave home some day. Plus, in Australia, Juan had to do his own laundry for the first time. Alba had spent her life making him breakfast and dinner and taking it to his room. That stopped after Australia.

With all this preparation behind her, Alba was alarmed when, as the 2003 fall semester began, Juan informed her that after graduating in December he planned to work at IBP to buy a car. He said he'd work until the 2004 fall semester began, then enroll at Dodge City Community College on the soccer scholarship Adam Hunter was offering him. But Alba was adamant. She insisted he enroll at the community college immediately after high school. As the season progressed, she secretly set about saving twenty-five hundred dollars so he could buy a car without working at the meat plant.

"I don't want him to leave school to go slaughter cows," she said.

"I've seen that they'll start liking the money and working and prefer that to studying. I'm afraid that if he goes to work, he won't go back to school."

Late in October, as the soccer season ended and the team headed into the playoffs, the issue of how Juan would spend the nine months after graduating still had not been settled between them.

Garden City finished its 2003 season a glorious 15–1–1. The team's only misstep was to tie a mediocre Wichita Southeast High School toward the end of the year. A soccer buzz began that no one could remember before. Attendance topped a hundred people at every game. The bleachers were packed. On campus, the team began to get the special treatment reserved for football players—though this was not always a good thing.

Rey Ramírez was far behind in his statistics class, partly from missing school to travel far to away games. His teacher gave him a midterm A anyway.

"I'm not going to argue with it," Rey said, "but I haven't done nothing in the class.

"Last year, if I was walking down the hall, a teacher would have stopped me and asked me why I wasn't in class," he said. "But if I was a football player, it'd be, 'Hey, good luck on Friday.' Now if I'm wearing a soccer sweater, she'd say, 'Good luck on Thursday' or something, even though it's obvious I'm ditching a class. It's not good. It's sending a message to me that schoolwork is secondary and sports is first."

The team's success had created gleeful anticipation on campus about the upcoming playoffs. That anticipation reached another level when Garden City won its first soccer playoff game ever, barely sweating to beat Wichita North 5–1.

Now Garden City prepared to play a much tougher opponent: Maize High School—a white school from Wichita—for the Southwest Kansas Regional Championship.

The game was played in Garden City the day before Halloween, under an aluminum-gray sky, and accompanied by a mercilessly cold northern wind. Maize showed up tall and in red, white, and black uniforms. White soccer teams in Kansas adopt many of the traits of football teams. Maize players did organized drills before the game, and its coaches drew up plays on an erasable board. Garden City's warm-up, meanwhile, was ragged and desultory. As the team warmed up, some of the freshmen on the junior varsity team played squirrelly games of keep-away. Padilla put on a tape and for ten minutes, ranchero singer Vicente Fernández sang "El Rey" (The King), his classic hymn to

Mexican machismo, over and over to a cold field of Latino soccer players and white players who probably didn't get the point.

The way soccer is played in the United States and Mexico reveals a lot about the two cultures. Americans have a more in-your-face style, using their strength and height, and tending to brashly blast the ball downfield into the opponent's side. Mexican soccer, on the other hand, is self-effacing, involving lots of quick passing and darting, indirect attempts at pushing the ball forward, as if the players are mortified at their own effrontery.

This describes the first minutes of the game between Maize and Garden City high schools. Maize tried to boom the ball downfield over the Garden City defense. Garden City packed Juan Torres and Luis Posada in around the defense. Later, Garden City players would acknowledge that Maize was the better team. Their players were stronger, taller, and faster. Maize players outjumped Garden City's and spent the first half breaking onto Garden City's side of the field.

Defense saved Garden City. With each breakaway, Maize ran into one of the Hernández boys, an unlikely pair of defensemen: Servando Hernández and Rudy Hernández, who are not related. Rudy had had his troubles in school, but, wanting to graduate and play soccer, was now going to class, making up what he'd missed, and his grades and interest in school were improving. Servando, one of the league's best defenders, had arrived a year ago from a small village in Guanajuato and still spoke no English.

Again and again, the Hernándezes repelled Maize attacks. When Maize players got through the Hernándezes, they collided with impenetrable Miguel Benítez in his lime green goalie shirt. Miguel is a big, thick kid, whose parents are from El Salvador. Miguel himself was born in Queens before his parents moved to Garden City. As the 2003 football team's kicker, he routinely kicked field goals of more than forty yards and was the only top college prospect the football team produced that year. As the soccer team's goalie, he dominated the game against Maize High School.

The goalie on a soccer team has a lot in common with the field-goal kicker on a football team. Both endeavors are solitary and essential to their teams. Neither one participates in the action for more than a few tense moments during the game. Both positions require nerve and the mental ability to ignore crowds and pressure.

This is what Miguel Benítez displayed against Maize. Maize players would streak down the field and rocket a shot at Garden City's goal that no one in the crowd believed would miss, only to have it freeze in Benítez's gloves. Over and over Miguel stopped the ball. He ran at Maize players to smother loose balls. Or he leaped, stretching his body lengthwise in the air in front of the goal to deflect a shot. The students on the sidelines would chant "Por-te-ro! Por-te-ro!"—Goalie! Goalie!—with each save.

As all this was going on, Garden City had trouble even getting off a shot at Maize's goal. So midway through the first half, Garden City began to boom the ball downfield as well, and the game changed. Now it was as if two tornadoes grappled. Up and down the field they went. Each team threw ferocious and desperate attacks at its opponent, who found just enough strength to blunt it.

Facing a superior opponent, Garden City players reached a higher level of play. They put on a sublime demonstration of feints, speed, no-look passes, and the footwork of tap dancers. As they raced down the field, at times they seemed to find a place similar to where jazz musicians go when they lose awareness of their instrument and technique and express perfectly what their minds imagine. Garden City's players twisted and faked and did three scissors in a row to leave a Maize defender behind. Yet when they got shots, which was not often, they missed. Several times, Hugo Blanco broke away down the left flank, only to have a Maize defender deflect the ball out of bounds.

The timidity with which Garden City had started the season was gone. Players elbowed Maize opponents and slid magnificently to steal the ball. But in this, Maize players matched them, diving into the path of their Garden City opponents again and again. These tackles, performed with a combination of abandon and precision, became the metaphor for how both teams played the game. In a rugged ballet, bodies flipped and flew. Garden's midfielder, Carlos Reyes, tackling so often, seemed to spend the entire game on the ground.

Meanwhile, a stream of students, parents, and teachers moved through the gray, numbing cold to the bleachers to watch. By halftime, more than three hundred people were in the stands. Never had that many people shown up for a Garden City soccer game. The cold froze reporters' pens and dug deep into bone marrow. Children and grown men shivered in the wind, but the game was electric, so no one left. From afar, the bleachers seemed to undulate, as lines of young men hopped in place, bellowing with each attack, rooting on Rey Ramírez and Pablo López as they sped down the near side of the field, and chanting "Ru-dy! Ru-dy!" when Rudy Hernández would blast a Maize ball away from the Garden City goal. Packs of girls shrieked and broke into chants of "Por-te-ro! Por-te-ro!" after each miraculous Benítez stop.

The game seemed to go on forever. Through the first half and then the second half, the game was scoreless, and so it remained as players ran and ran through one overtime period and then another, and a third, and, finally, a fourth. Neither team hit a wall of exhaustion; at least no player asked to be replaced. Yet neither team could score. Finally, after 110 minutes of soccer, playing time ended with the teams tied 0–0.

In Kansas high-school soccer, when two teams are tied when the game ends, they play an overtime. After the overtime, if they are still tied, they play another, and if the score doesn't change, a third overtime, and then a fourth. After the fourth overtime during the regular season, the game is officially tied. But when the game is a playoff game, and one team must move on and another must go home, then the matter is settled by a shoot-out.

Shoot-outs consist of each team taking turns firing penalty shots at the other's goalie. Each player tees up the ball and aims like a rifleman at the goal, the target, twelve yards away, with a jittery goalie standing between the shooter and jubilation. This tension is only released by a split second of joy or agony, which the crowd endures or enjoys only momentarily before it's the next player's turn and the ordeal begins again. If after five shots the teams are still tied, they continue on, battering each other in deliberate strikes to sudden death: when one team makes a shot and the other one misses.

So it came to this, a frigid shoot-out on the grass under the darkening sky. The crowd poured from the bleachers and streaked down the sidelines to be beside the field's east goal, gripping themselves and hopping in place from the cold. Young men bellowed bilingual cheers, "Let's go, Miguel. Es tuya. Es tuya! He's got nada." Wrapped in blankets, mothers shivered, covered their mouths, and looked about to cry.

During a shoot-out, the goalie's job reduces to guessing which way the opponent will fire and hoping to guess right. On the first ball of the shoot-out, and for the first time all day, Miguel Benítez guessed wrong. He dove left, the ball went straight and into the goal, and the Maize players jumped to their feet, jubilant. A second Maize shot went over the net. But Garden City missed its first two shots. With each shot, the crowd grimaced, stomped and kicked the grass, and doubled over in agony.

On Garden City's third ball, down 1–0, up came little David Villegas. David is a plucky ninth grader, born in Mexico City. He is also thin and one of the shortest players on the Garden City team. David's presence is impish, a look aided by a massive smile that winds around his face and reveals a mouth of big teeth. Murmurs swept the crowd, as people wondered what Padilla was thinking placing little David on the list of kickers. Still, David's presence is deceiving, for in practice he'd shown himself to be one of the team's fiercest penalty kickers. He put the ball down. He calmly backed up. Then he ran forward and shot a rocket into the net, tying the shootout at one goal apiece and sending the crowd into delirium.

The shoot-out now became a war of attrition. On the next ball, Maize scored, but Garden City kept pace with a score of its own. On the fifth ball, Maize shot wide of the goal, giving Garden City an opening. But Rudy Hernández, his legs shaking from the nerves and the fatigue that comes with almost two hours of soccer in the cutting cold, banged a ball over the goal. With each shot, the crowd reached another kind of frenzy. Maize put its sixth ball past Miguel again, and defeat loomed. But Juan Torres answered, tying the shoot-out at three goals apiece.

Then came the seventh ball. The Maize player lined it up, raced at it and kicked it hard, and directly into the hands of Miguel Benítez, where it froze. A Garden City goal would win it. The crowd went berserk, screaming, bellowing, pleading for the team to end it.

The game now rested on the foot of Elbin Palencia. Elbin is tall and thin—a likeable, soft-spoken fellow, whose parents are from El Salvador. He was born in Los Angeles. His parents split up when he was two, and his mother remarried. Elbin's mother and his stepfather had moved the family to Garden City from Los Angeles when he was in the seventh grade. His mother and stepfather worked on the cutting line at IBP. In the plant, his mother lost a lot of weight and often came home with her fingers frozen in a knife-gripped position. Seeing this made Elbin want something else for his life. He wanted to go to college and study architecture.

On the soccer field, Elbin's play sometimes reflected his demeanor. It was distracted at times, and many were the games when from the sidelines Padilla could be heard yelling "Palencia!!," which usually meant that Elbin had let a ball go, or failed to be aggressive enough.

But Elbin could kick, so Padilla put him on the shoot-out list. "It could have been somebody else, better than him," Padilla said. "But it was just him, him and the goalie, and that was it."

Night was closing in as Elbin stood there on the frigid field. He looked down and placed the ball on the ground. Before him the desperate Maize goalie waved his arms and hopped in place to keep limber. Brought to a fever, the crowd now pleaded with Elbin to put an end to it. Elbin backed up, stopped, said a little prayer, and ran at the ball.

The Maize goalie guessed correctly and dove to his right, but Elbin's kick was too hard, low, and toward the corner to be stopped. As Elbin Palencia's ball skipped into the net just under the goalie's outstretched arm, a frozen mass of students and teachers, children and parents, exploded in cries and tears, and raced onto the field. And from midfield, his teammates came running at Elbin, arms outstretched, like lovers too long apart.

Late the next night, Elbin's stepfather, Maurelio García, who'd raised him since he was two, died of a heart attack.

Five days later, Garden City was to play Wichita Heights High School to decide who would advance from western Kansas to the state soccer championships in Topeka.

Shortly before noon, an announcement over the high-school intercom called the team to a special meeting in the locker room with their coach. The players left class and met in the locker room. As they did, they heard another announcement, requiring all students to come to the big gym. So relegated had soccer been at Garden City High School that even after this announcement, some of the players still didn't realize what was about to happen.

In the locker room a few minutes later, they heard the band start up "Hail to the Buffalo." The team walked out, and before them sat the entire student body, packed to the rafters in the gym. For the next half hour, Garden City High held its first pep rally for the school's soccer team.

Pep rallies at Garden City High School, as in most high schools, amount to a secular mass. They consecrate what the school holds dearest. Up to then Garden City had reserved rallies for the annual anointing of the football and basketball teams. But things were different now. The football team hadn't had a good year since winning state in 1999. This soccer team, made up mostly of children of meat-plant workers, was the best thing Garden City had going.

Aware of what was now about to take place, the players stood dazzled and nervous and pumped with pride. They had sat in the stands of this gym and watched many pep rallies dedicated to the adoration of the football team. Here before them were the great hallmarks of high-school sports glory: cheerleaders, school band, teachers, and fellow students.

Hernán Macías's knees began shaking. Carlos Reyes's heart pounded, and butterflies were making him weak. He was almost sick and was not the only player hoping not to trip when he trotted out before the crowd. He looked at Juan Torres. Finally! they said to each other.

For the next fifteen minutes, a gym teacher named John Ford, with a voice made for monster-truck rallies, boomed out the players' names, taking five to ten seconds in the windup and delivery of each one: "Meeeguel Montohhhhyyya," "Loooooowwweees Posaahhhda." The school had brought out the inflatable tunnel that the football team uses to run onto the field at home games. As his name was called, each soccer player now ran out through the tunnel and onto the basketball court, high-fiving teammates. The students packing the bleachers received each of them with a roar. Walking out through the tunnel, assistant coach Anselmo Enríquez remembered his years playing soccer for Garden City High School and thought, "We never got anything like this."

Ford continued priming the delirium, making up with energy what he lacked in the subtleties of Spanish pronunciation. With a machine-gun "r," he crowed "RRRaaay RaMIIIrez" and "RRRuuudy Hernaaandez." He continued on through the roster. The junior-class section stood and gave Carlos Reyes, a junior, an ovation when his name was called. "Elllbin PalENNcia," Ford announced, reminding the crowd that it was Elbin's goal that had beaten Maize a few days before. Elbin's stepfather was to be buried the next day, but there was no way Elbin was missing this. It just felt so great.

Ford finally crescendoed with "the man with the golden glove... Meeeguel Beniiitez" and ended by introducing Juan as "a great student athlete... Juan Torrrrrres.... Here they are, your regional champions and after next weekend, your state champions."

In her seat in the sophomore bleachers, Vanessa Ramírez was giddy. "It was like this excitement, that we are something in this world," she said later. "For once the whole school sees what we're doing. They see what we've accomplished."

Thus fired with optimism and giddy dreams of going to the state championship in Topeka, the Garden City High School soccer team took the field a few hours later.

The steely cold and low clouds remained from the week before. Another tall, white soccer team in red and black uniforms—Wichita Heights—had come early and was already well into its warms-ups when the Garden City players showed up.

Now, the full range of American sports symbols were laid before the team. Six cheerleaders, white and Asian girls all, arrived to urge the Buffaloes to "S-C-O-R-E, Score!" and again to "F-I-R-E, Fire up!" The bleachers filled with parents and students. Four white students showed up wearing no shirts in the painful cold. Each fellow had painted on his chest a different school initial: "G," "C," "H," and "S." The athletic trainer was there. The entire band and drum line came, too, and at half time they played "Brick House," the Commodores' 1970s disco hit. For the first time, the soccer team had what the football team had every Friday night.

The game shaped up at first as a replay of the Maize ordeal. To several players, it seemed that Heights wasn't as talented as Maize. Still, neither team gave an inch, neither team could score, and in the gray cold, they went up and down the field. The half ended scoreless.

It was twenty minutes into the second half when Garden City scored. Servando Hernández whistled a free kick from thirty yards out. The Wichita

Heights goalie bobbled the ball, and it bounced before Luis Posada, who smacked it into the goal.

The stands roared, and the shirtless guys with the GCHS letters on their chest ran the school flag back and forth before the crowd.

At this point, Garden City fell back, and there was the slightest perceptible passion. It seemed as if, ahead 1–0, the team didn't run as hard for loose balls. They stood a bit more, even though nineteen minutes remained.

This letup now stung them. Garden City defenders didn't get back to cover a Heights breakaway in time, leaving a Wichita Heights player alone with Miguel Benítez. The Heights player chipped a ball over Miguel's head to score.

Now tied 1–1, the game rocketed back and forth across the field. Wichita Heights, feeling the momentum was theirs, laid siege. The Garden City crowd pleaded with its players, chanting "Si Se Puede! Si Se Puede!" (Yes, We Can!). Girls began to pray for another goal. Yet after relenting a bit while ahead, Garden City had trouble digging up that extra vehemence once the game was again tied. Finally, a Heights player scored again.

In a Hollywood movie, the game would have gone on until Garden City tied it, then won it in overtime. Instead, time ran out two minutes after Wichita Heights scored for the second time.

Garden City's soccer season slammed to an end. The crowd deflated visibly. Players collapsed, pounding the cold grass. Others stood on the field with their heads down. The tricky footwork, the dazzling dribbles through three and four defenders, Miguel Benítez's miraculous saves. They had been so close, and so good.

Silence covered the field, broken only by the yelps of Wichita Heights players as they ran to their bus and left. Garden City's cheerleaders, band, and much of the white crowd trailed off for the parking lot. The players walked off the grass and slumped down around their bench on the far side of the field. Seeing this, Vanessa Ramírez and some of her friends broke through the fence built especially for this game to keep spectators off the field. Groups of Latino students began a slow pilgrimage to the far sidelines. There, they came to a stop in a semicircle around the team, as if to protect them. Vanessa began to cry. No one could think of anything to say, but no one wanted to leave, either. So they stood like that for a long time. Miguel Benítez looked out glumly at the field, comforted by his girlfriend. Carlos Reyes saw people crying and wondered if he should be crying, too.

They had gone further than any other soccer team at Garden City High School. Their success was the success of the Mexican and Salvadoran students whose parents worked in the plants. The Latino half of the student body stood a little taller around school each time the team won. Facing Maize, a better, stronger team from a big city, which trained all year long, they'd drawn strength from the hundreds of students and parents who cheered them, and hung in to win. Beyond that, the team had galvanized a part of the population of meat cutters and packers that the beef industry had drawn from La Piedad, Michoacán, and La Unión, El Salvador, to the High Plains of southwest Kansas.

To one side stood Alba Torres. "Well, it's sad," she said, "but they are regional champions."

Padilla gave a brief, dispirited speech, lauding the seniors, saying the team would be back next year. Still, the players had also come to hope for so much more from this year. It was heartbreaking to think that now it wasn't going to happen. Their parents and friends had planned trips to Topeka for the weekend championship tournament. The first pep rally Garden City High School ever held for soccer, for Mexican and Salvadoran immigrants, had been for them.

Juan Torres sat staring at the grass. "I can't imagine that this would have ended here," he told the *Garden City Telegram* later. "Nobody was prepared to have it end."

Seven months later, one bright Saturday afternoon in May 2004, the sun was again beginning its decline in the west over the flat plains of southwest Kansas as the 301 members of the 117th class of Garden City High School prepared to graduate.

Had a strong breeze not blown in from somewhere, the field at the high school stadium might have been deadeningly hot, as May afternoons can be on the High Plains. Two days before it had been so cold that school administrators had to prepare the basketball gymnasium as a fallback venue, in the event of hail or rain.

As it was a sunny day, the ceremony was held on the school's stadium field, which, depending on your point of view, was now either the new soccer field or the new football field. The school had spent half a million dollars converting it from grass and football-only to an artificial turf that could handle soccer as well. White and yellow lines now traced the limits of both sports, creating a chaotic geometry across the emerald field. Football had made way for soccer in the cattle country of southwest Kansas. At Garden City High School, the sport would now finally be played in the stadium under the lights. The field seemed a lot like the heartland nowadays: a place that had once been simple and homogenous was now a bit more complicated, may be a bit more interesting.

Five Gonzálezes, five Nguyens, a Brookover, and an Irsik were in the graduating class. Up into the bleachers filed wizened grandmothers, toddlers, girls in heavy makeup, boys with Ramones T-shirts, and parents speaking Vietnamese, Spanish, and southern-accented English. They were from Zacatecas. They were from Da Nang. They were sunburned ranchers with baseball caps from Midwest Seed Genetics.

Students and administrators gave speeches expressing the clichés of graduation, though these were no less important for being clichés. They were about setting out in life, opportunity, about making choices, and about dreams and the importance of following them. This being Kansas, one student speaker urged his fellow graduates to have "a heart...a brain...and courage" and to remember, "there's no place like home."

As the sun was setting over a Garden City water tower, seniors filed across a stage on the field to receive their diplomas. John Ford, the teacher who had announced the soccer team's pep rally, was more subdued this time, but lapsed occasionally into his monster-truck voice when announcing the names.

He called the names of Hugo Blanco, Chuck Dodge, Armando González, and Miguel Benítez. Miguel, with his powerful leg, was not leaving to attend a university on a football scholarship, though he was a Division 1 prospect. He was staying to attend Garden City Community College. Miguel had fathered a son, and his girlfriend was only a junior.

Elbin Palencia had planned to move to Los Angeles. But after the death of his stepfather, he was staying to work to help his mother and attend Garden City Community College as well, hoping to take drafting classes, and one day to become an architect.

Tri Dang graduated with a 4.0 grade point average and Principal's Honors. He would leave soon for Middle Tennessee State University.

Rey Ramírez had accepted a soccer scholarship from Adam Hunter and would attend Dodge City Community College in the fall.

Alba Torres watched Juan receive his diploma. She was happy. "But it's not yet what I want," she said. "I'll be really happy when I see him with a diploma from a university. That's what I want."

Alba had been true to her plan and bought her son a car, a white Chevrolet Malibu, for six thousand dollars, so he wouldn't have to work in the meat plants. She took out a loan to buy it. As it turned out, Juan wasn't too interested in enlisting at IBP after all. It was hard work, and he liked his free time. He worked as a cook at the Lonestar Steakhouse in town.

Anselmo Enríquez and Álvaro Torres were still working at IBP. Álvaro and his wife had had a baby and bought a house. To Sylvia Trevino's great chagrin, her youngest son, Sergio, graduated from high school and two weeks later started work at IBP. Watching her sons sever their educations and rush to be fitted for the meat plant's corset made Sylvia ill, and more determined than ever to get her bachelor's degree in early child development.

"It started as a personal goal," she said. "It was something I had to have for myself. But I also want to show my children that I can do it, so you can do it."

A few weeks after the 2003 soccer season ended, the city officially named the field at Kenneth Henderson Middle School for the late Martín Esquivel. It was the first public facility in Garden City, or perhaps anywhere in southwest Kansas for that matter, named for one of the Mexican-immigrant meat-plant workers who extract the wealth from cattle and corn that sustains the region's economy.

Shortly before graduation, James Mireles was named principal of Garden City High School, becoming Kansas's first Hispanic high-school principal. Mireles, the son of a Mexican immigrant, was a school administrator and former football coach who spoke English with the accent of the Texas panhandle where he'd grown up. Like many of the Mexican Americans in Garden City, he spoke no Spanish, but Mireles got congratulatory e-mails from Latinos from across the state.

IBP had been bought by Tyson Foods and was called Tyson Fresh Meats, though everyone in Garden City called it IBP anyway. The Tyson purchase amounted to another consolidation of the U.S. meat industry. Based in Arkansas, Tyson now was the country's dominant producer of beef and pork, as well as chicken, and in dozens of small rural towns it ran plants of the kind Andy Anderson had devised. It was also one of the largest private-sector employers of Mexicans anywhere in the world.

Meanwhile, the boys' soccer team's success was still being felt on campus that spring. The girls' team had more than twice the player turnout than in its previous three years. Half the players were Latinas, many of them ESL students. Vanessa Ramírez was not among them. She was still fighting academic problems. But she had made the school's dance squad and was working to improve her grades so she could participate in it in the fall. The girls' team even won three games, which was more than it had won in the program's first three years combined.

Joaquín Padilla was expecting more boys to try out for soccer next fall.

Soccer in Garden City was facing some interesting challenges. One was whether the sport should leave the immigrant ghetto in which it resided. Padilla, the team, and the school will have to decide if they want soccer to be a racially diverse and consistently winning program or a segregated program designed to keep Latino kids in school. Doing both probably won't be possible. To be successful statewide, Garden City will have to beat the perennial winners: schools from Topeka, Kansas City, and Wichita, where players are predominantly white, tall, strong, and fast, and who train far more rigorously than Garden City. Without a few tall, strong white players of its own, Garden City may have trouble beating those teams. But that will require that Garden City make a prolonged effort to cultivate interest among white kids in the sport that Mexicans brought to town.

Like the Mexican enclave in America, soccer in Garden City will have to open itself to outside influences to fulfill its potential. In the same way that football shared its field and lights with soccer, Latino immigrants will have to share their sport and reach out to make white players who speak no Spanish feel comfortable on the team.

But that was for later. For now, the Garden City High School team had diverted the attention of a town obsessed with football. Immigrant kids had puffed with pride, and more than a sport emerged from the shadows on the High Plains.

A change occurred in the years that followed. Most of the players on the 2003 squad would go on to at least junior college. Several would go on to four-year colleges. They would look back and know the season, as Rey Ramírez put it, "opened the eyes of a lot of guys on the team, to let them dream a little bigger."

And nothing like that had ever before come out of a soccer season in southwest Kansas.

Gladys: An Immigrant Story

Ilan Stavans

I've known Ramona Gladys Pérez Lozano for years—how many exactly, I forget. I value her friendship dearly. Her story is at once common and perplexing, with an unfortunate dose of disaster.

Gladys is from El Salvador. She came to the United States in 1996 as an undocumented laborer, not speaking a word of English. She was thirty years old at the time. Her mother had died giving birth to her thirteenth child. The father got frightened right away. How would he take care of more than a dozen children, none of them yet fifteen? He had a propensity for alcohol. He would disappear late in the afternoon and would not come back until next morning. In one of his escapades, he disappeared for good. The kids were as good as orphans.

The poor are sometimes able to look fate in the eye and recognize in themselves exceptional strategies of survival: they don't easily give in to depression ("the action of lowering, or process of sinking"). Gladys's oldest siblings took charge. Everyone who was capable of it got a job. Gladys was nine years old at the time. She quit school. She never completed first grade. She is still barely able to read and write. When she sends me a note, it is in preteen handwriting.

In time Gladys herself gave birth to three kids: Oscar, Fanny, and Elizabeth. She never married her children's father. They lived together for a couple of years. Then he, too, disappeared.

Two of Gladys's siblings left El Salvador for Massachusetts. They each took three weeks to make the move. The United States–Mexico border is notoriously harsh. But their trouble began in the border between Guatemala and Mexico. The Mexican border patrol caught them and beat them. A *coyote*—from the Nahuatl *coyotl,* traditionally understood as a carnivorous, canine animal smaller than the wolf, but in this usage a smuggler of undocumented immigrants into the United States—was helping Gladys's siblings. They promised him $1,500. Part of the deal was that they would attempt the crossover

---

"Gladys: An Immigrant Story." Copyright © 2005, Ilan Stavans. Reprinted from *Dictionary Days: A Defining Passion,* with the permission of Graywolf Press, St. Paul, Minnesota.

three times. After that, they would be on their own. Fortunately, they crossed the Guatemala–Mexico border on the third try. They successfully crossed the United States–Mexico border on their second attempt.

Years later, already settled down—one worked at La Veracruzana, a small-town ethnic restaurant owned by a former gang member from Los Angeles, the other at a Howard Johnson's—they sent for Gladys. It took her thirty-six days to make the transnational journey. She walked, took rides, hid in trains and trucks, and ate thanks to the mercy of strangers. She assured me she spent the equivalent of $65 overall. She finally made it to the outermost point of Mexico. In the dead of night, she shrank under a fence, at the coyote's instructions, and desperately ran for almost a mile across a desert. Gladys heard gunshots behind her, but didn't look back. Someone was waiting for her in a blue Chevrolet. They drove her to Douglas, Arizona. A couple of days later she was taken to Phoenix. From there she took a flight to Hartford. She had never been on an airplane in her entire life. As the plane took off, she peed in her pants.

Gladys lived at first in her sibling's one-bedroom apartment. A total of eight Salvadorans lived there, six male and two female. She worked in a pizza parlor, a hair salon; she cleaned people's houses, swept floors at a Holiday Inn, and worked as a dishwasher in an Italian restaurant called Pinocchio's. It was around then that I met her.

Before going to work, I used to stop at a café called Rao's that sells strong, freshly brewed Colombian coffee. It's the type of place where artists, students, and misfits hang out—not your typical immigrant parlor. But it was on Gladys's way to the bus station, so she often stopped to get an espresso to go. I would hear her communicate with the person behind the counter. Gladys would use a maximum of three words: "espresso, please" and "*tenkyu.*"

I exchanged a smile with her and then, the next day, I said something in Spanish. Her eyes sparkled. She was relieved to hear someone use her native tongue. She immediately became talkative. Gladys told me where she was from, the number of hours she worked cleaning houses, and so on.

The next time we saw each other she told me more. I also told her about my own upbringing, my two kids, and about my students.

We became friends.

She also worked for a while at La Veracruzana. I would go for breakfast there every so often with my friend Martín. Gladys would prepare delicious *huevos rancheros* and *chilaquiles* for us. If the clientele wasn't too demanding, she would come sit for a few minutes at our table.

Eventually I convinced Gladys, after some months, to attend English lessons. I found a place conveniently located—the second floor of the Fleet Bank—where free classes were offered to immigrants. I once went to visit a class. The majority of the students were from China and Malaysia. I also saw some Haitians. I was surprised not to see more Latinos—only three or four in a classroom of roughly fifteen students.

Gladys began to go every Wednesday. But she had a terribly rough time. "Ay, Ilan, *no puedo pronunciar las palabras,*" she would tell me in a Salvadoran-accented Spanish. Pronouncing the most basic English words was excruciatingly difficult for her. "The teacher says I need to study harder. But I don't have time.... Last time I was in school I was a *chipota*. My mother, before she died, told me always to go to school. But I haven't been able to. It's hard!"

I help Gladys as much as possible. We repeat words together and we go over her spellings. *Gur morne, ticher. Ai am fain. An jau ar yu?*

Whenever I see Gladys, I think of my own odyssey as an immigrant across the Rio Grande. But lately I've been reflecting less at a personal level. I have been compelled to see the broader canvas before me. How do immigrants become Americans? By what innate, unfathomable metamorphosis do we cease being the people we were upon arrival and go about acquiring altogether new selves?

I am particularly attracted to the subject from the perspective of language. America has always benefited from languages other than English. Since the first polyglot encounter between Pocahontas and John Smith, the Puritans and Indians in the sixteenth century figured out ways to interpret—to translate, to reinvent—one another. The miraculous aspect of the endeavor, though, is that no matter what the circumstances were, the English language always prevailed. It was, is now, and is likely to remain the great, undefeated equalizer. This is, needless to say, a good thing; for the nation to remain one, homogeneous yet pluralistic, the mastering of the vernacular is the only viable step in the process of assimilation. *Parlez-vous anglais? Mai oui.* Okay, so please join the party.

Gladys's journey is not unlike that of millions before her. They arrived speaking Swahili, Creole, Cantonese, Italian, Yiddish, Portuguese... and, years later, they, or more often their children and grandchildren, have left the immigrant parlance behind.

Is the situation changing? In the small Massachusetts town where Gladys lives there are barely enough Latinos to make a soccer match happen. But that isn't the case in the rest of the nation. Plus, the number of Asians is also growing rapidly. These waves of newcomers are learning English at a rapid speed. And yet, they—I'll change the pronoun now: *we*—are arriving in such gargantuan numbers that the capacity to assimilate, to become American in the traditional sense, is being subverted. Spanish for sure has become the country's unofficial second language. To handle yourself well in numerous parts of the United States today, you need Cervantes's tongue as much as you need Shakespeare's.

The desire to incorporate others into the so-called Melting Pot results in impatience toward non-English speakers. Billy Wilder said: "I don't object to foreigners speaking a foreign language; I just wish they'd all speak the same foreign language." Increasingly for the gringos any interest in the rest of the globe has been reduced to a condescending attitude best represented by my good ol' Uncle Stanley of Long Island. Once, after he congratulated me for having learned the English language, I said: "It's now your turn, *Tío Estanli*. You have to learn Spanish now." His was a laconic response: "But why should I, Ilan, when you can already talk with me rather nicely?"

My initial reaction to attitudes like Uncle Stanley's is always one of pity. *Tío Estanli* is clearly all the poorer for his monolingualism. Or is he? Then I remember that he himself is a child of Jewish immigrants from Poland. When he was a child Stanley spoke English in the street and at school. His parents also made every effort to use English at home, although their English was half baked and they made mistakes. Yiddish was heard in the household when the parents didn't want the kids to understand something. It became a forbidden language.

Years later, it remains forbidden, not only Yiddish but any other foreign tongue. A well-known joke asks: How does one refer to a person who speaks four languages? Tetralingual. A person who speaks three languages? Trilingual. Two? Bilingual? And only one language? An American.

America is an international power but, curiously, it is a culture allergic to foreignness.

In fact, my dialogues with *Tío Estanli* once led us to a fascinating *Via Crucis*. So much distress goes into another language. If English is the *lingua franca* of the twenty-first century, why not turn it—officially, that is—into a *lingua universalis?* Why, in his own words, "doesn't everyone in the world just come to their senses and switch to American English? Can you imagine the amount of business and diplomatic hurdles that would solve?"

I pretended to be gung ho about it. "Yeah, yeah, it's a brilliant idea...!" The end of communication that often leads to warfare, the end of disparity that frequently results in famine.

Okay, so my uncle's suggestion isn't altogether new. The objective he's after is a sensitive one whose roots go back to... well, think about it: Isn't the Tower of Babel to be blamed for all the confusion around?

Before Babel, we are told, there was a universal language. Then humankind became conceited and tempted the Almighty. In return, G-d sent us as punishment the multiplicity of languages that has defined human endeavors ever since. Babel points to a simpler, purer origin. The resulting trauma is the initiation of a period of verbal plentitude. Today we live in a world with some 5,000 different tongues.

To me that plurality is exquisite. But not to *Tío Estanli.* So, as he puts it, why can't we return to the origin?

The attempt to return to a pre-Babelic period is deeply rooted in history. People have defined Hebrew (and at times, Latin, too) as a primal language. Also, people have sought to find a universal tongue capable of abolishing all others. In the nineteenth century, an age known for its romanticism, the desire acquired the form of several ur-languages, including Esperanto. The product of the Polish linguist Dr. L. L. Zamenhof, Esperanto was established mathematically in 1887 after years of research. Zamenhof proposed it was a second language that would allow people who speak different native tongues to communicate. This meant that no linguistic and cultural identity would be under threat, but a common verbal code would be established to bring an end to violence. Esperanto, it is said, is four times easier to learn than other languages.

Earlier in time, efforts to codify a universal language entertained European thinkers, among them Francis Bacon, René Descartes, Athanasius Kircher, and Gottfried Wilhelm Leibniz. Another one of them, arguably the most intellectually sophisticated, was John Wilkins, a seventeenth-century Briton who was a member of the Royal Society and the author of, among other books, *An Essay*

Towards a Real Character and a Philosophical Language, published in 1668. The premise is straightforward: there is a universal grammar and a universal lexicon with which a universal phonology can be connected. The yearning to see reason as the ultimate unifier is a product of the Encyclopedic age and it has a religious background. Before the building of the Tower of Babel, in what language did people—Adam and Eve, Cain and Abel, Noah and his wife, et al—communicate? The answer is the pristine, original (e.g., universal) language of Paradise, the one G-d used to make himself understood to his progeny.

Four years before his *Essay,* Wilkins wrote:

> As men do generally agree in the same Principle of Reason, so they do likewise agree in the same Internal Notion or Appreciation of things. That external Expression of Mental notions, whereby men communicate their thoughts to one another, is either to the Ear, or to the Eye.... So that if men should generally consent upon the same way or manner of Expression, as they do agree in the same Notion, we should then be freed from that Curse in the Confusion of Tongues, with all the unhappy consequences of it.

Wilkins suggested a relatively easy linguistic system. He organized words according to categories (which he also called classes). These categories were in turn divided into differences, and the differences were divided into species. Borges, in one of his sleepless nights, made a chart of Wilkins's approach. "He assigned to each class a monosyllable of two letters; to each difference, a consonant; to each species, a vowel. For example, *de* means element; *deb,* the first of the elements, fire; *deba,* a part of the element fire, a flame." Borges praised the system.

> Let us consider the eighth category: the category of stones. Wilkins divides them into common (flint, gravel, schist), modics (marble, amber, coral), precious (pearl, opal), transparent (amethyst, sapphire), and insolubles (coal, chalk, and arsenic). Almost as surprising as the eighth is the ninth category. This one reveals to us that metals can be imperfect (cinnabar, mercury), artificial (bronze, brass), recremental (filings, rust), and natural (gold, tin, copper). Beauty belongs to the sixteenth category: it is a living brood fish, an oblong one.

It makes sense, except that language... well, language doesn't always make sense. What about ambiguities? What about redundancies? One single aspect of language messes up the whole approach: *usage.* People first learn to use a word and then they adapt it to their circumstances. Could language be structured logically? It surely could, but it wouldn't make it too practical. Jacques Barzun of Columbia University once said that

> usage is not an agent but a result—the result of innumerable "votes" cast over the years for or against a particular word. The leaders in this popular choice are the men who write and speak professionally—the Roosevelts and Churchills, Hemingways and Audens. If, as often happens,

such a man is also a theorist about his own art, he will tell us his loves and his hates among vocables. As user and critic, he himself is the voice of usage, himself his own highest authority, with power of life and death over any current form. And as old words are not sacred and may be changed, so new ones are not sacred and may be liquidated. It is the one instance in which rational killing is no murder.

Plus, usage is what makes art possible. Could Wilkins's disciplined invention allow for the production of novels and plays? I doubt it. A language has to be malleable enough to be able to communicate the complexities of its age. And would a universal language that is shaped artificially, in the security of a laboratory, solve Gladys's problem? Not in the least.

And should *Tío Estanli* be turned into a prophet and English be imposed on the rest of humankind?

History holds the answer.

Gladys's urge to memorize the English vocabulary against all odds had made me think, time and again, of two books I read long ago. I cherish them enormously. They granted me a precious understanding of that most ethereal, evanescent human capacity: memory. (Flaubert, in his *Dictionaire des idées reçues,* said of memory: "Complain of your own; indeed boast of not having any. But roar like a bull if anyone says you lack judgment.") The volumes were both written by a Russian neurologist, who was professor of psychology at the University of Moscow, Aleksandr Romanovich Luria. (I've seen an alternative transliteration from the Cyrillic: Luriia). One of them was *The Man with a Shattered World: The History of a Brian Wound,* about a solider named Zasetsky who suffers a terrible injury in the battlefield in Smolensk in 1943 and loses his capacity to fully remember events as a result. He is able to recall his childhood but not his recent past. He also loses half of his field of vision. Plus, he has trouble writing, reading, and speaking. The other book is, in a way, a response to the first: *The Mind of a Mnemonist: A Little Book About a Vast Memory,* about a man—he is called S., a device, needless to say, reminiscent of Kafka—with a portentous memory, one of whose attributes is the incapacity to forget.

When I first switched to English in search of a literary language to better express myself, I wrote a long story set in the Czech Republic and Mexico and inspired by Luria. It was called "The Invention of Memory." (It is part of *The One-Handed Pianist.*) Its protagonist, one Zdenek Stavchansky, a freak with an enviable talent to remember is suddenly diagnosed with an illness that will erase his memory altogether. He chooses to travel to his mother's native home, Mexico, and attempt to re-create as frequently as possible, in the theater of his mind, the various episodes that constitute his life.

I also wrote an essay, "Memory and Literature," a meditation on books and remembrance. I'm not interested in rehashing the same ideas again. My interest has shifted to words. Doesn't the *OED* define *reason* single-mindedly as memory? What is the connection between words and memory? For one thing, it's clear that communication is impossible without the faculty to remember words at a precise time, and to fit those words into the mental train of thought. Brian-damaged patients, for instance, often have to relearn how to speak. They are taught how to slowly move their facial muscles again. But the effort often needs to go further. They need to retrieve words from their verbal reservoir. Is that reservoir still available? Have they forgotten it? If they have, the process will require becoming a child again, so to speak. They will be forced to enhance their memory banks by naming things one by one.

Gladys knows that a *tenedor* in Spanish is the word that refers to "an instrument with two, three or four prongs, used for holding food while it is being cut, for conveying it to the mouth, and for other purposes at table or in cooking." So the connection between object and sound has been established. Her objective is to move onward to the acquisition of *another* word for the exact same object: *tenedor, fork.*

When Gladys turned thirty-three, I gave her a bilingual dictionary for her birthday.

It was her idea. "The teacher showed us one. What is it?"

I told Gladys it's a list of words, with their respective meanings. The one she needed, I said, was a bilingual one.

"You look up a word in Spanish and it will give you the English." In my office in the third floor of my home, I showed her a Spanish/English lexicon.

She had no clue. "Look! Words and more words," I explained. "Every single one you'll ever need."

I forgot about the incident. Time went by. When I recalled that her *cumpleaños* was around the corner and asked her what she wanted for a present, she replied: *"Un diccionario."*

I got one wrapped. Gladys was excited. She opened it right in front of me, looked at it, and then said she needed to go back to work.

"Wait!"

I told Gladys we could look up a word. *"¿A ver?* Is my name in it?"

"I'm afraid not," I replied. "This dictionary doesn't include names."

I waited to see her reaction. Gladys was disappointed. I felt somewhat awkward. I was trying to help my dear friend handle an instrument that is useful only when one is able to handle oneself freely in a language. In a way, it was like showing a Mapa Mundi to someone who has never left his birthplace and does not suspect there's life anywhere but there. (In fact, in Flaubert's story "A Simple Heart," a scene exactly like that occurs.)

Then I said: "You could look for the word *tenedor...*"

She smiled but felt a little ashamed, too. *"¿Cómo le hago,* Ilan?"

I shouldn't have been surprised by her response. A person with a limited education doesn't know what to do with a dictionary. He might understand what it is, but to use it he would need lots of practice. The mere idea that words are organized alphabetically is a challenge. Gladys, it became clear to me, knew the alphabet, but it is hard for her to go automatically to the letter *P*. She has to recite the alphabet in her memory a letter at a time, then browse through the lexicon pages. It's a considerable effort, to say the least.

The next day when I saw Gladys she said: "I don't know why to use the dictionary you gave me. I already know the words in Spanish. Everybody does..."

"But you don't in English."
"*Sí*, I don't," She said. "But I can ask my teacher."

Some eighteen months ago, Gladys paid a coyote $3,500 to bring her son Oscar from El Salvador to Massachusetts. The travel took him three weeks. He also works at Howard Johnson's now.

Oscar's language fascinates me even more. Unlike his mother, he graduated from high school in El Salvador, so the Spanish tools he arrived with in the United States were more helpful. Still, his English-language skills were primitive. Oscar could say *hello, good-bye, how much does it cost?, where is the restroom?,* and other similar expressions, but little in the way of complex conversation.

He began attending Gladys's classes and learned much faster than his mother. He also enrolled in a public technical school twice a week. It is in a town some twelve miles away. As a result Oscar began to socialize with other Latinos. His linguistic pattern, thus, has moved in directions different from Gladys's.

He mixes Spanish and English much more. This is an important aspect that recalls my conversations with *Tío Estanli*. Oscar is starting to speak in Spanglish, the mixture of English and Spanish. A jargon? Carl Sandburg described *slang* as the "language which takes off its coat, spits on its hands, and goes to work."

In the last decade or so, I've spent countless hours studying Spanglish. How does it evolve? Is it a recent verbal phenomenon? Are there precedents in the United States? Elsewhere in the globe, what are the similarities between Spanglish and say Franglais, Portuñol, Hebrabic, and Chinglish? Is Spanglish a dialect? And does it appear to be evolving syntactically in such a way that might lead to the formation of a full-fledged language? I even compiled a lexicon of some 6,000 of its terms.

Spanglish has a long and rich history. Its roots are traceable as far back as the Guadalupe Hidalgo Treaty of 1848, when, after the Mexican-American War, two-thirds of the Mexican territory was sold to the United States for $15 million. Those territories were mostly inhabited by Spanish-speaking dwellers who abruptly found themselves exposed to English and an Anglo-Protestant way of life. In newspapers and legal documents of the period there are traces of Spanglish words and syntactical formulations.

Another time of intense linguistic experimentation occurred during the Spanish-American War of 1898, when Spain finally ceded its colonies in the Caribbean Basin. Cuba and Puerto Rico entered the orbit of influence of the United States, thus embarking—each of them in different fashion—in a cultural life in which English formed an integral part.

It is difficult to establish precisely how many people use Spanglish, as well as when and how often they use it every day. Unquestionably, it is used on a regular basis in Puerto Rico (population 2 million) and the United States–Mexico border (approximately added population: 25 million). But it is also heard in major urban centers such as Miami, New York, Los Angeles, San Antonio, Chicago, Dallas, Boston, and so on. You hear it used primarily in the home, the street, the community center, the classroom, and the office.

Studies have established that Spanglish speakers can be bilingual (English and Spanish) and also monolingual (either English or Spanish). They belong to different social strata: low-income workers, middle-class professionals, upper-class entrepreneurs, etc. This means that Spanglish is neither defined by class or by race or ethnicity. Latinos and other speakers of every background use it.

In my travels I've come to recognize three verbal strategies used by Spanglish speakers: [1] codeswitching, e.g., the free-travel from English to Spanish and vice versa ("Yo went to la store"); [2] automatic and simultaneous translation (e.g., expressions like *"Te llamo pa'trás!"*); [3] and the coining of new terms (*marqueta* for market, *grincar* for green card, *rufo* for roof). Depending on where geographically and temporally Spanglish speakers might use it, the syntactical foundation is either English- or Spanish-based.

As more detailed scholarship accumulates, it is clear that there isn't one Spanglish but a whole variety. Each Latino national group has its own variety. Thus, there are Pocho, Pachuco, and Chicano forms of Spanglish; you can find Cubonics, Nuyorrican, Dominicanish, and so on. This is because the Spanish in Latin America isn't homogeneous: each country has its own distinct type (Ecuadorian Spanish, Peruvian Spanish, Venezuelan Spanish, etc.). As immigrants from the Hispanic world move to the United States, they bring with them their own national syntax and vocabulary, which in turn influences the way Spanglish evolves. But the multiplicity of Spanglish is also defined by location: Chicano Spanglish in El Paso, Texas, is different from Chicano Spanglish in Portland, Oregon.

The growth of Spanglish, I believe, is, to a large extent, the result of a number of factors: an unabated Hispanic immigration to the United States; the triumphs and pitfalls of Bilingual Education; the spread of multiculturalism as an ideology; and globalization as a cultural pattern at the beginning of the twenty-first century.

Yes, there are many other hybrid languages in the world: for example, Portuñol (a mix of Portuguese and Spanish spoken in the border of Spain and Portugal as well as Brazil and countries like Venezuela) and Franglais (the cross between French and English, spoken on both sides of the English Channel, in the Caribbean and parts of Africa). But Spanglish is a far more complex verbal way of communication, mainly because, unlike other border dialects, it is surely used by a huge number of speakers (more than the total population of Spain or Argentina).

Some argue that Spanglish is but a middle step in the process of English-language acquisition. This means that as soon as Latinos abandon Spanish completely and become fully fluent in English, Spanglish will disappear. These specialists use as evidence the experience of previous immigrants to the United States. Among Jewish immigrants from Russia and Eastern Europe, for instance, Yiddish gave place to Yinglish, which in turn gave place to English. Roughly a century after the first Yiddish-speaking Jewish immigrants arrived to American shores, the vast majority of American Jews speak no Yiddish. A similar pattern was followed by Germans, Italians, and other immigrants.

This argument is flawed. Latinos immigration, for one thing, has been constant for over a century and doesn't show signs of diminishing. Plus, the closeness of the immigrant's old home (Mexico, Guatemala, Puerto Rico, the Dominican Republic...) and the relatively inexpensive travel fares make mobility back and forth relatively easy. This means Spanish doesn't disappear from the landscape like other immigrant languages have done.

Oscar's ordeal has allowed me to appreciate, in an immediate way, the use of Spanglish as a form of communication.

Once I saw Oscar at a baseball game where my son Josh was playing for the Reds in the Babe Ruth League. I was seated in the bleachers when Oscar showed up with other teenagers. He saw me and came to say hello. We talked for a few minutes. I mentioned that I was quite impressed by his use of English. "You're really learning it fast, my friend," I said. I also told him I was spellbound by the way he—like myself—sometimes intertwined words from both languages.

"*A Gladys no le gusta,*" he said. "But she does it, too." And then Oscar asked, "Why is it wrong if what ya' sayin' is clear?"

Oscar is a sharp young man and that was a sharp question. Yes, why is it that the mixing of two perfectly circumscribed languages is forbidden? Why do people in Berlin take offense when German and Turkish are intertwined, immediately decrying impurity? Why don't the French like using English terms in their speech?

The image that crossed my mind as Oscar went back to his peers was of a dictionary like the *OED* that would include, in a major soup of backgrounds, words from scores of languages. Not a bilingual lexicon, not even a multilingual one, but one defined by chaos. Why not?

Why do we create barriers between tongues? How has it come to be that children are taught to speak and write in a particular language and not to borrow from another linguistic bank? American English is astoundingly elastic. Words from other tongues—called loan words—are always being incorporated into its verbal bank. Dozens, for instance, come from Algonquin dialects, including *moccasin, pecan, powwow, skunk, squash, totem,* and *wigwag.* Or else, think of more recent acquisitions from French, German, Italian, Spanish, etc., such as *divorcée, media, lasso, libretti, paparazzi, parfait, piñata, sauerkraut, soprano, taco,* and *virtuoso.*

I believe I have the answer: language is a ticket to identity. To mix languages is to appear confused. The Hungarians speak Hungarian, the Italians Italian, the Czechs Czech, and the Russians Russian. If and when a Russian introduces Chechen into his Russian speech, he is called a double agent, a conspirator, maybe even a defector. Language is infused with nationalism. Like the flag and the national anthem, it is the stuff that makes a nation unique. And uniqueness means rejection—or at the very least, separation—of other people's heritage.

And yet, languages have intermingled with one another since the moment the first Sumerian, Phoenician, and Babylonian merchants offered their goods to others: to interact is to let one's language be exposed to change, to enrich oneself through the speech of others. What is Early English if not the outcome of the jumbled parlance used by the Celts, the Romans, the Saxons, the Vikings, and the Normans? Isn't that part of the magic of the kennings in *Beowulf*? And how did Yiddish come to be if not by using German morphology and Hebrew characters? Didn't Spanish in the eleventh century evolve from vulgar Latin and the incipient dialects of the Iberian Peninsula? People lament the death of a language in Africa, South America, and India. But how about applauding the birth of cross-fertilized tongues? These are born in the modern world thanks to globalization, the exact same globalization that kills aboriginal speech.

It has been a difficult battle but interracial marriages are more a norm than ever before. Folklore, food, and culture are also juxtaposed. Might language follow the same road then? Will the intercourse of different tongues ultimately be accepted?

Oscar at times talks a mumbo jumbo like the one tourists use. That, too, is a consequence of his late-in-life northbound immigration and his socializing with other Latino kids. In fact, as I listen to him I wonder if anyone ever attempted a dictionary of "immigrant-speak"? On the other hand, there is also the jargon improvised by tourists as they struggle to communicate in countries whose language they hardly speak. A dictionary of *tourisms*? By this I don't mean a lexicon that tells a traveler how to say the simplest expressions—"Where's my change?" and "Is there a lavatory?" Instead, I'm referring to the way tourists think they know how to utter these expressions in Swahili and Tagalog. I don't know if there's a bundle to be made there, but at the very least, there is a possibility for plenty of laughter.

In an e-mail exchange with a student of mine who lives in Japan, I told her about Oscar and about my interest in tourisms. She immediately sent me back, in an attachment, a compendium of what she called "gems of Japanized English." It included the following sentence found near an out-of-service elevator at Narita Airport: "An escalator avobe this notice is under repair hoping to be savoured with yours use of northern escalator or elevator." The attachment also had this line, which, according to my student, first appeared at Expo '70: "WARNING Gentlemen! Please do not carry your wallets in rear pocket for your backside is easily attacked." But probably the best example she e-mailed me was a sign posted on a road in Kansai: "WEL COME TO JAPAN THE SEA MEN YOU GENTLEMEN DROP IN THE BAR KING AT GIRST: LADIES ARE READY. *In boxes and stands.*"

One day I heard Oscar announce: "Drink a note." I asked him what he meant. He said in El Salvador people say *"Tome nota."* In Spanish the verb *tomar* might be translated as either *take* or *drink*.

I mentioned this to the executive of the National Book Foundation, who happens to be a close friend. A great talker, he reacted by giving me several instances in which, while abroad, he had come across one restaurant menu after another that simply used dictionary terms without understanding them. For instance, in Port Bou, Spain, in 1979, he came across a dish called *Rape a la marinera*. This was a reference to monkfish (or angler-fish) in tomato sauce. He also remembers an item called *Rape, sailor-style*. Then he said that a non-English-speaking Catalan friend of his once came across an English-language learning manual from the twenties and forever afterwards used such phrases as *Dat's de cat's meow* and *Dat's de cat's pihamas*. Finally, he recounted the extent to which tourist expressions have embarrassed him—even though he sometimes had his own dictionary on the side. He was once in Jakarta. Just before going shopping, he looked up in the lexicon the word for *looking*. But when he made it to the store and a sales clerk asked him if he needed help, the word he looked up meant *searching*. He then mispronounced it, and it came out as, "No, thanks. I'm only stealing..."

It would be easy to ridicule Oscar's jargon but it would also be wrong. Embedded in that jargon are the linguistic structures he maneuvers in order to communicate in English. His language might sometimes be impure but it is never impractical. He is able to make himself understood far better than his mother Gladys.

By far the most mystifying episode in Gladys's journey of assimilation took place in March 2004. It started in the early days of March. Gladys told me she had once again saved enough money to bring one of her children to the United States. Her daughter Fanny was already fifteen. Gladys hadn't seen her since she left El Salvador. Fanny and her sister Elizabeth were living with one of Gladys's siblings. Fanny is an average student. By all accounts she is also timid, perhaps even naïve. She isn't a big talker. Unlike Oscar, she also doesn't know any English. Gladys wanted Fanny to be with her and Oscar.

So she sent $4,000 to another coyote. Again, he promised three tries. Fanny left El Salvador on a Thursday. She was supposed to cross the Guatemala–Mexico border three days later and the United States–Mexico border one week after that. The trip was arranged so that Fanny would not go alone, but with a twenty-year-old cousin and her five-year-old son.

Gladys asked the cousin to give Fanny a piece of paper with Gladys's telephone number. She said she would.

The path to Sonora, the northern Mexican state, was long. It took an entire month. The cousin kept Gladys informed of their whereabouts by using a phone card. She would always call at 10 P.M. Eastern Standard Time.

By mid-May the three were ready to cross the Rio Grande. Regrettably, they were stopped by the border patrol and sent back. They spent some more days in Ciudad Juárez. The cousin had some money. But judging from the telephone calls, the behavior of the five-year-old was becoming increasingly difficult. He missed his bed and friends. He wanted to go back home.

It is hard to know what transpired in the early hours on the morning of May 24. The day before the cousin had called Gladys to tell her they would attempt a second border-crossing at 5 A.M. the next day.

For the next twelve days Gladys didn't hear a single word. Her phone remained silent. Then she got a call from a relative living in Virginia. The cousin and her five-year-old were already there. But somehow Fanny had been left behind.

Gladys was shocked. How could Fanny not make it with them? The cousin told Gladys that, at a given juncture, the coyote asked people to run to a bus parked across a highway. They all did. It took them forty-five minutes to run across unseen by passing motorists. Then, when everyone was seated on the bus, another man came on and asked everyone to leave the bus. People complied—but not the cousin. Fanny asked her to come down, but the five-year-old just didn't want to move.

In retrospect, it was the right choice. Once everyone was off, the man sat in the driver's seat and drove the bus to a neighborhood in El Paso where the original coyote was waiting. The coyote arranged for an airplane ticket for the cousin and the child for the next day.

As it happens, the cousin never gave Fanny Gladys's telephone number. She also had no money left.

The cousin did say that the day before they separated, the coyote got them false IDs. By then, Fanny was upset and ready to go back home if necessary. When the coyote took a passport photograph and asked each and every one for their name, Fanny didn't want to use her real one. Instead, she said she was called Ramona Gladys Pérez Lozano—her mother's full name.

Three weeks went by. The real Gladys had not heard a word from her daughter. Nobody in El Salvador had heard from her either. Gladys kept on calling everyone she knew: relatives in Los Angeles and Virginia, an on-and-off cellular phone number the coyote had given her at some point.

I saw my friend Gladys at La Veracruzana one afternoon. She told me the entire story. *"Fanny no habla ni una sola palabra de inglés,* Ilan...."

She also said she wished she could give her the dictionary I gave her for her birthday. "She'd probably use it far more than I do."

The choice of her name on the ID was potentially disastrous. My friend Gladys had benefited from a moratorium on undocumented Salvadoran laborers signed by the presidents of the two countries after El Salvador suffered a tragic earthquake that killed many people and left many more homeless. But she and Oscar were back to square one—illegal again—after the moratorium ended. There was a remote possibility of filing for a Green Card under special privileges, but the details of those privileges were lost in judicial fine print. It might take years to sort out.

Fanny's disappearance pushed her mother to despair. Ciudad Juárez is known as a town from hell, a drug-trafficking center, filled with Maquiladoras, where young girls, almost three hundred of them, have been kidnapped and assassinated. Their dismembered bodies are disseminated throughout the Sonora desert, where the corrupt Mexican police, whose complicity in the kidnappings is undeniable, find them later in a state of decay.

Gladys could not sleep and lost a lot of weight. Would her daughter be okay? Could someone be taking advantage of her sexually? She called me at all hours of the day seeking advice. I posted a notice in a missing persons' Internet web site. But everything needed to be done with extreme care. If the girl was found by the authorities on this side of the border, she would be sent back to El Salvador. If instead she had gone back to Mexico, her chances of survival were noticeably slimmer.

I told Gladys I was ready to take a plane to Phoenix and look for her. I didn't know what good this would do: Where would I start my search? To whom would I talk? Contacting the police was out of the question. But I knew

Gladys would find some comfort in my suggestion. After all, she wasn't able to book a flight herself and go. Her English was insufficient. Maybe Oscar could go. But then again, he was undocumented. As for Gladys's siblings in town, they did everything they could, but they needed to work from dawn to dusk every day.

The whole affair was terribly emotional. Language and memory—what are we without them?

Then, out of the blue, Fanny—aka Ramona Gladys Pérez Lozano—sent word from Ciudad Juárez to El Salvador that she was all right, in the home of a Good Samaritan. (As it turned out, it was a Mexican woman whose energy in the past few years has gone to help "disoriented *señoritas*" like Fanny). The Good Samaritan would try to cross her to the United States in a few days.

Was it a ploy? Gladys appeared full of joy. She wired $800 to Ciudad Juárez. And she talked to the Good Samaritan on the phone a number of times. Fanny was fine, she told Gladys, but she hardly ever spoke. "*Como si un gato le hubiera mordido la lengua,*" she said. It's a Mexican saying, though I've heard a similar expression in the United Kingdom: silent as if a cat ran away with her tongue.

When Gladys told me this, the next day, she laughed. "No cat would do it, Ilan. *¿Qué piensa?* She'll need that tongue. In this country you're a *donnadie*"—a nobody—"if you don't open your mouth."

Fanny crossed the border for the final time on June 28. This was done in an unlikely fashion. The Good Samaritan drove her by car. They showed their IDs to the customs officer. It turns out that the last name of the Good Samaritan is also Pérez. She told the officer Fanny was her daughter. Then the officer asked the girl: "Yes, *ella es mai moder.*"

Fanny is now living in Los Angeles with an uncle.

"Headed North" and "The Runner"

Ramón "Tianguis" Pérez

HEADED NORTH

In another half hour of walking, I'll arrive at the highway where I'll catch a bus to take me to Oaxaca City. From there another bus will carry me to Mexico City, then yet another one will take me to Nuevo Laredo, on the border. My plan is to go to the United States as a *mojado*, or wetback.

It didn't take a lot of thinking for me to decide to make this trip. It was a matter of following the tradition of the village. One could even say that we're a village of wetbacks. A lot of people, nearly the majority, have gone, come back, and returned to the country to the north; almost all of them have held in their fingers the famous green bills that have jokingly been called "green cards"—immigrant cards—for generations. For several decades, Macuiltianguis—that's the name of my village—has been an emigrant village, and our people have spread out like the roots of a tree under the earth, looking for sustenance. My people have had to emigrate to survive. First, they went to Oaxaca City, then to Mexico City, and for the past thirty years up to the present, the compass has always pointed towards the United States.

My townsmen have been crossing the border since the forties, when the rumor of the *bracero* program reached our village, about ten years before the highway came through. The news of the *bracero* program was brought to us by our itinerant merchants, men who went from town to town, buying the products of the region: corn, beans, coffee, *achiote, mescal,* eggs, fabric dye, and fountain pen ink. The merchants carried these items on the backs of animals, or sometimes, on their own backs, until they reached the city of Oaxaca, about a three days walk from home. On their return trips, they brought manufactured products, like farm tools, cooking utensils, coarse cotton cloth, ready-made clothing and shoes, candies and so on. They sold their goods from house to house, town to town. One of them came with the news that there were

---

"Headed North" and "The Runner" are reprinted with permission from the publisher of *Diary of an Undocumented Immigrant* by Ramón "Tianguis" Pérez (© 1991 Art Publico Press–University of Houston). Used by permission of the publisher.

possibilities of work in the United States as a *bracero,* and the news passed from mouth to mouth until everyone had heard it.

To see if the rumor was true, a merchant and two others went to the U.S. embassy in Mexico City. The only document the embassy required them to provide was a copy of their birth certificates, for which they came back to the village. On their return to Mexico City, they were contracted to work in California.

From the day of their departure, the whole town followed the fate of those adventurers with great interest. After a little while, the first letters to their families arrived. The closest kinsmen asked what news the letters contained, and from them the news spread to the rest of the villagers. Afterwards, checks with postal money orders arrived, and their families went to Oaxaca City to cash them. The men's return home, some six months later, was a big event because when they came into town they were seen carrying large boxes of foreign goods, mainly clothing.

Their experience inspired others, but not all of them had the same good fortune. Some were contracted for only short periods, because each time there were more people waiting for the same opportunity at the contractors' offices. That's when some men smelled a good business; the men called *coyotes,* the forerunners of today's alien smugglers. They were men who, for a sum of money, intervened in the Mexican offices where contracts were given to make sure that their clients were included in the list of men chosen.

The contractual system came to an end with the *bracero* program, in the mid-sixties, but ending the program didn't end Mexican desires to cross the border. People had learned that in the United States one could earn a wage much higher than the standard Mexican wage, even if to do it one had to suffer privations, like absence from one's family. So when the *bracero* program ended, the *coyotes* kept working on their own. They looked for employers in the U.S. and supplied them with workers illegally.

I, too, joined the emigrant stream. For a year I worked in Mexico City as a nightwatchman in a parking garage. I earned the minimum wage and could barely pay living expenses. A lot of the time I had to resort to severe diets and other limitations, just to pay rent on the apartment where I lived, so that one day I wouldn't come home and find that the owner had put my belongings outside.

After that year, I quit as night watchman and came back home to work at my father's side in the little carpentry shop that supplies the village with simple items of furniture. During the years when I worked at carpentry, I noticed that going to the U.S. was a routine of village people. People went so often that it was like they were visiting a nearby city. I'd seen them leave and come home as changed people. The trips erased for a while the lines that the sun, the wind and the dust put in a peasant's skin. People came home with good haircuts, good clothes, and most of all, they brought dollars in their pockets. In the *cantinas* they paid for beers without worrying much about the tab. When the alcohol rose to their heads, they'd begin saying words in English. It was natural for me to want to try my luck at earning dollars, and maybe earn enough to improve the machinery in our little carpentry shop.

During my infancy, I always heard people say "*Estadu*," because that's the way that "*Estado*," or state, is pronounced in Zapotec, our language. Later on, people simply said "*El Norte*," "The North," when referring to the United States. Today when somebody says "I'm going to *Los*," everybody understands that he's referring to Los Angeles, California, the most common destination of us villagers.

But I'm not going to Los Angeles, at least not now. This time, I want to try my luck in the state of Texas, specifically, in Houston, where a friend of mine has been living for several years. He's lent me money for the trip.

THE RUNNER

The waiting room at the bus station in Nuevo Laredo is spacious and well-lit. It is full of people walking in different directions with bags in their hands. Some are just coming in, some are leaving. Some are in line to buy tickets, and others are seated in the terminal, nervous or bored. A tattered beggar has laid some cardboard sheets on the floor of one corner and he's sitting there, chewing on a piece of hardened bread, his supper before retiring for the night. The waiting room clock marks nine P.M. My traveling companions seem content to have arrived, but I notice them yawning from tiredness; the trip took fourteen hours. Some of them try to comb their disheveled hair and others rub their red eyes. On seeing them, I decide that I probably have the same appearance.

Disoriented, I take a seat in the waiting room, hoping to shake off my own sleepiness. I know what I should do next. I should go out onto the street, take a taxi to a hotel, rest a while and then look for a *coyote*, or alien smuggler. Before setting out, I take my belongings and head towards the restroom, thinking that a stream of cold water across my face will help me wake up.

With the first steps I take towards the restroom, a dark-skinned guy comes up alongside me. He's short and thin and he's dressed in a t-shirt and jeans. He greets me familiarly, with a handshake. After looking him up and down, I'm sure that I've never seen him before. I give him a stern look, but he smiles broadly at me, anyway.

"Where are you coming from, my friend?" he says.

"From Mexico City," I answer.

"From Mexico City!" he exclaims. "Well, man, we're neighbors! I, too, am from Mexico City."

He reaches out and shakes my hand again.

I already know the type from memory. It's not the first time that a stranger has come up to me, saying almost the same things. I am waiting for him to tell me that he had suffered such and such instances of bad luck and that he had a relative in danger of dying and that he had to go to the relative's bedside and that, though it pained him to be without resources, he at least felt encouraged to have come upon a townsman who could give him a little money. But instead of saying that, the stranger keeps walking at my side.

"Where are you headed?" he asks.

I keep silent and without breaking my pace I give him an inquisitorial look, trying to figure out why in the devil's name he's trying to insert himself into my affairs. Still smiling and talking, he repeats his question, as if I hadn't heard him the first time.

"To Houston, I hope to arrive in Houston, with luck, and I'm going to have to find a *coyote,*" I tell him, because, given his insistence, I suspect that he might know something about the border-crossing business.

"Are you looking for a particular *coyote*? Has somebody recommended one?" he asks with growing interest.

"I don't know any and nobody has recommended one, and in just a minute, I've got to begin looking for one."

"Well, you're in luck, friend!" he exclaims, adopting the mien of a happy man, content to have brought good news. "You don't have to keep looking, because I"—he points to his chest with the index finger of his right hand—"work for the best and the heaviest *coyote* in Nuevo Laredo.... The heaviest," he repeats, emphasizing every syllable as if pronouncing the word really was a task of heavy labor.

After entering the restroom, I go up to the urinal, an earthen-colored, tiled wall with a narrow drainage canal at its foot. I start making water and my stranger friend does the same.

"A Mexican never pisses alone," he says, recalling an old saying.

"Right now we have forty *chivos* ready to leave in the early morning, and they're going precisely to Houston, your same destination, my friend."

I'd later learn that they call us *chivos,* or goats, because of the odor we exude from lack of bathing facilities and clean clothing. I am surprised by the ease with which I've run into at least the assistant of a *coyote,* but I don't show much interest in knowing more about his work. After urinating, I go to a sink, open a faucet, and with cupped hands I wet my face a time or two. My friend follows me to the sink and plants himself nearby, without pausing in his praises of his *coyote* boss.

"How much is it going to cost me?" I ask, without raising my head from the sink.

"Four hundred and fifty dollars, plus four thousand pesos for the boat," he answers.

"Good, if that's all, paying will be no problem."

"Very good!," he exclaims with a triumphant gesture. "Well, my friend, in less than eighteen hours you'll be in Houston."

"That's even better," I say, holding back my happiness.

Then my unexpected friend takes a couple of steps and thinking, he says to me, "There's something missing. We've got to be sure that you'll pay that amount or that it will be paid for you."

"That's no problem. You will be paid when I get to Houston."

I'm carrying the money, but my distrust tells me that I shouldn't let the stranger know. The money is a loan of $650. I've got $100 in my billfold. The other $550, in bills of $50 each, is sewn into the lining of my jean jacket.

"Oh," he says, answering himself, "you've got a relative who is going to pay for you in Houston. It's incredible how everybody has relatives in the United States."

Without my asking, he has told me what my answer should be, should anyone else question me about money. I'll say that my friend will pay in Houston. Nobody will know that I'm carrying the money myself.

"It's not really a relative that I've got, it's a friend," I say, to get the story rolling.

"You should give us the phone number of your friend so that we can make sure that he really knows you and will pay for you."

"That's no problem," I tell him, just for the moment. The telephone number could be a problem because my friend has asked me to use his name only if it's urgent. He also asked me not to carry his telephone number and address with me. I have complied with his requests. I memorized his name and address. The only problem I can foresee will be to find a way to tell him that if the *coyotes* call, he should promise to pay for me.

The friendly stranger doesn't stop trying to convince me that his boss is a powerful man. He says that his boss is invulnerable because he has paid-off the police.

"On top of that," the stranger says, "he treats the *chivos* better than anyone else, because he gives them a house to stay in while they're waiting. The other *coyotes* put people out in the brush without jackets and a lot of times, without food. Not to mention the way he treats me," the guy adds. "He doesn't pinch pennies when we're out drinking."

I'm more interested in what he says about payment than in his endless homage to his boss.

"Do I have to pay for the boat every time it crosses the Rio Grande, or only to cross without incident?" I ask him, while I'm drying my face with the sleeve of my jacket.

"Oh, no!" he says, as if scolding himself for having forgotten an important detail. "If *La Migra* catches you ten times, we'll put you across ten times for the same money. And what's more"—his face brightens as if with surprise—"my boss is right here in the station. Come on, I'll introduce you!"

We go walking towards the station's cafeteria, and the stranger who says he's my townsman points towards a group of three men seated at a table, each one in front of a can of beer.

"Do you see that dude who's wearing the cowboy hat? Well, that's Juan Serna, he's my boss," he tells me, with the pride and arrogance of someone who has introduced a Pancho Villa. "All you have to do is say that you're a client of Juan Serna, and the police will leave you alone, because—let me tell you—if you go outside to the street right now and you take a taxi at the next block, or if you catch a city bus, the Judicial Police will grab you—and forget it!—they'll let you go on the next corner, with empty pockets. They'll rip-off your change, man. But if you tell them that you're with Juan Serna, they themselves will take you to the house where we keep the *chivos*."

"Wait for me here," he says when we've come within a prudent distance of the table where the three men are chatting. "I'm going to tell the boss that you're going to Houston."

He walks towards the table and speaks to the man named Juan Serna, then looks towards me. With a movement of his hand, he tells me to come nearer.

Juan Serna is dressed in an orange, nylon t-shirt with black lettering on its frontside that says, "Roberto Duran #1." He's dark-complexioned with somewhat fine facial features. His eyes seem very deep in their sockets. He's clean-shaven, with a wispy moustache. Beneath his eyes are the wrinkles of a man bordering on fifty. Several tattoos adorn both arms, most prominent among them is the head of Jesus, dripping blood from his crown of thorns. Juan Serna doesn't waste good humor like his assistant. He remains rigid, as if preoccupied with other affairs. He leans forward a little, supporting his body upon the table with his forearms, his hands clasped around a can of beer. He makes no gesture and gives no greeting when his assistant introduces us, only a rapid look, a look as indifferent as if he'd been handed the next can of beer. His two companions are seated in front of him, and they're saying something that I can't hear. My "townsman" stands, waiting expectantly at Juan Serna's side.

"Where are you going?," Serna says to me in a northern accent and in a voice so dry that it sounds like he's formed his question not in his mouth, but in his throat.

"To Houston."

"Do you have someone to pay for you there?"

"My friend who lives in Houston."

"So should I take him?" my townsman says.

Juan Serna gives his consent by nodding at my townsman, but he nods without moving a single muscle of his face. I follow my townsman, with the impression that behind us Juan Serna is still nodding, like the branch of a tree that sways involuntarily after somebody has pulled on it.

Outside the bus station, the townsman leads me to a station wagon. He and I get into its back seat.

"We have to wait until the driver arrives," he says.

From the floor of the vehicle he picks up a six-pack and hands me a can.

"What's your name?," he asks.

"Martín," I say, just to give a name.

"My name is Juan, just like the boss," he says without my having asked him. "And I won't give you my last name because I don't know you, but I'll gladly tell you my nickname. You can call me Xochimilco, just like everybody here does."

While I sip on my beer, Xochimilco drinks one, then another, and a third, chatting all the while.

He says that he was a taco vendor in the Xochimilco district of Mexico City, and that was the reason for his nickname. The taco business had been a good one because his boss had lent him a car to go to places where people amassed, like soccer games. But things went bad when the boss had to sell his car. Xochimilco says that he found himself first without work, and then without money. He found it necessary to ask a friend for a loan of five thousand pesos.

Xochimilco began to worry when his friend put twice the amount he'd asked for into his hands. He accepted only after making long declarations of gratitude. A month later, that same friend came to his house in a luxurious new car. "When from the doors to my house I saw him pull up," Xochimilco says, "I immediately thought about the loan he'd made me, and I was really relieved when he said that I should forget about it, because I still didn't have anything in my pockets."

His friend told him that if he was still in need, he'd help him get past his troubles, on the condition that he cooperate with the friend's plans. When Xochimilco asked in what way he could help, his friend laid a .38 caliber automatic pistol in his hands. Xochimilco didn't know what to say, but he looked with fascination upon the gun given to him.

"At first, it frightened me," Xochimilco tells me, "because I'd never shot a pistol, much less shot at a human being."

"Who said that you're going to kill anybody?" his friend said when Xochimilco expressed reservations. Xochimilco decided to trust his friend in the hopes that he, too, would someday have a car like his. His friend and another guy had planned a hold-up.

"Five hundred thousand pesos for only one simple hold-up!" Xochimilco bragged after a long swig of beer. "Your nerves make you tremble after the first job."

But Xochimilco's money troubles were finished. After the first job came others. The gang's biggest and last hit came after they had gotten to know the son of the owner of a slaughterhouse. The son was firmly resolved to rob his father, who he said was swimming in money but was so cheap that he wouldn't spend a cent, not even on himself. And the son, who knew his father's routine, conspired with Xochimilco and his friends. The four of them went into the father's office just as he was counting bills on his desk with the company safe open. When he realized that he was being robbed, the father reached for a pistol that he kept in his desk, but the bandits all opened fire, even the son. They made off with four million pesos; Xochimilco's cut came to half a million. Time passed and investigations began. When the son was arrested, Xochimilco decided to flee to *El Norte*.

"I had enough money to pay a *coyote*," Xochimilco says, with a slight and fleeting expression of nostalgia. After two attempts, he managed to reach Houston but he only stayed a month because one night, on leaving a beer joint drunk, the police stopped him and turned him over to agents of *La Migra*, the Immigration and Naturalization Service. A couple of days later, he was taken back to Nuevo Laredo. Now with only ten thousand pesos to his name, he could neither return to Mexico City nor cross the border again. He asked the man who is now his boss to give him a job.

"And here you have me," Xochimilco says. "I'm a runner. They call us that because we're always running behind guys that we suspect are headed to the United States."

I ask him how much he earns. He says that of the four thousand pesos that I'll pay for the boat, two thousand are for him. "I make that much for every *chivo* I take to Juan Serna's house."

"I imagine that you're not exactly poor," I tell him.

"Well, okay," he says, teasing, "I've made enough to have money, but I don't have it saved, because...well, what good is money? Huh, my friend?" His eyes open into an interrogatory look as he leans closer to me. "To spend it! If not, what good is it?"

His job, he says, pays him different sums on different days, especially because he isn't the only runner.

"You can ask for 'Shell,' for the 'Mosquito,' or for the 'Dog.' Anybody can tell you about them, they're in the same business as me. Today I can pick up ten clients and tomorrow, none. That's the way this job is."

Xochimilco interrupts his explanations to point out a car that has parked in front of the terminal.

"That car without license plates belongs to the Judicial Police, and I can assure you that it won't be long before Juan Serna comes out to talk to them."

Just as he said, a minute later Juan Serna comes out of the terminal and walks directly up to the car without plates.

"Do you see it! Look at that!" Xochimilco exclaims. "What I tell you is no lie. That son-of-a-bitch is well-connected."

A few minutes later, a middle-aged man sits down in front of the steering wheel of the car where Xochimilco and I are waiting. Without saying a word, he starts the motor and we pull off.

"That idiot," Xochimilco says, pointing to the driver, "is the one they call 'Shell.'"

The car passes over paved streets, and for a few minutes, bumps down dirt streets full of chugholes. Meanwhile, I'm thinking that my circumstances are like those of a fugitive. To avoid being stopped by the police I have to keep company with thieves and maybe murderers, who, oddly enough, enjoy police protection. If the police stop me, I could argue that I'm a Mexican citizen, with a right to be in any part of the Republic, and I could point out that the police don't have the right to suppress my rights unless I'm committing a crime. To be a wetback, to go into the United States illegally, isn't a crime that's mentioned in our Constitution, but whether or not it is, it's not important. Here, he who's going to be a wetback, if he has money, will have trouble with the police, and if he doesn't have money, he'll have even more trouble. The idea that the police watch over the social order is an old tale that's true only in my village, where we name the policemen from among our own townsmen. If they find you drunk, they're likely to drag you home. If you deserve a punishment, the worst that can happen to you is a night in jail.

Conversations with Ilan Stavans

Rubén Martínez

Rubén Martínez (USA, b. 1962) is the author of The Other Side/El Otro Lado: Fault Lines, Guerrilla Saints, and the True Heart of Rock 'n' Roll *(1992),* Crossing Over: A Mexican Family on the Migrant Trail *(2001), and* The New Americans *(2004). This interview took place in Boston, September 2003, as the paperback edition of his second book was released.*

IS: How many people cross the U.S.-Mexican border annually?

RM: Impossible to say. All we know is how many people are apprehended at the border by the border patrol and turned back, and then there are some estimates of how many people are living undocumented in our cities. But I would have to say about 2 million, 3 million maybe, every year.

IS: Three million people?

RM: Yes, a year.

IS: How is it that we know so little about who they are?

RM: Because we simply don't pay attention. The media doesn't know how to pay attention. It's a bias of the mainstream U.S. media. I'm talking about radio, print, TV... The undocumented Mexican laborer who's omnipresent in a colloquial way on the street, whether it's a day laborer or somebody painting your house, somebody nannying your children. Somebody helping with your groceries, helping you get your groceries to your car at the supermarket. So in one way there is an omnipresence of the immigrant laborer in the United States, but that doesn't get translated into the media image.

First published in "Crossing the Border: Rubén Martínez," in *Conversations with Ilan Stavans* (Tucson, Arizona: University of Arizona Press, 2005, 123–131). The interview aired on PBS-WGBH in the program *Conversations with Ilan Stavans* on January 17, 2004. Courtesy of Ilan Stavans.

IS: Why are we so afraid to talk about it?

RM: It's a hand grenade. American consciousness historically splits right down the middle between the American that receives with generosity through the Statue of Liberty: "Give me your tired, your poor, your huddled masses yearning to be free..."

IS: Emma Lazarus, "The New Colossus."

RM: Exactly. And the other side is the one that simply rejects, closing borders.

IS: Yet with nostalgia for a mythical land of opportunity that is always open...

RM: Ellis Island on the one hand, receiving the stranger with open arms and the possibility of becoming a Horatio Alger on the streets of America, and on the other hand intense vitriolic xenophobia, which in its extreme forms has led historically to lynchings of Chinese laborers in Los Angeles and in recent times to the deaths at the hands of paramilitary groups of Mexican laborers on the U.S.-Mexico border.

IS: Is the situation with those millions of Mexicans that are crossing the border, and Central Americans too that are crossing the border every year, different from the Italian immigration or the German or the Irish?

RM: A fundamental difference.

IS: How so?

RM: The most obvious one is that the old-world European immigrants who arrived at Ellis Island in the middle of the nineteenth century and then again in the early part of the twentieth century—an ocean separated them from their homeland. Many of them talked about returning home; the first generation, the zero generation immigrant, would yearn to go back to Italy, go back to Germany. But the reality was that most of them ended up staying here. The impossibility of travel or going back, swimming against the tide of immigration coming across the ocean this way. Latin American immigrants are within reach of their homelands, especially Mexican immigrants. The U.S.-Mexican border is the longest single frontier in the world between a first-world nation and a developing world or third-world nation. This makes the relationship of the United States to Mexico—and of the Mexican immigrant laborer vis-à-vis American society overall—absolutely unique in terms of American immigration history.

IS: In a science fiction twist, imagine one year without these million Mexicans crossing the border. What would happen to the United States?

RM: The immediate impact would be going to the supermarket when strawberry season starts in March and April—there wouldn't be any strawberries. Because strawberry picking is a labor-intensive, manual labor-intensive proposition, and if you didn't have the seasonal flow of undocumented—we're talking about undocumented labor, the vast majority of strawberry pickers in northern California strawberry fields...

IS: You have a chapter called "Strawberry Fields Forever."

RM: Everybody in California—the growers, the politicians, the labor unions, the supermarkets, the corporations—everybody knows this to be true. It is just a fact of life. But do we talk about it? No. Just like one of these open secrets, it's wink, wink. A politician can rail at election time against "illegal immigrants," but when we go to the supermarket we're all enjoying the fruits of that labor.

IS: Is it only the supermarkets? Okay, so for a year we won't eat strawberries...

RM: Not just the strawberries, of course. In the seasonal sense of labor, migratory flow, the immediate impact would be in foodstuffs, the produce sections in our supermarkets. But beyond that, say in my home state of California, in the skyscrapers downtown the trash would start piling up in all the offices. Drywalling, all the new developments going up—because the drywallers are mostly undocumented immigrants now—there will be nobody to tack the drywall in the developments.

IS: Mexico needs to allow those immigrants to come north...

RM: Oh yes. Mexico must have it that way.

IS: So both economies depend on this coming and going from people south to north.

RM: Just to mention the other side of the equation: It's crucial for the Mexican government to have the flow going northward as much as it benefits the United States. It benefits Mexico to the extent that Mexico does not have enough jobs to give to its people, and the number three source of income right now for the Mexican, the Mexican economy, is the amount of dollars sent from laborers in the United States to their family members back home. And that's after tourism and oil; then comes the Mexican laborer in the States sending money back home to their mom and dad. That's a huge contribution to the economy.

IS: You begin *Crossing Over* with the death in a car accident of a number of immigrants. Every so often the media gives us news of immigrants that have died in the desert of thirst, immigrants that are beaten down by the border patrol. Do you have an estimate of how many people are killed or die that way?

RM: It's a conservative estimate because many of the dead, their bodies will never be found. The bones are at the bottom of the Rio Grande, they're out in the middle of the desert in southern Arizona or in Texas.

But we have found many bodies over the years. The University of Houston has done a study that tallied from coroners' reports on both sides of the line some 3,000 people over the last decade, and that study is a few years old now, so we can calculate that it's probably closer to 3,500 to 4,000 people.

IS: That's more than those that died on September 11.

RM: A huge amount of people, and yet on a daily basis the media coverage given to the deaths is usually relegated to border newspapers: the *El Paso Times,* the *Arizona Daily Star.* There will be a small notice: another undocumented immigrant found in the desert looking for shade died of thirst.

IS: It isn't only the media and the politicians. In our capital, there are monuments for the Holocaust, there is a proposal to build a memorial or a monument for slavery and the place that it has in the United States. Should there be a point, not so distant hopefully, where we should have a monument, a museum, a memorial in Washington to remember all the many crossing from south to north and whose presence is at the very heart of the American dream?

RM: There won't be such a monument to undocumented Mexican laborers in my lifetime, I'm sure. We have a plethora of memory sites that celebrate immigrants throughout American history. But Mexicans are a dirty secret. It's an open secret, always with that wink for the corporate moguls and the politicians and everybody who knows that this is the way things work. They can have their cake and eat it too. It isn't something that you could acknowledge aboveboard, because to do so is to implicate yourself morally in the deaths of thousands—not just of thousands of people but the destruction of millions of people's lives, stripping the dignity from these people's lives for generation after generation after generation, because this story is not new. People have been dying and being exploited and being spit upon as greasers or spics for generations now, and there hasn't been a whole lot of change in that story because we're not willing to fess up.

IS: With the slow but obvious move of Latinos from the margins of society to the middle class, and with a sense that Latino culture eventually will become an essential part of American culture, could there be this vision that the Mexican immigrant, the South American immigrant, will play a larger role in our psyche in the way we perceive things?

RM: I don't know...

IS: Too optimistic?

RM: It depends what time of day you speak to me.

IS: Not now?

RM: Generally speaking, the fact that Carlos Santana has won a dozen Grammys in the last couple of years and sold a billion albums and that Ricky Martin was shaking his bonbon and then J. Lo and Ben are going out—I really don't think it makes any difference whatsoever to the lives of the millions of people in this country who are living in the shadows. Jennifer Lopez, Carlos Santana, and Ricky Martin aren't saying, Now that I have the eyes of millions, it's about time for us to address this terrible immigration policy.

IS: You are speaking out.

RM: This is personal.

IS: How so.

RM: I'm the son and I'm the grandson of immigrants from El Salvador and from Mexico to the United States. When I see my brothers and sisters, not just from Mexico but from Central America, from China, Korea, central and eastern Europe, when I see any immigrants' dignity stripped from them because of some exploitation in the labor situation, my own humanity is diminished as an American. Because we have these ideals here; we have the Statue of Liberty that says this, and we have the Constitution that says this—it's there on paper. Our mythology is supposed to be part of the way we live, the way we act in the world.

IS: In the end, literature has a limited impact in a society. Is your voice doomed to be lost? What can be accomplished through reportage like yours?

RM: To reach a wider audience, I would have to shake my bonbon like Ricky Martin. How many people have read this book? 20,000? Would I like to be on the Oprah Book Club? Of course. Anyway, there's nothing else that I can do.

IS: Oprah won't be interested...

RM: It's a messy subject, not sexy. The book begins with the mangled bodies of nine young men crushed under a truck after a chase effected by the border patrol and winding up in the hills of Temecula. Now somebody might think, oh, maybe we can turn that into a Hollywood movie, but let's face it, when we get Hollywood renditions of Latinoness, it's something completely different from this scenario. This is a little bit too gritty, and yet I can do no other thing than to write about it.

IS: Are things worse after September 11?

RM: Yes.

IS: How have things changed?

RM: Since September 11 more people are dying on the U.S.-Mexican border this year. The summer of 2003 will be the deadliest season on the border in recorded history: close to two hundred people will have died by the end of this summer, most of them in southern Arizona in a very forbidding and terrible part of the desert called the Camino del Diablo, the Devil's Road, where migrants have to cross some seventy miles of desert without a single water source. And that's where they're dying. Why are they dying? Even before September 11, and even more so since September 11, the border patrol has had a strategy of trying to close down the major crossing points, that is, San Diego, Nogales, El Paso, McAllen, Texas, trying to divert the migrant flow, keep it back. The border is two thousand miles long. Most is open. You could skip across it. The water only goes up to your knees. I was there a couple of weeks ago as a matter of fact. Even though people maybe don't cross at San Diego anymore, they cross in the mountains east of San Diego. They don't cross at Nogales; they cross in the open desert, and that's what's becoming deadly. I'm afraid that the United States, everyone, all American citizens are complicit in the deaths of the migrants to a certain extent.

IS: We are guilty, all of us?

RM: Yes. The Mexican government is guilty. And the migrants have to take some responsibility, and the smugglers have to take some responsibility too. There's plenty of responsibility to dole out here. I'm not just pointing the finger at Uncle Sam in a self-righteous way. We need to come together on this. Ours is the era of globalization. Some people think that we can go it alone in a complex world like this, but even in the regionalized sense of looking at the way the world is, there's no way we can come up with an immigration policy that would be humane without involving all parties, without having a direct conversation...

IS: Just before September 11, though, there was this debate between the two administrations, the one of President Bush and the one of President Fox, about legalizing. The numbers would fluctuate between 3 million and 5 million undocumented immigrants in the United States, and there was even tension within the Latino community of why the Mexicans are getting this preferential treatment. But then September 11 came and all that kind of discussion vanished.

RM: Right in the paranoia of the times. Understandably so in the wake of 9/11. Nobody knew where the threat to the United States was coming from. But I can tell you one thing: if there's a threat to the United States on the U.S.-Mexican border today, the terrorists, what kind of terrorists are they? Are they guys with dishrags and leaf blowers coming across to terrorize our cities? I've been on the U.S.-Mexican border; there is not a single shred of evidence that Al Qaeda has used the border to ship missiles across or anything of the sort. There's zero evidence of that. As you said earlier, we do have some evidence on the U.S.-Canada border, but right now the U.S.-Mexican border is not a place of national security threat in terms of Al Qaeda. It's a threat to our moral standing before ourselves and the rest of the world in terms of human rights and dignity for the U.S. and for the Mexican laborers crossing that border.

IS: What is it in the border that is in Rubén Martínez, and vice versa?

RM: I grew up in—or perhaps on—it. Los Angeles is 120 miles from the border. The border splits us along racial and economic lines. East Los

Angeles was Mexican, west Los Angeles was white, south Los Angeles was black. As kids we'd go down and go across the border and go to Tijuana with my family. Once again Mexicans are within reach of Mexico in the United States. An hour and a half drive from LA and we cross the border, and it would be for me like going into the land of Oz. All of a sudden the neon and the color and the streets that weren't sanitized, safe, straight lines like those in San Diego. It was a whole other world. I loved leaping back and forth over that line. It's not as if one side is better than the other. I loved both. They were just so different... So I grew up with the border in me. As an adult the drama of the border has just drawn me for political and moral reasons. It's a place that, after I finished this book, I told myself, I'm not going to deal with the border or immigration anymore. I've done it for twenty years. And I'm about to start work on a new book that's about the southwestern desert. And it *will* have several chapters about the border.

IS: You can't get away from it.

RM: No, I can't. It's also the landscape of the Southwest. The desert west and the issue of water—water is the only metaphor in the west. Whether you use it as the metaphor for the migrants crossing the River Jordan into Canaan, or to talk about water and gold. When you're thirsty and lost, water is the primordial trope.

IS: In a haunting scene in *Crossing Over,* immigrants that have made it to the other side in Arkansas, Missouri, or to California, in their homes they actually replicate the way they lived—the homes, the landscape that they had in the place they left behind. It is as if they needed to move north to look for paradise. And yet they carried the little home with them. Not just Mexicans do it, of course.

RM: The Little Italys, Little Saigons, Little Moscows that we have in the United States throughout our history are testament to the need of the zero and first generation of immigrants to have that cultural hearth, to bring it with them, because to deal with the newness of America, the language issues and the different cultural rites, without having that little piece of home with you—it would be impossible. There is something in human nature about it. Mexicans are particularly adroit at establishing Little Mexicos in the modern era of immigration, precisely once again because we're so close to Mexico and because the Southwest was Mexico and still is in so many different ways. To re-create the homeland, you could do it with the snap of a finger. The first time a Mexican arrives in Wisconsin, well, there are the tortillas and all the other signage that comes with them and establishes the beginning of the migrant's new life. Which doesn't mean that they're not going to Americanize in some way, of course they are. What Americans fear about Mexicans is precisely this historical memory: oh, we vanquished them 150 years ago; they probably still hate us, and we can't trust them. Well, young Mexican migrants are as enamored of violent Hollywood flicks and McDonald's and rock 'n' roll and hip-hop as any other young immigrant, as any other young global kid these days.

IS: You traveled with different members of a Mexican family from one state to another, miles and miles time over time. You chronicle what is going on in their minds, in their souls, a tension that exists between the various members. Does it ever come to a point where you feel that you're part of that family, and do you also have the sense that you're losing your subject, that they are using *you*?

RM: I've been a journalist, but I never ever subscribed to the ideal of objectivity in journalism.

IS: Writing is subjective?

RM: Yes. It's amazing to me that people like the networks, Dan Rather, look straight at the camera and say, I'm objective. Absurd. About seventy-five years of quantum physics and literary theory have done away with the idea of objectivity. It does not exist even though American media runs on that for its moral authority. I subscribe to the idea that subjectivity reigns in my realm of writing.

Selected Bibliography

Alba, Richard, with Victor Nee. *Remaking the American Mainstream: Assimilation and Contemporary Immigration.* Cambridge, MA: Harvard University Press, 2003.

Aranda, Elizabeth M. *Emotional Bridges to Puerto Rico: Migration, Return Migration, and the Struggles of Incorporation.* Lanham, MD: Rowman & Littlefield, 2007.

Elliott, Bruce S., with David A. Gerber and Suzanne M. Sinke, eds. *Letters across Borders: The Epistolary Practices of International Migrants.* New York: Palgrave Macmillan, 2006.

Gabaccia, Donna R., with Colin Wayne Leach, eds. *Immigrant Life in the U.S.: Multi-Disciplinary Perspectives.* New York: Routledge, 2004.

Gerber, David A., with Alan M. Kraut, eds. *American Immigration and Ethnicity: A Reader.* New York: Palgrave Macmillan, 2005.

Lee, Taeku, with S. Karthick Ramakrishnan and Ricardo Ramírez, eds. *Transforming Politics, Transforming America: The Political and Civic Incorporation of Immigrants in the United States.* Charlottesville: University of Virginia Press, 2006.

Mobasher, Mohsen M., with Mahmoud Sadri, eds. *Migration, Globalization, and Ethnic Relations: An Interdisciplinary Approach.* Upper Saddle River, NJ: Pearson Prentice Hall, 2004.

Montero-Sieburth, Martha, with Edwin Meléndez, eds. *Latinos in a Changing Society.* Westport, CT: Praeger, 2007.

Portes, Alejandro, with Rubén G. Ryumbaut. *Legacies: The Story of the Immigrant Second Generation.* Berkeley: University of California Press and the Russell Sage Foundation, 2001.

Suárez-Orozco, Marcelo M., ed. *Crossings: Mexican Immigration in Interdisciplinary Perspectives.* Cambridge, MA: Harvard University Press and the David Rockefeller Center for Latin American Studies, 1998.

Waters, Mary C., with Reed Ueda and Helen B. Marrow, eds. *The New Americans: A Guide to Immigration since 1965.* Cambridge, MA: Harvard University Press, 2007.

Ueda, Reed, ed. *A Companion to American Immigration.* Malden, MA: Blackwell, 2006.

Index

Affirmative action, 62–63
African Americans: affirmative action and, 62–63; in black/white racial dichotomy, 60, 67; demonization of, 65; employment of, 64; Hurricane Katrina and, 97–98; immigration policy shaped by, 59; in Los Angeles riots, 55–56, 61–62, 64–66
Alien Nation (Brimelow), 57
American Dream, 17–18, 28
Americanization, 60, 68, 97
Anderson, Andy, 133–36, 165
Animal metaphor: deixis and, 41–42; inherent logic of, 35; instances of, 30–34; interpretation of, 45–48; ontology of, 34–37; racism of, 45–48; testing of, 37–41
Anti-immigrant sentiment: antipathy toward non-English languages, 62; assimilation arguments of, 4, 96–98; cultural arguments of, 6–12; current rise in, 3; economic arguments of, 13–14, 17–18, 26–28, 30, 63–64; of Huntington, 3, 9, 12, 90–91, 96–97, 101, 107; in Los Angeles riots, 54–56; policies tilting against white Americans and, 62–63; public resources argument of, 63; voting bloc argument of, 12. *See also* Proposition 187
Asian immigrants, 3, 18; Chinese, 101; discrimination against, 60–61, 67; Korean, 56, 61–62, 64; in Los Angeles riots, 56; political involvement of, 67; Vietnamese, 127, 152–53

Assimilation, 168, 191, 194–95; anti-immigrant sentiment and, 4, 96–98; Latino Bloc and, 90–91, 96–98; of Latino immigrants, 3–4, 90–91, 96–98, 177–79

Balanced-budget conservatism, 43
Barrios, Eduardo, 137
Barzun, Jacques, 170–71
Baseball, 6
Benítez, Miguel, 126–27, 144, 157–59, 161–62, 164
Black/white racial dichotomy, 60, 67
Border fence, 120
Border Patrol, 19, 117, 120, 177, 192–93
Boxing, 39–41
Brimelow, Peter, 57
Burden metaphor, 20, 22, 27, 45
Businesspeople, metaphors of, 37–41
Byrd, James, 106

Calavita, Kitty, 42–43, 45
California, 18–19, 34, 36, 44, 100, 187, 190. *See also* Los Angeles; Proposition 187
Census Bureau categories, 94
Cercas, Daniel "El Chespiro," 121–22
Cercas, Luis, 121–23
Cercas family, 118–19, 121–24
Chespiro. *See* Cercas, Daniel "El Chespiro"
Chicanos, 95, 99, 108
Child metaphor, 44–45
Children, of immigrants, 13–14
Chinese immigrants, 101

Chivos, 183–84, 186
Civic involvement, 70–78
Class: Latino Bloc divided by, 105–7; race and, 97–98, 105–7; residential segregation and, 104
Colonization, 93, 96–97
Communities: in Los Angeles riots, 61–62, 67; multiracial, 61, 67; residential segregation and, 104
Coyotes: Cercas family, 118–19, 121–24; hatred of, 117–18; New-Jack, 120; runners, 182–87; walkers needing, 121, 166–67, 173, 177–79
Craven, W. A., 34
Criminal metaphor, 45
Cuban immigrants, 103

Dangerous waters metaphor, 20, 23–30, 47–48
Dang, Tri, 127, 145, 152–53, 164
Davila, Bill, 68
"A Day without Mexicans," 13
D-Day invasion, 21
Deixis, 41–42
Denny, Reginald, 54–55
Discrimination, 60–61, 67, 103
Disease metaphor, 20, 22, 27, 45
Disreputable people metaphor, 37
Domestic violence, 109
Dominant metaphors, of Proposition 187 discourse: animal, 30–37, 41–42, 45–48; dangerous waters, 20, 23–30, 47–48; ontology of, 25–26, 34–37
Dominican immigrants, 5, 77–79
Douglass, Frederick, 48

Earthquake relief, denial of, 36, 44
Economic immigrants, 102
Economy: anti-immigrant sentiment and, 13–14, 17–18, 26–28, 30, 63–64; Californian, post-WWII economic upswing in, 18; competition in, 63–64, 66; cycles of, 17–18, 63–64; immigration's positive impact on, 13–14, 189–90; Los Angeles riots influenced by, 63–64; nativism influenced by, 42; transformation of, 64–65
Education: of immigrants' children, 13–14; quality of, 106; soccer scholarships for, 146–50, 164

Ellis Island, 189
El Moreno, 122–24
El Negro, 122–24
El Salvador, 78–79, 83, 103, 105, 127, 157, 166–67, 176–77
Enemy metaphor, 41, 45
English: antipathy toward non-English languages and, 62; learning of, 7, 167–73; as *lingua universalis*, 169; in Spanglish, 173–75
Enríquez, Anselmo, 149–50, 161, 164
Esquivel, Martín, 141, 164
European immigrants, 3, 60, 68, 101, 189
Evolution, 33–35
Expansionism, 93

Family values, 8
Feed yards, 133–34
Fence. *See* Border fence
Football, 138–40
Foreign policy, Latino organizations not targeting, 9

Gangs, 104–5. *See also* Coyotes
Garden City High School soccer team: ascent of, 140–43; challenges to, 165; coach of, 126–30, 138, 148, 150, 156, 160, 163, 165; first, 149; games played by, 125–26, 137–38, 156–63; graduation and, 163–64; kickers on, 125–26, 157; money and, 154–55; in Southwest Kansas Regional Championship, 156–60; unequal treatment of, 139–40
Gender, Latino Bloc divided by, 108–9
Globalization, 63–64, 66, 97, 107
Gonzales, Alberto, 110
Gould, Stephen Jay, 33–34
Great Chain of Being, 33, 35
Great Experiment, 48
Guadalupe Hidalgo Treaty, 17, 173
Guatemalan immigrants, 36, 103

Hacker, Andrew, 60
Hermetismo, 144
Hernández, Rudy, 157–59, 161
Hernández, Servando, 157, 161
Holman, Currier, 134
Holyfield, Evander, 40
Home-country political involvement, 70, 75, 77–78, 84

Home town associations (HTAs): activities of, 9–12; establishment of, 9; Mexican officials pursuing, 9–10
Hoover, Herbert, 56–57
HTAs. *See* Home town associations
Human smugglers. *See* Coyotes
Hunter, Adam, 146–51, 164
Huntington, Samuel, 3, 9, 12, 90–91, 96–97, 101, 107
Hurricane Katrina, 97–98

IBP. *See* Iowa Beef Packers
Illegal immigrants. *See* Undocumented immigrants
Immigrants: children of, 13–14; civic involvement of, 70–78; demographic characteristics of, 72, 76; discrimination against, 60–61, 67, 103; economic, 102; European, 3, 60, 68, 101, 189; exploitation of, 192; in immigrant *v.* citizen narrative, 36; long-term, 69; marches of, 90; in media, 188–89, 191; organizations of, 9–12, 67, 71, 77; public benefits and, 13–14, 19; reactions of, against nativism, 67–68; remittances of, 11, 13–14, 102; as scapegoats, 56, 65, 102; undocumented, 31, 68, 103, 105, 173. *See also* Anti-immigrant sentiment; Asian immigrants; Latino immigrants; Naturalization; Proposition 187; Walkers
Immigration: economy positively influenced by, 13–14, 189–90; policy regarding, 59, 69–70; quota system of, 18; self-interested attitude toward, 17–18; self-interested immigration attitude toward, 17–18. *See also* Proposition 187
Immigration and Naturalization Service (INS), 31, 73
Imperialism, 93
INS. *See* Immigration and Naturalization Service
Invasion metaphor, 20–22, 32
Iowa Beef Packers (IBP), 133–36, 141, 150, 152–56, 159, 164–65

Jordan, Barbara, 58–59

Kansas: history of, 130–37; IBP in, 133–36, 141, 150, 152–56, 159, 164–65; Latino immigrants in, 125–30, 140–52, 162–63; *The Wizard of Oz* set in, 137. *See also* Garden City High School soccer team
Keating, Charles, 39–41
King, Rodney, 42, 54, 106
Knox, W. H., 58
Korean immigrants, 56, 61–62, 64

Lakoff, George, 43–45
Language: antipathy toward non-English, 62; intermingling of, 173–76. *See also* English; Spanish
Latin America: Latino immigrants' views of, 9; U.S. relations with, 7–8
Latino Bloc: assimilation and, 90–91, 96–98; class dividing, 105–7; construction of, mapped in negation, 92–93; cultural exchange and adaptation marking, 96–99; gender, sexism, and sexuality dividing, 108–9; heterogeneous population of, 94–96; homeland and national origin issues dividing, 99–101; internal political and social contradictions marking, 110; as late capitalist phenomenon, 93; not feeling at home in U.S., 107–8; terminology of, 91–92, 94–96; as transitional, 91; as urban population, 104–5; utility of, 110–11; xenophobia faced by, 101–3
Latino immigrants: assimilation of, 3–4, 90–91, 96–98, 177–79; baseball played by, 6; civic involvement of, 70–78; Cuban, 103; demographic characteristics of, 3, 72, 76, 90, 101–2; discrimination against, 60–61, 67; Dominican, 5, 77–79; Guatemalan, 36, 103; in high end professions, 13; in Kansas, 125–30, 140–52, 162–63; as latest immigrant group, 60; Latin America viewed by, 9; in Los Angeles riots, 55–56, 61–62, 64–65; meat packing by, 133–37, 147–50, 152–56, 159, 164–65; migratory waves of, 101–3; national identity and, 3–4; organizations of, 9–12, 67, 71, 77; political involvement of, 6–12, 14, 67, 77–80, 83, 110; popular culture

shaped by, 4–6, 14, 27–28, 192; religion important to, 8; residential attachment of, 76–78, 81; Salvadoran, 78–79, 83, 103, 105, 127, 157, 166–67, 176–77; Spanish not spoken by, 95; terrorism and, 8, 105; values of, 6–12. *See also* Latino Bloc; Mexican immigrants
Liberal individualism, 66
Liberal nationalism, 66
Lind, Michael, 66
Living standards, 27
Los Angeles, 18–19, 61, 193–94. *See also* Riots, Los Angeles
Los Angeles Times, 19, 20–22, 30, 36–39, 43–45, 47
Los Polleros. *See* Coyotes
Lott, Eric, 66
Lozano, Ramona Gladys Pérez: assimilation of, 177–79; English lessons of, 167–68, 171–73; family of, 166–67, 173, 175–79
Luria, Aleksandr Romanovich, 171

Maize High School, 156–60
Mamitis, 148
Meadows, Dave, 139
Meat packing, 133–37, 147–50, 152–56, 159, 164–65
Mehan, Hugh, 41–42, 45
Memory, 171–72
Metaphors, of Proposition 187 discourse, 19–20; animals, 30–37, 41–42, 45–48; burden, 20, 22, 27, 45; businesspeople and, 37–41; Calavita's analysis of, 42–43, 45; child, 44–45; criminal, 45; dangerous waters, 20, 23–30, 47–48; disease, 20, 22, 27, 45; dominant, 20, 23–37, 41–42, 45–48; enemy, 41, 45; implications of, 26–28; influence of, 46–47; inherent logic of, 26, 35; invasion, 20–22, 32; invisible, 48; Lakoff's analysis of, 43–45; Mehan's analysis of, 41–42, 45; nation as body, 43; nation as family, 43–45; nation as house, 28–30, 43; occasional, 20, 22–23, 32; secondary, 20–22, 27, 32, 37, 45, 48; soldier, 42; sports and, 37–41; Suárez-Orozco, C. and Suárez-Orozco, M. analysis of, 42, 45; tax burden, 42–43

Mexican immigrants: as biologically suited to stoop labor, 58; in *bracero* program, 180–81; in "A Day without Mexicans," 13; demographic characteristics of, 78–79; as dirty secret, 191; economic, 102; entertainment contributions of, 6; first-generation, 99; food of, 6, 98; in Kansas, 125–30, 140–52; labels of, 95–96; numbers of, 3, 5; political involvement of, 77–80, 83; walkers, 117–24, 180–88
Mexico, 9–10, 128, 157, 190, 193
Miles, Robert, 46
Miner, Craig, 131–32
Mireles, James, 164
Moi, Don, 118–19, 123–24
Morrison, Toni, 60
Musick, Andy, 143–46
Musick, Sidni, 143–46

National-origin identification, 99–101
Nation metaphors: body, 43; family, 43–45; house, 28–30, 43
Native Americans, 97
Nativism: economy influencing, 42; immigrants' reactions to, 67–68; in Los Angeles riots, 54–56; Proposition 187 and, 18–19, 56–57; racism and, 57–60; resurgence of, 57–58
Naturalization: administration of, 73; demographic characteristics influencing, 72, 76, 78–83; incentives to, 73; increased rates of, 68, 69–70, 73; INS and, 31, 73; predictors of, 82, 84; propensity toward, 72–73, 79; transnationalism influencing, 74–75, 77–84
New-Jack Coyote, 120
Nurturing Family model, 43

Obesity epidemic, 136
Occasional metaphors, of Proposition 187 discourse, 20, 22–23, 32
Omi, Michael, 58

Padilla, Joaquín, 126–30, 138, 148, 150, 156, 160, 163, 165
Palencia, Elbin, 159–60, 161, 164
Pan-ethnic organizations, 67
Patriarchal structures, 108–9

Pep rallies, 160–61
Police corruption, 187
Political involvement: of Asian immigrants, 67; home-country, 70, 75, 77–78, 84; Latino Bloc and, 110; of Latino immigrants, 6–12, 14, 67, 77–80, 83, 110; measures of, 70–75
Popular culture, Latino immigrants shaping, 4–6, 14, 27–28, 192
Pro-country of origin lobbyists, 9–10
Professional jobs, 13
Proposition 187: drain of public resources and, 63; as nativist reaction, 18–19, 56–57; naturalization incentives influenced by, 73; political values underlying, 43; unconstitutionality of, 19. *See also* Metaphors, of Proposition 187 discourse
Puerto Ricans, 75, 77–79, 103

Quota system, of immigration, 18

Race: black/white dichotomy of, 60, 67; class and, 97–98, 105–7; importance of, in social conflict, 59–60; recent scholarship on, 59
Racism: of animal metaphor, 45–48; cultural and structural forces shaping, 65–66; of dangerous waters metaphor, 47–48; definition of, 46, 58; discourse of, 46–47; evolutionary progress and, 34–35; examples of, 36; Hurricane Katrina and, 97–98; nativism and, 57–60; in 19th-century U.S., 17; political boundaries of, 57–58; rootlessness and, 107; soccer and, 144–45; stereotyping and, 103
Ramírez, Rey, 127, 138, 140–41, 144, 156, 161, 164–65
Ramírez, Vanessa, 142–43, 161, 165
Rape of Nanking invasion, 21
Raza, 95–96
Reagan/Bush era, 65
Reeves, Frank, 48
Religion, 8
Remittances, 11, 13–14, 102
Residential attachment, 76–78, 81
Residential segregation, 104
Riots, Los Angeles, 42; as anti-immigrant, 54–56; communities in, 61–62, 67; destruction of, 55–56; economy influencing, 63–64; nativism in, 54–56; participants in, 55–56, 61–62, 64–66
Rockhurst High School, 125–26
Rohrabacher, Dana, 44
Rucker, Juan, 144–46
Runners, 182–87

Salvadoran immigrants, 78–79, 83, 103, 105, 127, 157, 166–67, 176–77. *See also* Lozano, Ramona Gladys Pérez
Sasabe sign, 117–18
Scapegoating, 56, 65, 102
Secondary metaphors, of Proposition 187 discourse: burden, 20, 22, 27, 45; disease, 20, 22, 27, 45; disreputable people, 37; invasion, 20–22, 32; weed, 37, 48
September 11, 192–93
Serna, Juan, 184–85, 187
Service jobs, cheap labor in, 13–14, 27
Sexism, Latino Bloc divided by, 108–9
Slavery, 35
Smith, Anna Deveare, 54
Soccer: in Mexico, 128, 157; racism and, 144–45; scholarships for, 146–50, 164; U.S. and, 130, 140, 157; youth teams playing, 143–46. *See also* Garden City High School soccer team
Social security system, 13
Soldier metaphor, 42
Southwest Kansas Regional Championship, 156–60
Spanglish, 173–75
Spanish: Latino immigrants not speaking, 95; linguistic isolation of, 6–8; as second language, in U.S., 14, 168; in Spanglish, 173–75
Sports: baseball, 6; boxing, 39–41; football, 138–40; metaphors of, 37–41. *See also* Soccer
Stavans, Ilan, 188–95
Stereotyping, 103
Strict Father family model, 43
Stull, Don, 135
Suárez-Orozco, Carola, 42, 45
Suárez-Orozco, Marcelo, 42, 45

Tamayo, Guillermo, 147–48, 155
Tax burden metaphor, 42–43

Terrorism, 8, 105
Texas, 180–87
Tonk, 31
Torres, Alba, 150–51, 153–56, 163
Torres, Álvaro, 153–55, 164
Torres, Juan, 125–27, 138, 144–45, 150–51, 153–57, 159, 161, 164
Tortillas, 98
Transnationalism, 9; measures of, 77–78; naturalization influenced by, 74–75, 77–84; scholarship of, 73–74
Treaty of Guadalupe Hidalgo. *See* Guadalupe Hidalgo Treaty
Trevino, Sylvia, 145, 154–55, 164
Trickle-down theory of social advancement, 65
Tyson Fresh Meats, 164–65
Tyson, Mike, 39–41

Undocumented immigrants, 31, 68, 103, 105, 173. *See also* Walkers
Unions, 134–35
United States: cultural make-up of, 4; diet in, 133; expansionism of, 93; fragmentation of, 90–91; inequities in, 17; Latin America's relations with, 7–8; Latino Bloc not feeling at home in, 107–8; Mexico's relations with, 10; 19th-century, racism in, 17; positive orientation to, 8; self-interested immigration attitude of, 17–18; soccer and, 130, 140, 157; Spanish as second language of, 14, 168; states with largest Latino populations in, 5, 18

Values: family, 8; of Latino immigrants, 6–12; political, underlying Proposition 187, 43
Van Teeffelen, Toine, 45–46
Vietnamese immigrants, 127, 152–53
Villegas, David, 159
Voting bloc argument, 12

Walkers: as *chivos*, 183–84, 186; coyotes needed by, 121, 166–67, 173, 177–79; from El Salvador, 166–67; fatalities of, 121–23, 190–93; from Mexico, 117–24, 180–88; number of, 188; smuggling of, 117–24; to Texas, 180–87
Weed metaphor, 37, 48
White Americans: in black/white racial dichotomy, 60, 67; policies tilting against, 62–63
Wichita Heights High School, 160–63
Wilkins, John, 169–71
Wilson, Pete, 23–24, 27, 29, 31, 56–57, 63, 68
Winant, Howard, 58
The Wizard of Oz, 137

Xenophobia, 101–3, 189
Xochimilco, 185–87

Yuma 14 catastrophe, 121–23

About the Editor and Contributors

EDITOR

Ilan Stavans is Lewis-Sebring Professor of Latin American and Latino Culture and Five College Fortieth Anniversary Professor at Amherst College. He is the author, among other books, of *The Hispanic Condition* (1995), *The Riddle of Cantinflas* (1998), *On Borrowed Words* (2001), *Spanglish: The Making of a New American Language* (2003), *The Disappearance* (2006), and *Love and Language* (2007); editor of *Growing Up Latino* (1993, with Harold Augenbraum), *The Oxford Book of Latin American Essays* (1997), *The Poetry of Pablo Neruda* (2003), *Encyclopedia Latina* (2005), *Lengua Fresca* (2006, with Harold Augenbraum), and *César Chávez: An Organizer's Tale* (2008).

CONTRIBUTORS

Rodolfo O. de la Garza is Eaton Professor of Administrative Law and Municipal Science, Columbia University, and vice president of research at the Tomás Rivera Policy Institute. He is editor, coeditor, and coauthor of numerous books including *Muted Voices: Latinos and the 2000 Elections* (2004), *Sending Money Home: Hispanic Remittances and Community Development* (2002), and *Bridging the Border* (1997).

Louis DeSipio is associate professor of political science and Chicano/Latino studies at the University of California, Irvine. He is coeditor and coauthor with Rodolfo O. de la Garza of *Awash in the Mainstream: Latino Politics in the 1996 Elections* (1999) and *Making Americans, Remaking America: Immigration and Immigrant Policy* (1998) and, with Carole Jean Uhlaner, the article "Immigrant and Native: Mexican American 2004 Presidential Vote Choice across Immigrant Generations," in *American Politics Research* (2007).

Rubén Martínez is associate professor of creative writing at the University of Houston. He is author of *The New Americans* (2004) and *Crossing Over: A Mexican Family on the Migrant Trail* (2002).

Ramón "Tianguis" Pérez is the author of *Diary of an Undocumented Immigrant* (1999) and *Diary of a Guerilla* (1999).

Beatrice Pita is professor of literature at the University of California, San Diego. She is coeditor, with Rosaura Sánchez, of *Conflicts of Interest: The Letters of María Amparo Ruiz de Burton* (2001) and *Who Would Have Thought It?* by María Amparo Ruiz de Burton (1995).

Sam Quinones is a reporter for the *Los Angeles Times*. He is the author of *Antonio's Gun and Delfino's Dream: True Tales of Mexican Immigration* (2007) and *True Tales from Another Mexico: The Lynch Mob, the Popsicle Kings, Chalino, and the Bronx* (2001).

George J. Sánchez is professor of history and director of the program in American studies and ethnicity at the University of Southern California. He is the author of *Becoming Mexican-American: Ethnicity, Culture and Identity in Chicano Los Angeles, 1900–1945* (1993).

Rosaura Sánchez is professor of Latin American literature and Chicano literature at the University of California, San Diego. She is the author of *He Walked in and Sat Down and Other Stories* (2000) and *Identities: The Californio Testimonios* (1995).

Otto Santa Ana is associate professor at the César E. Chávez Center, Department of Chicana and Chicano Studies, University of California, Los Angeles. He is the author of *Brown Tide Rising: Metaphors of Latinos in Contemporary American Public Discourse* (2001).

Luis Alberto Urrea is professor of creative writing at University of Illinois–Chicago. He is the author of, among other books, *Across the Wire: Life and Hard Times on the Mexican Border* (1993), *By the Lake of Sleeping Children: The Secret Life of the American Border* (1996), *The Devil's Highway: A True Story* (2004), and *The Hummingbird's Daughter* (2005).